C0-GMY-670

A
COMPREHENSIVE
HISTORY OF THE
PROGRESSIVE MISSIONARY &
EDUCATIONAL
BAPTIST STATE
CONVENTION
OF FLORIDA, INC.

Reverend H. T. Rhim
President

A COMPREHENSIVE HISTORY OF THE PROGRESSIVE MISSIONARY & EDUCATIONAL BAPTIST STATE CONVENTION OF FLORIDA, INC.

by
Altermese Smith Bentley

Published for
The Progressive Missionary & Educational
Baptist State Convention of Florida, Inc.
By

The Mickler House, Publishers
Chuluota, Florida 32766-0038

RECEIVED DEC 18 1997

Copyright 1996
by Altermese S. Bentley
All Rights Reserved

ISBN 0-913122-58-0
Library of Congress
Catalog Card Number
LC 96–75042

TABLE OF CONTENTS

ACKNOWLEDGMENTS

The manuscript for the History of the Progressive Missionary and Educational Baptist State Convention of Florida, Inc., evolved from a diverse community, with few untapped areas. It was important that such extensive range of involvement be included. This diversity was found within the local churches and in fellowship with the Convention. These churches are the keepers of the oral history, collectors of various statistical, descriptive and biographical materials. The richness and diversity of sources provided a wealth of information for developing the manuscript. Materials gathered, soon unfolded, revealing a rich history. In the process new relationships were formed and old ones revived.

For their invaluable help, I am deeply and greatly indebted to many people in the local churches, district congresses, associations, the General Baptist Convention of Florida, Inc., the Progressive Missionary and Educational Baptist State Convention of Florida, Inc., Florida Baptist (Southern Baptist) Convention, and Dr. E. Earl Joiner, Curator of the Florida Baptist Historical Society. My thanks to the many pastors in particular, who shared their time and information, and to the moderators who released the histories of their Associations. A special tribute to the late Lula Owens, Elizabeth Baptist Church, Arcadia, Florida, who gave an interview on the first president, the late Robert B. Pittman. Hazel Hall, St. Matthew Baptist Church, Clearwater, Florida, contributed a picture, and an interview on the late Reverend Lawrence N. Anderson, Essie Wilson, Shiloh, Orlando, Florida, shared family history about the late First Vice and Interim President, Dr. F. G. Hilton.

Several pastors and the laity stood as "anchormen," fielding information and providing photographs. My thanks to the following: Dr. Rudolph McKissick, Bethel Baptist Institutional, Jacksonville, Mr. and Mrs. Alexander Heard, Second Missionary Baptist, Jacksonville, Rev. J. J. McGriff, Mt. Calvary Baptist, Lakeland, Dr. N. S. Sanders, Greater St. Paul Baptist, Lakeland, and Pastor Lewis Lampley, Southside Tabernacle, St. Petersurg. Mrs. Annie Doles, First Missionary Baptist, Winter Haven, graciously gave her total collection of Souvenir books, funeral programs, minutes and news clippings. Estelle Dickson, preserved notes from the Senior Women's Conventions. Also, thanks to Mrs. Carrie Fields, Epiphany Baptist Church, Jacksonville, for followup calls made to several individuals and churches.

I also want to thank the Seminole County Library System, the Florida Department of State and the Division of Historical Research, Stetson University, Deland, Florida Memorial Library and Archives and the Florida Historical Society.

My sincerest appreciation to Felecia Robinson Geuka, Seminole Community College and Pat Janis of Spinnaker Publishing for technical assistance, including a prepared disk of the manuscript. Kelly Mitchell provided invaluable service by typing and producing copies of the manuscript. Dr. Stephen Caldwell Wright gave special guidance and encouragement.

I would also like to acknowledge a very special group of people who willingly consented to support an application for funding to the Florida Endowment for the Humanities. They are: Reverend Lester T. Whitelock, Florida Memorial College, Miami, Dr. Stephen Caldwell Wright, Seminole Community College, Dr. Rebecca Walker Steele, Bethune Cookman College, Mr. Charles Rowe, Community Development Director, City of Sanford, Dr. Randolph Bracey, Jr., Pastor, New Covenant Baptist Church, Orlando, The Honorable Emmerson R. Thompson, Jr., Fifth District Court of Appeals, Dr. Storm L. Richards, Archaeologist, Sanford, Dr. Kimberly M. Jones, Seminole Community College, Dr. Harry D. Rucker, Sr.,

First Shiloh Baptist, Sanford, Professor Annye Louise Refoe, Seminole Community College and Mrs. Jackie Perkins, Orlando.

Too much cannot be said in words of thanks to Gretchen Debose Mason for her clerical help. Thanks also to Patricia Hutchinson for keeping the President updated on developments, and to Barbara Wright for skillfully coordinating and steering the activities of the overall operation affecting the office of historian. These efforts moved the Annual Report of the Historian into prime time.

My sincerest appreciation to Dr. Walda Metcalf, Associate Director and Editor in Chief, University Presses of Florida for reviewing the first draft of the manuscript, and referring me to Dr. Maxine D. Jones, Associate Professor of History at Florida State University, Tallahassee.

And to Dr. Jones for accepting me as her protégé, traveling to Sanford for group conferences and work sessions, rather than the reverse. Whatever success or credit that comes from this endeavor will be the outcome and quality of performance and professional standards that Dr. Jones set, as we worked to produce this document.

The Author

FOREWORD

The *History of the Progressive Missionary and Educational Baptist State Convention of Florida, Inc.* is designed primarily as a documented instrument to follow our heritage. It is a reference tool to familiarize ourselves with how we came to be. Great toils and pains have been taken to bring this book to fruition.

Today there is a new wind blowing—we want to ***reveal*** the hidden mysteries of our past, as a group of churches under the banner of Progressive M & E.

Altermese S. Bentley has included in these pages reports of Associations and sessions of the Convention and its Auxiliaries. The book has been designed to make it attractive to the reader. We want it to be, not simply a history book, but rather a pleasing presentation that will invite readers to turn to its pages for enlightenment and inspiration. It is my prayer that each member of our Convention will proudly acquire a copy of this book.

As the current leader of Progressive M & E we do give God all praise and glory for this publication that has helped us to discover our past. If the worthiness of this publication will arouse and propagate interest then the effort in preparing **The History of the Progressive Missionary and Educational Baptist State Convention of Florida, Inc.** will be more than repaid.

Yours in His Service,
H. T. Rhim, President

INTRODUCTION

The history of the Progressive Baptist State Convention is interwoven into the internal affairs of our local, state, and national government, and is influenced greatly by the impact of world events.

Between 1917 and 1918, the United States entered World War 1. To many Floridians this was a great sacrifice; to some war came as an opportunity to gain a profit and to become mercenaries. Florida soon became a military center to train men for the field of aviation. The climate was very well suited for the operation.

> Shipbuilding at Jacksonville and Tampa attracted many new residents to Florida. Major military and naval training centers were established at Jacksonville, Pensacola, and Arcadia. They drafted thousands of Floridians, some five thousand from Duval County alone, and almost fifty thousand from the state as a whole.[1]

Eartha Mary Magdalene White, humanitarian and a notable citizen of Jacksonville, was active with the Women's Department of the Progressive Baptist Convention. A member of the Bethel Baptist Institutional Church and an alumnus of the Baptist Academy, White served as Camp Community Service Director and Recreation Coordinator for service men in Savannah during World War I. She was the only African American to attend President Woodrow Wilson's Council on National Defense at the White House.[2]

> To the masses of Floridians, however, World War I seemed far away, and few hardships were found in the rising prices and scarcity of some consumer goods. Material prosperity of the farmer and other producers was almost beyond previous imagination.[3]

Sarah A. Blocker also aided in the war effort. Long associated with the educational work of the black Baptists in Florida, Blocker was a member of the faculty at Florida Institute in Live Oak. In 1892, she transferred with Rev. M. W. Gilbert and Rev. J. T. Brown to Jacksonville to establish the Baptist Academy. Although the Baptist Academy was in a transitional stage of relocating to St. Augustine between 1917 and 1918, Miss Blocker became involved in a community service.

> During World War I Miss Blocker extended her services to the YWCA and the War Camp Community Work at Newport News, Virginia, assuming as one of her responsibilities alleviating housing conditions exacerbated in the area as a result of the war efforts. Although the War Camp Community agency requested her to remain, Miss Blocker gave up that work to return to the Institution which she evidently felt was her major responsibility. They can hardly measure the impact she made upon the thousands of students whom she touched during her tenure.[4]

Common necessities for daily survival were scarce and often over priced. To control and encourage conservative use of these products, Tallahassee appointed a board to oversee the distribution of consumer goods. These were real life situations that pastors and struggling churches had to face. The increase in pay for the ministers and missionary workers did not rise in proportion to the inflated economy. These hardships were encountered by pastors as they marshaled their forces to earn an income to support missions and education and to provide benevolent aid to the membership and community.

Stewardship among black Baptists had not kept pace with programs in other areas. Meeting the demands to underwrite the expenses, several kinds of patterns were set. They became the traditional vehicle for supporting the church. These patterns were all familiar, and were etched and ingrained into individual self-discipline, as contributing resources for sharing material possessions. Traditional fundraising activities such as ice cream socials, box parties, fish fries, and church dinners were held. More important sociologically than theologically, these events were, in addition to raising money, used to build a bulwark to buttress the periods of inactivity that often led to social isolation. Therefore, the pastor was looked upon as the pivotal point within the community to sustain the political, economic and social life of the people.

At the end of World War 1 an influenza epidemic swept the country. The death toll in the larger cities was very high, and the rate in the smaller towns was equally as ravaging.[5] These life-threatening situations were directly related to the ministries of the church and affected the role of the convention in the community. The epidemic held sway over the entire community. Public meetings, including schools, churches and other gatherings were restricted, canceled, or prohibited. A crisis existed, especially in the black community. The African American community, stricken by a widespread illness, had to deal with closed facilities and segregated accommodations such as hospitals, and clinics. The limited number of nurses and black doctors in a given area supported, most forcefully, the distinct role of the Negro minister.

> " . . . Any religion that professes to be concerned with and ignores the social and economic conditions that cripple the soul is a spiritual morbid and dead religion only waiting to be buried. It is the duty of all ministers to make the gospel relevant, and in almost every community, it is the Negro minister who is at the forefront of protest."[6]

Thus, pastors led the crusade to provide and help staff the facilities for the temporary care of the ailing community. The schools, churches, and lodge halls were used as sites for treatment. These sites were necessary because of segregated hospitals and clinics. Public Health or Visiting Nurses were often not available in the black community. Therefore, black doctors and nurses traveled around the rural areas helping to relieve suffering.

Churches in the earlier history of the Convention were a cross-section of a community of believers, with a diversity of skills, talents, and abilities, committed to building a fellowship. They fortified themselves in the belief that the church was not made for Paul or Apollos or Cephas, but these were given for planting, watering, and culture.[7]

The first three presidents, Robert H. Pittman, John E. Ford and Lawrence N. Anderson, steered the organization through the social changes caused through world events and the aftermath of the post-war period.[8]

Endnotes

INTRODUCTION

1. Merlin G. Cox and J. E. Dovell, *Florida, from Secession to Space Age* (St. Petersburg: Great Outdoors Publishing Co., 1974), p. 153.

2. Charles E. Bennett, *Twelve on the River St. Johns* (Jacksonville University of North Florida Press, 1989), pp. 142-143.

3. Cox and Dovell, *Florida, from Secession to Space Age,* p. 154.

4. George P. McKinney and Richard I. McKinney, *History of the Black Baptist of Florida, 1950-1985* (Miami: Florida Memorial College Press, 1987), pp. 148-149.

5. Cox and Dovell, *Florida, from Secession to Space Age,* p. 154.

6. Felicia Kessel, "The Fighting Black Clergy, The Evolution of the Black Ministry in America," *Crisis* (June/July 1990), p. 52.

7. Corinthians 3:22.

8. Pittman, Ford, and Anderson shared a combined nine years in office. There are no records to document the length of tenures of these men.

Chapter 1

Slave Trade and Religion

There were two State Conventions before the Progressive Baptist State Convention of Florida, Inc., was organized. They were the General Baptist State Convention of Florida and the Educational Baptist Convention of West Florida.[1]

We must set a background for the churches that emerged to form the fellowship known as a convention. This backdrop must extend into the history and development of a State discovered and first governed by a nation that planted its religious roots. Including a study of the secular history is also important because it describes the economic structure of the State's dependency upon slave labor and the early importation of the Negro. We need to see or know the number of flags flown over the territory before it became a State.

Slaves were introduced into Florida when the area was claimed by Spain as part of her vast colonial empire in America. As early as 1580, colonial officials had requested permission to import African slaves to be used as a work force in St. Augustine. Negro slave trade into Spanish Florida did not increase in any significant way due to the rigid restriction of the Spanish crown prohibiting the use of slave labor in Florida.

Thus, a labor shortage prevailed in Florida during Spanish control between 1565 and 1763. This greatly hampered the development of crop production, and the colony never became self-sustaining, having to import its staples from Havana, Cuba, and abroad.[2]

When the United States took possession of Florida in 1821, it was virtually as wild and undeveloped as it was when Ponce de Leon landed. There were about 58,560 square miles of land, extending 447 miles south from the St. Mary's River to Key West, and 361 miles from the Atlantic to the Perdido River. At that time, there lived in Florida only 12,000 people, half of whom were Indians. The other 6,000 dwellers were a diverse group: plantation owners who had settled along the St. Johns during the British and Spanish occupations; farmers and cattlemen from Alabama, Georgia, and the Carolinas; free blacks and slaves; survivors of the Minorcan colony at New Smyrna; and runaway slaves, many of whom lived with or near the Indians. The Seminoles lived in the wilds of the interior, while they restricted the white, slave, and free-black populations to the area of Pensacola and northeast Florida.

Around 1824, the interior began to draw settlers after Congress set aside $23,000 to build a highway from St. Augustine to Pensacola. The route followed the old Spanish Trail from St. Augustine to the former Spanish settlement of San Luis, the site of Tallahassee. Many towns soon sprang up along or near the St. Augustine Road: Tallahassee in 1824, Quincy in 1825, Monticello in 1828, Marianna in 1829, and Madison in 1831. Federal authorities in 1823 forced a treaty on the Seminoles that required them to give up their land in northwest and north Florida and move into an area of sand hills, flatwoods, and swamp south of Gainesville, covering nearly five million acres. With this came an influx of settlers. By 1830, the population increased from 34,735 to 54,477. One reason for this influx was the very large number of wagon roads the military built in nearly every part of the peninsula and the erection of Forts for the protection of settlers. At the conclusion of the Seminole war in 1842, settlements grew up about the vacated military sites and kept the names of those Forts such as: Fort Pierce, Fort White, Fort Myers, Fort Meade, and Fort Lauderdale.[3]

Most of Florida's growth between 1830 and 1840 took place in the panhandle which experienced a boom in cotton, lumber, and naval stores during those pre-Civil War years. The rapid expansion and increase of cotton culture in Florida would not have happened without slavery. Without the use of abundant cheap labor, they could never have achieved the process of winning new lands from a wilderness. The plantation and its development in Florida exemplified the manner in which settlers pushed into virgin lands to create new slave-holding societies based upon an enforced labor system. The heaviest concentration of plantations, slaves, and cotton production were centered in Jackson, Gadsden, Leon, Jefferson, and Madison Counties.[4]

It was only after 1840 that settlers with their slaves spilled over into Alachua and Marion Counties to develop new lands. In South Florida sugar plantations developed as early as the 1820's. After 1840, a new migration to South Florida along the Manatee River resulted in the rise of a few large sugar plantations, but sugar in Florida was in no way comparable to cotton as a money crop, and after 1850 its importance declined.[5]

The institution of slavery was dehumanizing, degrading, and exploitative. A group of people was brought to a new land, separated from its cultural heritage, and forced to adapt to an environment which inflicted upon it images of inferiority. Many families were separated. Husbands and wives were sold to different masters, and children were snatched from mothers and sold as chattel. Many families living on the same plantation were not always housed together. Women who were house slaves worked and lived with the owner and family. Younger girls and older youth became the caretakers of the master's children. The same was true for male slaves who were chosen as house boys and butlers. The handwork and back bending labor supplied by slaves, without benefit of the smallest comforts or human treatment, created an economic status for their owners.[6]

There was a common and acceptable view among slave owners that the Negro was largely dependent upon his emotional stability to reinforce acceptance of his bondage. Some owners justified their holding slaves on biblical interpretation. Based upon these views, slave owners permitted slaves to receive limited religious teaching, which reflected their beliefs.[2]

Endnotes

CHAPTER 1

1. McKinney and McKinney, *History of the Black Baptists in Florida,* p. 5.

N. H. Pius, *An Outline of Baptist History* (Nashville: National Baptist Publishing Board), pp. 22–23.

2. Julia Floyd Smith, *Slavery and Plantation Growth in Antebellum Florida 1821–1860* (Gainesville: University Press of Florida, 1973), p. 9.

Ibid., pp. 10-11.

3. Carter G. Woodson and Charles H. Wesley, *Negro Makers of History,* (Washington, D.C., Associate Publishers, 1968), 6th Edition—Revised, pp. 116–120).

4. Langston Hughes and Milton Meltzer, *A Pictorial History of the Negro in America,* Third Revision by C. Eric Lincoln and Milton Meltzer, (New York: Crown Publishers, 1973), pp. 62–63.

5. Gary W. McDonough, ed., *The Florida Negro: A Federal Writers' Project Legacy* (Jackson and London: University Press of Mississippi, 1993), p. 27.

6. Albert J. Raboteau, *"The Secret Religion of the Slave," Christian History,* 11 (1992), p. 44.

Chapter 2

The Slave Preacher

The slave preacher, a leader among his people, bears a heavy responsibility. He was seen as a moving force. Since he influenced the lives of slaves in many ways, the slave master looked upon the preacher with distrust and suspicion. Preachers of this era were often illiterate and unschooled in the church doctrine, less trained in public and human relations. They were truly empowered through divine guidance to distance themselves from the conflicts of the social order of the day. Often foiling the efforts of the master to dictate the text of the message, they were skilled enough to use signs and symbols to communicate the true burning message of the gospel. There was a mind set and determination to lead and be a force for good in the lives of God's children.

The legacy of Negro spirituals, folk songs, and ballads illustrate that the followers of the Negro preacher knew and understood the restrictions and hardships under which he proclaimed the redemptive message of salvation and deliverance. They accepted his authority, not because the master gave free time to "Steal Away," but because the authority was from God, and the gospel was good news. It was given with power. The place where it was delivered did not lessen its effectiveness. Sometimes it convicted; other times it was uplifting. In whatever place the worshipers found themselves, the message was like a spring of water in a desert.

For a black man "to stand and preach with eloquence, skill, and wisdom"[1] though was evidence of competence and intelligence, and most certainly, a gift from God that the injustices of slavery were not able to alter or destroy.

> Unable to read the Bible for themselves and skeptical of their masters' interpretation of it, most slaves learned the message of the Christian gospel and translated it into songs about their own experiences. John Dixon Long observed, 'many of them could state the cardinal doctrines of the gospel in the language of song.' It was in the spirituals, above all, that the characters, themes, and the lessons of the Bible became dramatically real and took on spiritual meaning for blacks.[2]

There is no vocation with a more noble or higher calling than that of the "Old Time Negro Preacher." Slave sermons provided the benefit of the healing balm that soothed the burning desire of slaves to have a place where they could express their feelings without the listening ears of their owners.

God inspired slave ministers. They were given keen perception, alert minds, and insight to discern the hidden mysteries of His Divine Word. They preached with power, stirred the hearts of men, and shook the consciousness of man's injustice with the ringing sound that penetrated the courts of Pharaoh, with the command, "Let my people go!" Floridian James Weldon Johnson wrote:

> The old-time Negro preacher has not yet been given the niche in which he properly belongs. It was through him that the people of diverse languages and customs who were brought here from diverse parts of Africa and thrown into slavery were given their first sense of unity and solidarity. He was the first shepherd of this bewildered flock. His power for good or ill was very great. It was the old-time preacher who for generations was the mainspring of hope and inspiration for the Negro in America.[3]

There was one Negro sermon that in its day was a classic widely known to the public. People came from areas far and near Richmond, Virginia, to hear John Jasper preach his popular sermon on the subject, "The Sun Do Move." Born in 1812, in Fluvana County, Virginia, Jasper began preaching after his conversion in 1839."[4]

> I tol' yer in de fust part uv dis discose dat de Lord Gord is a man uv war. I 'spec by now yer begin ter see it is so. Doan' yer admit it? When de Lord cum ter see Joshwer in de day uv his feers an' warfare, an' actu'ly mek de sun stop shine in de heavuns, so de fight kin rage on tel all de foes is slain, yer bleeged ter und'rstan' dat de Gord uv peace is also de man uv war. He kin use bofe peace an' war ter hep de reichus, an ter scattur de host uv de ailyuns. A man talked ter me las' week 'bout de laws uv nature, an' he say dey carn't possi'bly be upsot, an' I had ter laugh right in his face. As if de laws uv ennythin' wuz greater dan my Gord who is de lawgiver fer ev'rything. My Lord is great; He rules in de heavuns, in de earth, and doun und'r de groun'. He is great, an' greatly ter be praised. Let all de people bow doun an' worship befo' Him![5]

Better known for his many hymns that are found in our New National Baptist Hymnal, than for his sermons was the renowned Charles A. Tindley, pastor of Tindley Temple, Philadelphia, Pennsylvania (named in his honor). Born a slave in Maryland in 1851, Tindley worked at menial jobs and attended night school in Philadelphia where he learned to read at age 17.[6] He took a correspondence course from the Boston School of Theology and in 1902 accepted the office of the pastor at Calvary Methodist Episcopal Church. There he preached to great crowds of people, both blacks and whites. Church leadership was diverse and included many from mixed ethnic backgrounds. Tindley wrote the lyrics and music for many gospel songs including "Nothing Between," "Leave It There," "Beams of Heaven," and "Stand by Me." His song, "I'll Overcome Someday," composed at the turn of the century, "served as a basis, more in spirit and thought than in actual words or melody," for the theme song of the Civil Rights Movement, "We Shall Overcome."[7]

Richard Henry Boyd (1843–1922) was born a slave in a log cabin in Mississippi. His master moved his family, possessions, and slaves to Texas in 1849. Richard H. Boyd fought in the Civil War and gained his freedom. As a free man he became a cowboy and traveled across Texas. While working in rodeos and at riding and herding cattle Boyd taught himself to read and write during spare times with the help of the Bible that he kept in his saddlebag. Boyd eventually became an ordained minister and urged congregations to read and act for themselves. He tried to instill in the people a sense of black pride and a willingness to take control of their own destinies.[8]

Dr. Boyd realized that existing religious literature was not relevant to the black experience in America. Blacks were using what was available to them, but Boyd was convinced there had to be a better and more meaningful way for blacks to be nurtured and trained effectively with an African American emphasis. Reverend Boyd opened an office in San Antonio, Texas, where he supplied religious books and materials to black Baptist Sunday Schools. The National Baptist Publishing Board originated in the state of Texas around the year 1894 when Reverend Richard Henry Boyd was elected Superintendent of Missions of the General Baptist Convention of that State. It is a matter of record that as early as 1891, in a meeting of the Negro Baptists from all over the country, plans were formed for a Baptist Publishing Society.[9]

According to James Weldon Johnson, "the old-time preacher was generally a man far above the average intelligence. He was, frequently, a man of positive genius." Often forced or required to attend white churches, many of the first preachers memorized sections of the Bible that they heard preached from the white pulpit and reinterpreted them for their black listeners.[10] Black preachers were great interpreters and dramatized scriptures and brought to life the many passages of the Old Testament. According to Johnson:

> The old-time Negro preacher of parts was above all, an orator, and in good measure an actor. He knew the secret of oratory that at bottom it is progression of rhythmic words more than it is anything else . . . He was a master of all the modes of eloquence. He often possessed a voice he could modulate from a sepulchral whisper to a crashing thunder clap. His discourse was generally kept at a high pitch of fervency, but occasionally he dropped into colloquialisms, and less often, into humor. He preached a personal and an anthropomorphic God, a sure-enough heaven and a red-hot hell. His imagination was bold and unfettered. He had the power to sweep his hearers before him; and so himself was often swept away. At such times his language was not prose but poetry.[11]

The unique style of preaching attracted the attention of the public generally. Also, we must recognize that, other than the black family, the single most important institution in the black community was the church. The type of structure was not the most important factor; what mattered was that it existed. The black pulpit, then, as today, wielded a great influence upon its people. Much of African-American culture and heritage has been traced and maintained in the black Church. The black Church continues to provide progressive leadership for the black community.

Endnotes

CHAPTER 2

1. Raboteau, "The Secret Religion of the Slave," pp. 42–44.

2. Ibid.

3. James Weldon Johnson, *God's Trombones* (New York: The Viking Press, 1927), pp. 2–3.

4. J. Alfred Smith and Charles O'Neal, *Baptists and Our Nation's Story, Condensed History of American Baptists, Southern Baptists and National Baptists in America* (Fullerton, California: Christian Printing Service, 1986), p. 23.

5. William E. Hatcher, *John Jasper: The Unmatched Negro Philosopher and Preacher* (New York: Fleming H. Revell Company, 1980), pp. 138–139.

6. William J. Reynolds, *Hymns of Our Faith* (Nashville: The Boardman Press, 1964), p. 423–424.

7. Reynolds, *Hymns of Our Faith,* p. 423–424.

8. "R. H. Boyd, Publisher and Banker", in *The Baptist Leader Adult Quarterly,* VI (April, May, June 1988), pp. 14[–]15.

9. Ibid.

10. Johnson, *God's Trombones,* p. 4.

11. Ibid., p. 5.

Chapter 3

The Black Baptists in Florida, The Early Years

> Black Baptist beginning in Florida dates back to 1582, when the first slaves arrived. To one of these families living in St. Augustine a son was born and baptized a Christian in 1606, the first documented baptism of a black in what is now the United States. Blacks and whites worshiped together at that time. Blacks retained few vestiges of their own African religious heritage.
>
> The Pigeon Creek Baptist Church in what is now Nassau County, was Florida's only known Protestant Church when the territory became part of the United States in 1821.[1]

Other white churches were started afterwards. Two of the earlier churches were established in 1825 in Jackson County: the Bethlehem Church (later the Campbellton Baptist Church near Marianna) and the Sardis Baptist Church. Four years later the Ebenezer Baptist Church was organized in Jefferson County.[2]

Black churches flourished and white ministers founded many of them. In 1834, Reverend Peter Nateal organized the Shiloh Baptist Church in Brooksville.[3] On a Sunday morning in 1838, six people gathered to worship in the government block house used for security against Indians. The log building was a pedestal so sentries could fire on attackers. In this atmosphere of siege, four white people and two slaves met to remember the Lord's Day with James McDonald, a white missionary, who organized the group to form Bethel Baptist Church (now Bethel Institutional), Jacksonville.[4]

Black Baptists founded their own churches before and after the Civil War. Being apart from a society that could not see the woes and injustices of slavery gave the worshipers a desire for freedom of self-expression. Singing and preaching added a special vibrancy to the church services. After emancipation, blacks withdrew from white churches in large numbers to form their own. For instance, ninety black members left the First Baptist Church, Ocala, in 1867 and formed the Mt. Moriah Baptist Church. First Baptist Church, St. Augustine, predates the white Baptist church which was organized in 1872. First Baptist was the first congregation of Baptists to organize in St. Augustine. Mt. Tabor, Palatka, was used as a Federal headquarters during periods of the Civil War. The church was founded September 15, 1869.[5]

After the Civil War a new era dawned. The black religious experience, marked by the institution of slavery, plantation stereotypes, and the aftermath of the Civil War, began to fade. There was an awareness that blacks, both slaves and free, had gained under the worst of situations, and they used this awareness to build a new society with viable cultural changes in their religious, social, and home life.[6]

Black Baptist Associations

After emancipation, Blacks, north and south, stepped up the process of organizing new churches while molding a cooperative movement among churches. Preachers saw the need for affiliation and cooperation for the edification of all and the general spread of the gospel throughout the world. As a result, general missionary societies and associations were soon organized.

> The earliest Associational movement developed out of independent church movement of the Ohio black Baptists. The early history of the Baptists of this state will show how a mixture of a missionary motif with a general desire for racial progress gave birth to the first Association among black Baptists.[7]

The associational concept spread rapidly among the states, moving east of the Mississippi to South Carolina and Georgia. However, the movement had not developed in Florida. A call was made to pastors and churches to band for the mutual benefit of support for the mission of the church. "To this end, messengers from a few of the leading Florida churches were called to attend meetings of the Georgia and South Carolina Baptists jointly in one or the other of these states two or three years in succession. However, the rapid growth of the work in each state, the long distances, and the inconveniences of travel, as well as the poor financial conditions of the churches, soon convinced the Floridians, at least, of the impracticality of this arrangement."[8]

Reverend James Page of Tallahassee, issued a call to Black Baptist churches to send their ministers and representatives to a meeting at the Bethel Baptist Church in Tallahassee on October 7, 1869, at 10:00 a.m. to organize the black Baptist Churches into an Association. Nineteen churches were represented at this meeting.[9]

Associations Founded Between 1869 and 1879

The First Regular Baptist Association of Tallahassee, Florida. (The name was later changed to the Florida Bethlehem Baptist Church Association.)

Bethlehem
Jerusalem
Second Bethlehem

It was during one of the annual meetings of First Baptist Association that a request by letter for dismission and the privilege to organize was granted. In 1874, Second Bethlehem was organized with a representation of 12 ordained ministers, 24 messengers, and 16 churches with a total membership of 1,038.

Second Nazarene. (Nazarene later merged with the Second Bethlehem and 'Nazarene' was dropped.)

Central (Columbia, Hamilton, and Suwannee Counties)

First West Florida Association (Escambia and Santa Rosa Counties)

Second West Florida Association (Jackson and Gadsden Counties)

History of Church Associations

AFFILIATED ASSOCIATIONS AND KNOWN DATES ORGANIZED

First South Florida Missionary Baptist—November, 1888 (First Session 1889, convened with the Mt. Gilboa Missionary Baptist Church, Bartow)
New Gulf Coast, 1941
East Florida and Bethany 1893 (First Session 1894)
Progressive
Union Foreign—1908 (First Session, 1909)
Equal Rights
Mt. Pilgrim—1912 (First Session, 1913)
Union—1909 (First Session)
South Florida Progressive—January 27, 1916
Second West
New Central—1945 (First Session, October, 1946)
Kissimmee Valley
Greater South Florida
Middle Florida and Clay County
Greater Union
Gulf Coast Progressive[10]

Endnotes

CHAPTER 3

1. Allen Morris, *The Florida Handbook 1989–1990* (Tallahassee: The Peninsular Press, 1989), pp. 289–90.

2. Edward Earl Joiner, *A History of Florida Baptists* (Jacksonville, Florida: Convention Press, 1972), pp. 18, 19; McKinney and McKinney, *History of the Black Baptist of Florida, 1850–1985,* p. 10; Altermese Smith Bentley, *History of the First South Florida Missionary Baptist Association, 1888–1988* (Chuluota, Florida: The Mickler House Publishers, 1988), pp. 1–3.

3. Altermese Smith Bentley, *Centennial Celebration: History of the First South Florida Missionary Baptist Association, 1888–1988* (Sanford, Florida: The Celery City Press, 1989), p. 2.

4. Bentley, *Centennial Celebration,* p. 2; McKinney and McKinney, *History of the Black Baptist of Florida, 1850–1985,* p. 11.

5. Bentley, *Centennial Celebration,* p. 2.

6. Ibid.

7. Leroy Fitts, *A History of Black Baptists* (Nashville: Boardman Press, 1985), pp. 64–65.

8. McKinney and McKinney, *History of the Black Baptist of Florida, 1850–1985,* p. 37.

9. Ibid. pp. 37–38.

10. Baptist Church Association, Florida Collection. Files in Florida State Archives, Tallahassee, Florida.

Chapter 4

The District Association

The Baptist Association initially set its goals in response to the urgent needs of the member churches within the fellowship and the focus has not changed. That focus is "churches in Fellowship." However, when a church's needs are not satisfied, that church may withdraw to seek membership in a similar fellowship. When several churches are of like opinion, another association is organized.[1]

"Fellowship finds its strongest expression in our commitment to one another in the accomplishment of our mission."[2]

> An Association is a voluntary society formed and maintained for mutual help among the churches associated, and for the religious welfare of the file it occupies. It is of human, not divine authority; it grows out of the sympathies of Christian fellowship and the need of mutual help. No church is under obligation to affiliate with it, and any connected church can withdraw cooperation, at any time for any reasons which seem to itself sufficient, without prejudice to either its evangelical or its denominational reputation and standing. But while it remains associated, it must abide by the rules and regulations mutually agreed upon, by which the body is governed. Because an Association is not a representative body, and because a church cannot be represented in any

> other organization, and because a church cannot, even if it would alienate, or transfer its powers and responsibilities to any man, or body of men; therefore, an Association cannot legislate for the churches, exercise any authority over them, or bind them in any way by its own action. Whatever is done while in session, is of authority only to those who do it; that is, the members, pastors, and messengers. They make suggestions to the churches, or present appeals, and lay requests before them; to all of which the churches will give such attention as may seem to them right and proper.[3]

The District Association continues to serve the needs of the local churches in providing the fellowship for functioning within the Body of Christ.

Conventions

Against the background of the associational movement, black Baptist leaders soon sought even wider cooperation among their churches. They saw the need for a unified program even among the various associations, which gave rise to the founding of state conventions. Black Baptists in North Carolina were the first to set forth this concept of cooperative associational programs with the organization of the General Baptist State Convention in 1866. The idea spread to other states. Alabama followed in 1866, Virginia in 1867, Arkansas in 1868, and Kentucky in 1869. By 1870 the cooperative movement was spreading. The black Baptists of Georgia organized in 1871.[4]

The organization of a state convention among black Baptists in Florida was considered when in 1873 the Reverend James Page offered the following resolution at a meeting of the Bethlehem Baptist Association.

> Resolved, that there will be a convention on the Thursday before the third Sunday in March, 1874,

> commencing at 10:30 o'clock to meet with the Tallahassee Baptist Church, Tallahassee. The object of this convention will be, first, to form two Associations instead of one, as per report of the Committee and as per resolution approved by this Association.
>
> The name 'Florida Bethlehem Baptist State Convention.' In 1875 at the session of the Convention, the name was changed to the Convention of the Missionary Baptist Churches of the State of Florida.[5]

Although the Bethelem Baptist Association adopted Page's resolution no state convention was formed. The next convention was the Missionary and Education Baptist Convention of West Florida in 1905. The two organizations made up the representative affiliation of local churches.

A ministry can be enhanced when it moves out into the wider community and beyond the walls of the local church. John Wesley said, "The world is my parish."[6] This quote is inclusive; it covers both lay people and ministers. This effort reaches the farthest point of denominational life with which the church is allied.

> A convention is a fellowship of churches working together on a voluntary basis for the accomplishment of Kingdom objectives mutually acceptable to the churches of the convention. The churches can accomplish together what no one church could ever achieve alone.
>
> The Convention draws its life from the churches. They create it and sustain it. The committees, agencies, boards, and institutions are comprised of persons and tend to take on the essence of living organism within themselves.
>
> The churches support them financially by combining their resources. Conventional leaders also receive moral and spiritual support from their fellow Christians in the churches.[7]

The authority and freedom of the local church does not lock it into a separate affiliation with any one convention. Churches often move their memberships as they perceive the objectives of the convention and how they are accomplished. Some churches withdraw due to a local church's program, and what appears to be a financial burden to support the convention and the related ministries. Another church may enroll without commitment, participation, and representation.

A pastor's recommendations may also lead a church to change Conventions. Pastors may strongly desire to remain in fellowship with a present Convention. Upon being called to a new field of labor; or serving two churches in different Conventions, one could find it more convenient to have one affiliation. Less frequently, but it does occur, a pastor wants to retain office in a Convention when called to the leadership of a church outside of his present fellowship. The exercise of independence can divert and disrupt unless the church remembers the reasons for its freedom. "Personal values and concerns are always in danger of being lost in the institutional structure."[8]

As careful as we are to keep in check our ambitions, drives for promotional gains, and the exposure we experience as we climb to the height of our expectancy, conflict, and tension, can change our direction. When these crises arise, the maturity of church and convention leaders is put to a test. Often, the results are divisiveness, factionalism, and the emergence of a new Convention.

H. E. Dana suggests three reasons why Christian unity must be sought: One, tragic consequences have resulted from dissensions and divisions within the Christian body; two, the Christian message will be more effective throughout the world when presented by a unified force; and three, unity is clearly the revealed ideal of the founder of our religion.[9]

Endnotes

CHAPTER 4

1. E. C. Watson, *The Baptist Association* (Nashville: Convention Press, 1975), p. 33.

2. Lloyd Corder, *Churches in Fellowship On Mission in Their Settings* (Atlanta: Associational Administration Service Department, Home Mission Board), p. 1.

3. Baptist Training Union *The Baptist Leader Adult Quarterly,* V (Fourth Quarter, 1986), pp. 9–10.

4. Fitts, *A History of Black Baptists,* p. 66–67.

5. McKinney and McKinney, *History of the Black Baptists of Florida, 1850–1985,* pp. 45, 46.

6. Baptist Training Union *The Baptist Leader Adult Quarterly,* V (Fourth Quarter, 1986), pp. 9.

7. Baptist Training Union *The Baptist Leader Adult Quarterly,* V (Fourth Quarter, 1986), pp. 9–10.

8. Baptist Training Union *The Baptist Leader Adult Quarterly,* V (Fourth Quarter, 1986), pp. 9–10.

9. Baptist Training Union *The Baptist Leader Adult Quarterly,* V (Fourth Quarter, 1986), pp. 10.

Chapter 5

Conflict and Resolution 1880–1913

The shift in population and a growing economy brought great changes in Florida. The center of the State was progressively moving out of north Florida toward the south. The vast area between St. Augustine and Key West did not remain an uncultivated region. The Florida East Coast Railroad, built by Henry M. Flagler, opened new opportunities to newcomers. Earlier, Miami was a small fishing town, and West Palm Beach was originally known as Lake Worth. Ocala was the largest town in Central Florida until the building of the Florida Central and Peninsular Railroad. Only a few towns were found between Ocala and Tampa.[1] The "phosphate fever" swept Florida in the late 1880's and 1890's. Pebble deposits were located in the Peace River in 1885 and hard rock deposits at Dunellon in Marion County 1889. Ocala became the phosphate center for the state with an overflow as far as Bartow.[2]

The discovery of phosphate brought a great influx of people to the State which in turn brought about an awakening among the churches. Pioneer pastors in the Central Florida area saw the need to unite and organize churches in these new communities. Such men as the Reverends E. C. Jones, W. B. Mills, A. N. A. Johnson, Amos Lassiter, and J. B. Reese led in these home mission efforts.[3] Pastors formed their own teams and devised plans to preach and teach. Found in these new communities were ministers who had come with families or who were looking for new fields of labor. These men joined the network and started a movement that reached great proportion in founding new churches.[4]

Before the expansion of railroads, pastors and missionary workers (appointed by the Association) walked to and from these remote areas. Winding their way along the unbeaten paths, they often came upon streams. They had to remove their shoes and place them across their shoulders while they carried their baggage. When they had crossed, they dried their feet, put on their shoes, and continued their journey. Unlike the "seventy," they were not without purse—nor shoes—but apparently had accepted the charge to carry the message and the burden of the mission.[5]

The encounters the pastors had organizing churches in the new communities profoundly affected not only their lives but, also those of the people they served. And new associations were formed as new churches were organized. Among them were:

First South Florida Missionary Baptist—November 1888
East Florida and Bethany—1893
Union Foreign—1908
Mt. Pilgrim—1912[6]

There were two basic concerns among the ministers within the newly organized associations which led to unresolved differences:

(1) The establishing of the Florida Baptist Academy at Jacksonville, which gained support from some pastors and churches.
(2) The strong desire on the part of some of the ambitious men for certain positions of leadership; this desire was not being met in the existing organization.[7]

In 1892, a group of irate white citizens of Live Oak, Florida, fired into a dormitory at the Florida Baptist Institute. When a reoccurrence demonstrated the potential danger to students Dr. M. W. Gilbert, President and Pastor of Bethel Baptist Church, Jacksonville, Florida, began a movement to build a similar school in a more urban center with the possible potential to support a church-related school. Reverend J. T. Brown, pastor of the First Baptist Church in Fernandina and Professor at the Florida Baptist Institute assisted Dr. Gilbert in this effort. Later, Reverend Brown became Vice President to Dr. Gilbert and succeeded him upon his resignation. Despite the difficulties at the school at Live Oak, the majority of churches continued to support its work.[8]

The name change to Baptist Academy and relocation from an agricultural area to an industrial center greatly benefited the school. Jacksonville at the turn of the century had nearly 450 industries, including the largest naval stores yard and wholesale lumber market on the East Coast. Not only was the world's largest cigar factory in Jacksonville, but so was the State's only dry ice plant and glass factory.[9]

The industrial, commercial, and economic stability of the area gave the financial support to impart new life and growth into the institution. Jacksonville also had a thriving black business community that included restaurants, theaters, funeral parlors, and the Afro American Life Insurance company which had assets of a quarter of a million dollars. The Baptist Academy received support from several Baptist Churches ranging from the storefront type with a few dozen worshippers to substantial edifices with congregations of larger numbers.[10]

Ambition was another reason for the split of the convention. Several men vied for leadership positions which led to animosity and factionalism and played a large role in the secession from the parent organization. The ensuing bitterness exploded during the historic 1913 session in Tampa and resulted in Reverend F. W. Lancaster filing a lawsuit against the Reverend J. B. Hankerson for slander. A verdict of "not guilty" was rendered in the civil suit.[11]

The Progressive Baptist Convention of Florida arose in answer to a need felt by several pastors representing local congregations. While attending the 39th annual session of the General Baptist State Convention, April 1913, held at Bethel Missionary Baptist Church, Tampa, the Reverend Robert H. Pittman, pastor, and a group of ministers withdrew and formed a temporary organization which became the Progressive Baptist Convention.[12]

Ministers present were the Reverends:

C. J. Smith, Pastor,
St. John, Sanford
C. S. Daniels, Pastor,
Gethsemane, Bradenton
William Smith,
Jacksonville
Robert H. Pittman, Pastor,
Bethel, Tampa
William Smith, Pastor,
First Institutional,
Lake Wales
F. W. Lancaster,
Jacksonville
J. W. Sparks, DeLand
I. C. Nimmons, Pastor,
Mt. Moriah, Plant City
C. T. Darrah, Pastor,
Shiloh, Jacksonville
R. Thomas, Pastor,
St. Thomas, Jacksonville
C. W. Vaught, Pastor,
St. John, Jacksonville
H. C. Williams, Pastor Day
Spring, Jacksonville
J. B. Reese Pastor, Mt.
Hermon, Tarpon Springs
E. W. Lewter, Pastor
Bethel, Winter Park
W. B. Mills, Pastor,
Tabernacle, Jacksonville
G. W. Jones, Shiloh
Orlando
T. C. Collier, Pastor
Friendship, Ft. Myers
A. Arnett, Pastor, Shiloh
Orlando
John E. Ford, Pastor,
Bethel Institutional
Jacksonville

Missionary Sisters were:

Idella Cason
Eliza Lewis
Theresa H. Moore
Mary Lewter James
Lucy White
Hannah B. Miller
Chaney B. Smith

Temporary Officers were:

C. J. Smith, President
C. S. Daniels, Secretary
William Smith, Jacksonville, Treasurer[13]

The newly formed group met in a called session July, 1913, at the First African Baptist Church, Green Cove Springs, to organize permanently. At this called meeting the first officers were elected.

Reverend Robert H. Pittman, President
Reverend Y. A. Roberts, Vice President
Reverend C. S. Daniels, Recording Secretary
Reverend R. V. Lawrence, Financial Secretary
Reverend C. J. Smith, Treasurer
Reverend W. D. Vann, Statistical Secretary
Reverend F. W. Lancaster, Corresponding Secretary
Reverend John E. Ford, Editorial Secretary[14]

The first annual session of the Progressive Baptist State Convention was held in March, 1914, with the Mt. Gilboa Baptist Church, Bartow. (It should be noted that the program and constitution presented at this session made no reference to any bitterness that may have been apparent in April, 1913, at the historic session at the Bethel Baptist Church, Tampa.)[15] The newly formed organization based its purposes upon the urgency to respond to some of the unmet needs of district associations and local churches outside the fellowship of a convention. The move was made to resolve some of the issues:

1. Out of the 20 Baptist Associations in the State, comparatively few of them were enrolled in the General Convention.
2. There were 400 churches not affiliated with the General State Baptist Convention.
3. There were 35 District Sunday School Conventions with no affiliation with the General State Convention.

4. Fewer than 100 Women's Missionary Societies out of 690 were enrolled with the Women's State Convention.
5. There were 20 District Baptist Young People Unions, and a State Baptist Young People Union. Neither group reported to the General State Baptist Convention.
6. There were weak and struggling churches in the rural districts with poorly paid pastors, without proper church buildings which received no assistance or encouragement from the General State Baptist Convention.
7. We believe in the Great Commission of the Lord Jesus Christ as laid down in the New Testament to go into all the world.
8. Since the Great Commission is not being carried out by the General State Baptist Convention, and since it seems impossible to organize within the present structure to do this work effectively, and since we are a part of this great Baptist Army, we believe that God will hold us responsible because of our failure to carry out the mission.[16]

Unsettled conditions often arose within a denominational unity. Uprisings at other levels, lost battles, broken bonds in relationships, waning influence, and shattered hopes were some of the matters leaders often confronted. These factors appeared to be insurmountable roadblocks, but many times they were turned into steppingstones. These stalwart fighters felt empowered to carry out the mission of the church. Among the pastors who helped found the Progressive Baptist State Convention were those serving churches (two Sundays monthly) in remote areas without church buildings other than a meeting place shared jointly with the county public school and other community organizations. This meeting house often was provided by a lumber, phosphate, resin and turpentine, citrus, or general agriculture company. In some cases, the County School Board and churches worked out arrangements for day school and churches alternating Sundays and weekly services. Whatever the agreements, pastors were struggling servants and poorly paid. Poor facilities, however, failed to dim their vision. They were inspired to reorder their priorities and sketch a new agenda:

> At that moment there is a change in relationships. A person's priorities are given new arrangement. Old things pass away and all things become new. New direction for life is established, self is dethroned, and Christ is placed completely and supremely on the throne of one's heart and life. Only when that experience is real can a person assume readiness for mission . . . [17]

The new Convention faced many problems most of which could have become major obstacles. There were many small congregations without pastors. Other churches had pastors who could benefit from continuing education through the several departments of the Convention. The feeling of security brought about by belonging to a wider fellowship of believers, and the opportunity to share their gifts in a creative way would improve the overall development of a growing agency.[18]

The area beyond Moore Haven, Florida, had undeveloped highways and a few trains connecting to the main system. Pastors and appointed missionaries serving had to endure many difficulties to reach churches. Many were dependent upon rail for travel. Moreover, there was discrimination in public accommodations. Uncomfortable overnight stays in waiting rooms at the local train station, unless a brother or lay family would give them lodging was an added hardship. Rarely were visitors turned away. If a pastor was unable to offer a place for lodging, there was always an open door in the community. In the more developed areas and larger towns, with growing churches, parsonages were often provided for the pastor. These pastors and their families made provisions for those who came their way. There were no restrictions as to church, association, or convention.[19]

Lay members who attended associations and conventions had the same difficulties as they traveled and gave of themselves to promote the work of the convention. To name a few and omit the teeming numbers would be a disservice to their sacred memories and to their steadfastness and worthy contributions. However, there is no history, oral or written, that can overlook these lay persons who came and supported the work, unaided, by the church. They were: Auttrice Flemning, Bell Water, Essie Hightower, W. E. Dancer, Lula B. Young, Reva Mather, John and Lucy White, S. W. White, G. W. Scott, Claudia Graham, Mamie Maxie, Sarah E. Bighman, J. W. Canady, Mary White, Idella Smith, Jessie Wright Yarn, Harry Taylor, Charles Vaught, Robert Owen, Sr., and Joe Jones.[20]

The Convention grew as church enrollment continued to increase and as transportation became more available. New Associations enrolled. In most cases, the new units were formed from churches in an Association large in area and by new churches desiring to cut the distance for travel to each yearly site. Opportunities for leadership were greater in this new convention and there was also a commonality in objectives and purpose. Pastors and churches agreed to support the agencies and ministries adopted by the association and convention. Support was given to Home and Foreign Missions, Belleview Orphanage, Florida Memorial (Live Oak), Baptist Academy (later Florida Normal), the Florida Baptist Seminary, and the Jones Training Center.[21]

Endnotes

CHAPTER 5

1. Cox and Dovell, *Florida From Succession to Space Age,* pp. 88–91.

2. Ibid., pp. 93–94.

3. J. H. Brown, Historian's Report to First South Florida Missionary Baptist Association, November 1944.

4. Personal Recollection of Altermese Smith Bentley.

5. Personal Recollection of Altermese Smith Bentley.

6. J. H. Brown, Historian's Report to First South Florida Missionary Baptist Association, November 1944.

7. McKinney and McKinney, *History of the Black Baptists of Florida, 1850–1985,* pp. 251–252.

8. McKinney and McKinney, *History of the Black Baptists of Florida, 1850–1985,* pp. 105, 107, 109, 251.

9. Federal Writers Project, *Florida, A Guide to the Southernmost State* (New York: Oxford University Press, 1939), pp. 185.

10. Personal Recollection of Altermese Smith Bentley.

11. McKinney and McKinney, *History of the Black Baptists of Florida, 1850–1985,* pp. 252.

12. McKinney and McKinney, *History of the Black Baptists of Florida, 1850–1985,* pp. 251–254.

13. C. J. Smith, *1943 Report on the History of the Progressive Baptist State Convention.*

14. C. J. Smith, *1943 Report on the History of the Progressive Baptist State Convention.*

15. McKinney and McKinney, *History of the Black Baptists of Florida, 1850–1985,* p. 254; C. J. Smith, *1943 Report on the History of the Progressive Baptist State Convention.*

16. McKinney and McKinney, *History of the Black Baptists of Florida, 1850–1985,* p. 254–255; C. J. Smith, *1943 Report on the History of the Progressive Baptist State Convention.*

17. Baptist Training Union *The Baptist Leader Adult Quarterly,* 11 (Fourth Quarter, 1983), p. 9.

18. Personal Recollection of Altermese Smith Bentley.

19. Personal Recollection of Altermese Smith Bentley.

20. Personal Recollection of Altermese Smith Bentley.

21. C. J. Smith, *1943 Report on the History of the Progressive Baptist State Convention.*

Chapter 6

The Progressive Baptist State Convention Founded and Struggles with Change

The Presidency of Robert H. Pittman

1913–1915

Robert H. Pittman became President well aware that there were challenges to be met. His successful service as pastor of the St. John Baptist Church, Fort Myers, and Elizabeth Baptist Church, Arcadia, before moving to Bethel Baptist in Tampa, had well prepared him to deal with the split in the State Convention. Insight and divine guidance, equipped him for this special ministry. As early as 1911, while filling the position of financial agent for the Florida Baptist Seminary, he negotiated the purchase of forty-eight lots adjoining the Seminary at the cost of $4,800. He also raised funds and supervised the construction of the first administrative building and a large girl's dormitory on the Lakeland site.[1]

Reverend Pittman's services to the Convention helped to clarify purposes and goals, and to formulate guidelines for a Constitution, Boards, and Auxiliaries. Under his guidance, the main work of the local church was encouraged because it was largely in the interest of rural struggling churches that the Convention emerged. Also, the support of Mission and Education was very apparent in the aid given to Florida Memorial, Live Oak; Baptist Academy (Jacksonville); and the Florida Baptist Seminary in Lakeland.[2]

Before the Convention stabilized under Reverend Pittman's leadership there arose two major obstacles. However unrelated they might appear, each had specific meaning for the growth and continued progress of the Convention. The first was the great migration of African Americans from the south to the big cities of the north and west. "Some were drawn by the opportunities to work in the steel mills of Pittsburgh or Gary, the automobile plants of Detroit, the packing houses of Chicago and St. Louis, and the machine tool plants of Milwaukee. Some were attracted by the opportunity to breathe an air of greater freedom. Some were simply running away from terror that was a companion of their days and nights."[3] This migration limited the growth of churches within the Convention.

The second obstacle was the great schism of The National Baptist Convention USA in 1915 which arose over the legal ownership of the National Baptist Publishing Board. During the final year of Reverend Pittman's presidency of the Progressive Baptist State Convention a great division occurred within the National Baptist Convention, USA. The roots to this specific problem were enmeshed in legal procedure as to ownership of the National Publishing Board. The Progressive Baptist Missionary and Educational State Convention of Florida supported the National Baptist Convention of America, Inc. in the dispute over the ownership of the National Baptist Publishing Board.

> Documents reflecting the great cleavage of 1915 within the National Baptist Convention, USA tends to give conflicting evidence relative to the real issues involved. It is, therefore, important for understanding to evaluate the more significant

> documents from the period to get a coherent account of the controversy.
>
> Rev. R. H. Boyd, a powerful leader in the Convention, published a lengthy document stating his views relative to the cleavage within the National Baptist Convention, USA. He claimed that the original constitution of the Convention did not contain a clear provision for the establishment of the National Baptist Publishing Board. Rev. Boyd further argued that the Board was organized with little or no help from President Elias Camp Morris and other officials of the convention. The leadership of the parent body seemed more interested in other matters of Baptist work at home and abroad. The fact that the Convention played little or no attention to the organization of the Board was cited as a justification for the claim of an independent legal status for it from the National Baptist Convention's official structure.
>
> Presumably, Rev. R. H. Boyd had developed at the turn of the century, a specific strategy for the organization of the National Baptist Publishing Board which gave it independence so claimed.[4]

A lawsuit was filed to decide between those who followed Rev. R. H. Boyd's claim of independence for the Publishing Board and the popular policy of the conventional ownership of all Boards. In 1915, a Chicago judge declared the Boyd group a "rump" convention and dissolved an injunction which they had taken out against President Elias Camp Morris and other officers of the National Baptist Convention, USA.[5]

When the judge announced his decision the Boyd group did not immediately consider itself a separate body. However, before the convention closed, the group mobilized and moved to the Salem Baptist Church and organized the National Baptist Convention, Unincorporated, on Thursday night, September 9, 1915.[6]

In 1916, the newly organized National Baptist Convention published a document entitled, "Rightful and Lawful Ownership of the National Baptist Publishing House," stating:

> Of late there has been a great deal of controversy, first, about the ownership of the National Baptist Publishing House, its management and control; second, about the rights of the Publishing Board to make choice of what faction it will affiliate with. Let us here and now make a clear statement that no messenger attending this body may go away from here deceived or disappointed. "The National Baptist Publishing Board is a legal entity; it was created by the State of Tennessee on the 15th day of August, 1898, under the Acts of Legislature of 1875, Chapter 142.
>
> Accordingly, the National Baptist Convention, Unincorporated, held that the Publishing Board did not belong to any convention; hence, it had the right to affiliate with any convention it so desired. This was done to counter the opinion of a few delegates to the new convention who were still a little doubtful of the ethics of the Publishing Board's leadership.[7]

While both events had an impact, the migration in particular was significant. Pastors and lay people alike were seeking improved economical, political, and educational advantages for themselves and their families. Reverend Pittman, himself was a part of the migration. He had moved to Florida from Georgia where his earliest years of ministry were spent in churches near Valdosta. Upon leaving Florida, he accepted a call to service in Cambridge, Massachusetts, later moving on to Detroit, Michigan, where he developed a large productive ministry. After a 1946 evening worship service, his stewardship came to an end. Leaving the church en route home, he stepped from the sidewalk into the path of a moving car and was killed.[8]

Dr. John E. Ford

1915–1920

Dr. John E. Ford, the second President of the Progressive Baptist State Convention, came to this office with a distinguished background as a Bible scholar, educator, author, church administrator, and Gospel preacher. He was the nationally known pastor of the historic Bethel Baptist Institutional Church, Jacksonville, Florida.

Dr. Ford's published works include *Bethel Baptist Institutional Church* (published as directories in 1920 and 1924, 50 and 60 pages respectively) and *Points of Differentiation Between Baptist and Other Denominations,* 1936. Dr. Ford, whose education included attendance at Beloit College in Wisconsin, received a B.A. from the University of Chicago, an M.A. from the University of Denver, and a D.D. from Morgan Park Theological Seminary.[9]

Dr. Ford's educational background gave him impressive status in the state. However, education alone was not what gave him his historical importance. First, the office of the president is an elected position and not bestowed by decendency, nor is one elevated through a structure of ascendancy. The process may follow several procedures but the outcome represents the voice of the people. However, elections for this office can provide a forum for well-articulated debates, colorful drama, and caucuses planned and led by some of the best strategists in support of their candidates. This is not uncommon to a Baptist Fellowship.[10]

Even though the president assumes a position which appears to be separate and apart from his primary function as pastor, in reality, the position of president carries some striking parallels. An ineffective pastor elected president is not likely to be productive, or to adequately develop the organization to its fullest potential. However, Dr. Ford's administration was reflective of his strong qualifications. He had prior call and election of God, and made preparation by a closeness in communion and relationship.

Dr. Ford led the emerging organization to fill what he saw as unmet needs within the fellowship. He was noted for his compassionate spirit. Even though he was often observed in a weeping posture, he presided over the convention with clarity and firmness. Dr. Ford's leadership strengthened and encouraged the bond among the pastors, and he supported the auxiliaries in various ways. He appeared to have been very aware that the spiritual life and well-being of the Convention was largely dependent upon the vitality of the local church.[11]

Dr. Ford was elegant in style, but informal in approach. He often addressed his peers by surnames such as Smith, Brown, and Darrah without blocking communication or relegating the person to lesser status. His maturity defined much of his leadership style. He used "models for ministries," which were available at Bethel Baptist Institutional Church and which were many years ahead in Social Ministries.

During Ford's administration the Convention committed itself to education by adopting a plan of support for church-related schools. Dr. Ford had a wide range of influence in Jacksonville and nationally, which made him the most eligible person to serve as a Trustee of the Florida Baptist Academy. He helped significantly during the period of transition when the institution moved from Jacksonville to St. Augustine.[12] Following the split in the convention in 1913, the major educational appropriations of the New Progressive Baptist State Convention went to Florida Normal and Industrial Institute. In the interest of the school, President Collier or some other representative of the Institute regularly attended the Baptist General State Convention and its auxiliaries.[13]

Mrs. Viola T. Hill, President of the Women's Department of the General Baptist State Convention, also gave her full support to the Baptist Academy and endorsed its move to the new location. She became the first woman to serve on the Trustee Board of Florida Normal.[14]

In a 1917 sessions of the General Baptist Convention, Jacksonville, Florida, President N. W. Collier, with a

Board of Trustees representing both Conventions, Mrs. Viola T. Hill, representatives from Southern and American Baptists, alumni groups, and friends joined in a decision to move the Baptist Academy from Jacksonville to St. Augustine, Florida. The need to follow current trends in higher education set the wheels in motion to effect the transfer of the Baptist Academy to a site that would prove to have historic meaning for generations to come.[15]

> Negroes had an important place in St. Augustine's history. As slaves of the Spaniards, brought over in the late 1500's, they were the property of the king and required to accept his faith. In the first hospital in the United States, built here in 1507, a Negro woman waited on patients, including Negroes and Indians. During the Seminole War, many Negroes allied with the Indians, causing much concern among St. Augustine slave owners. Shortly before the war between the States, escaped slaves were aided in reaching Canada by a white family occupying a plantation near the city. This was the site chosen for the new location of Florida Normal and Industrial Institute founded in 1892.
>
> The new location for the school was adjacent to the Florida East Coast Railroad, running between Jacksonville and Miami. Within a short time it was marked as a regular stop, known as College Park . . . discharging and receiving passengers, mail, baggage, or such items in transit. The college was a part of a thriving Negro community with stores, churches, a school, and recreational center. The residents were employed in domestic service, as guides, unskilled laborers in small manufacturing plants and on the shrimp fishing docks, and in hotels.[16]

As the movement to transfer the institution became more of a reality and other on-going problems increased, Dr. Ford and the Progressive Baptist State Convention united behind the move to the 1,000-acre Hanson Plantation. Ford used his office effectively. As Chairman of the Board of Trustees of Florida Normal, he amassed and reinforced support of pastors and churches around the state and most notably along the East Coast from Jacksonville to Miami. Some of the pastors who supported the school were: the Reverends J. W. Drake, J. R. Evans, S. A. Thomas, S. A. Sampson, J. N. Stokes, James Massey, George O. Sumner, and McCoy.[17]

Dr. Ford was still Chairman of the Board in May 1941, when representatives of both the Progressive Baptist Convention and the Baptist General State Convention approved a resolution to merge Florida Normal Institute and Florida Memorial College. Florida Memorial moved to St. Augustine.[18]

There are no records that fully delineate Dr. Ford's tenure as president. However, his role in the growth and development of the educational program of the Baptist Academy, Florida Normal and its merger with Florida Memorial is one of the most involved and dramatic developments of the Convention. As a distinguished scholar and pastor, Dr. Ford's long years of service are etched in the annals of Baptist History. He died August 9, 1943.

Reverend Lawrence N. Anderson

1920–1922

The Convention under Reverend Anderson continued to develop its structure, and the office of president enjoyed high visibility, due largely to the creative skills and talents he brought to the office. This was evidenced when he designed a logo and gave a new direction to the Sunday Afternoon Mass Worship for Foreign Mission and designated Thursday night for education.[19]

Rev. Anderson was an artist. On canvas, with palette, paints, and brush he would illustrate themes and provide motifs to set forth the basic principles or truths to be taught. His innovative methods of using visual aids placed him in an era well ahead of his time. For evangelistic services he often presented a series of illustrated sermons at the invitation of pastors. The outreach from the president's office was invaluable to the churches visited. These skills had relevance. The rate of literacy varied from area to area, and the canvas communicated the non-verbal as well as appealed to the beauty that abounds in the souls of every individual. However, it was not a substitution for salvation or a regenerated heart.[20]

During Rev. Anderson's administration, the Foreign Mission Board started drawing wide attention with the Sunday Afternoon Service. Rev. T. C. Collier, a young minister and pastor of the Friendship Baptist Church, Fort Myers, became the central personality for the Mass Meeting. This special ministry had been started by President Anderson when he pastored the St. Matthew's Baptist Church, Clearwater (1912–1918, 1927–1930) and when he served with the First South Florida Missionary Baptist Association, and the District Sunday School and Baptist Young Peoples Union. The early introduction of child evangelism through Rev. Anderson's methods of presentation, was scarcely recognized and never really took roots or brought about change. He lacked adequate public relations, and without such support, his potential as an illustrator went unnoticed. Within the St. Matthew Church, he formed a team of Robert and Mamie Paul and Joe Jones to cover a Chautaugua Circuit as effectively as Billy Sunday with Homer Rodeheaver and Ira Sankey.[21]

Anderson brought the same intensity obvious in his church ministry to a wider range of auxiliaries of the Convention. Although assisted by Convention officers and moderators, the operations of the Convention were centered around the president's church or his home office. Anderson was the contact person for coordinating the programs. His activities brought him into contact with Northern (American) and Southern Baptists, as well as in the work of the Home Mission Board of the Southern Baptist Convention, Atlanta, Georgia.[22]

Visits by the Executive Directors of the Foreign Mission Boards of the National Baptist Convention of the U.S.A., Inc., and the National Baptist Convention of America were arranged jointly by presidents of the Progressive Baptist State and General Baptist Conventions. The pastors were receptive to the visits, some served churches in associations in both conventions. Pastors from Jacksonville to Tampa opened their doors to the representatives from the Boards as well as the educational institutions.[23]

Foreign Mission Executive Directors who visited Florida under joint sponsorship were Reverend James Edward East, National Baptist Convention U.S.A.; Dr. E. D. Hubbard, National Baptist Convention of America, Unincorporated; and Reverend D. B. Horton, National Baptist Convention of America, Unincorporated. In a letter dated September 30, 1992, Dr. Isadore Edwards stated: "... The date of origin of this Board is unknown to me at this time."

First Secretary Treasurer—Rev. J. P. Reeder, S. C.; Second Secretary Treasurer—Dr. E. S. Branch, TX, 1950–1975; Third Executive Secretary Treasurer—Dr. Robert H. Wilson, 1975–1987; Present Executive Secretary Treasurer—Rev. Isadore Edwards, Jr.; Present Chairman—Rev. Asa W. Sampson."[24]

> The first field of work was Sinoe County, Liberia. The coup in the late 1970s made it impossible for us to continue work on this field. Our last Superintendent there was Rev. Harold Cottman who spent twenty-five (25) years on this field.
>
> The second field of work was Jamaica which we continue to support.
>
> The third field of work was Panama which we continue to support.
>
> The fourth field of work was the Virgin Islands which we continue to support.
>
> The fifth field of work was Haiti which we continue to support.
>
> The sixth field of work was Cameroon, W. Africa. We supported this field until December of 1986. Lack of technical personnel caused our with-

drawal. Rev. David A. Rooks was our Superintendent on this field.

The seventh field of work was Ghana which we continue to support. This is our target field to complete the James Carl Sams Home for Children. Sixty Thousand Dollars ($60,000) is needed for completion of this project.[25]

In 1915, Dr. E. D. Hubbard had indicated his desire to serve in Africa under the board of the newly formed National Baptist Convention of America, Unincorporated. He labored in Liberia near Carysburg. He later visited the Mission Stations of the National Baptist Convention, USA, Inc., and applied and was employed under this board.[26]

In 1917, Mrs. D. B. Horton, wife of Reverend Horton, worked at the Baptist Industrial Academy at Grand Bassa, Liberia. Reverend Horton organized several small churches among the Bassa people. The largest church at which she worked was the St. Simon Baptist Church at Grand Bassa.[27]

The Home Mission Board gave aid to the local churches in time of emergencies. These needs varied from church to church. No aid was given with intent of divesting or controlling. Needy churches were being organized in Okeechobee, Hardee, Highlands, Charlotte, Collier, Hendry, and Indian River counties, new counties that were being formed in South and South Central Florida. The Home Mission Board supported their appeals for help.[28]

Rev. L. N. Anderson supported wholeheartedly the belief that:

> Mission is the sending forth of authorized persons beyond the borders of their immediate gospel influence to proclaim the gospel of Jesus Christ, and to establish functioning, multiplying local congregations who will bear the fruit of Christianity in that community and to that country.
>
> In the Great Commission found in all four gospels, the church has its divine charter of Christian Missions. It is in that commission we as the Body of

> Christ find our orientation, authority and direction. The task of the church is summarized in several statements which present the purpose of missions. She is placed under obligation to do the following:
>
> (1) To present Christ intelligibly and effectively to the world, and to the individual, as the Savior of God, the sovereign Lord of the universe, and the coming Judge of mankind.
>
> (2) To lead persons into a faith relationship with Jesus Christ to the end that they experience forgiveness of sins and newness of life.
>
> (3) To establish believers in Christian doctrine, principles, and practices of Christian living, fellowship and service, teaching them to observe all things.[29]

The end of Anderson's administration came during the March, 1922, Annual Session of the Progressive Baptist State Convention. The session met with Mount Tabor Baptist Church, Palatka, Reverend L. N. Anderson, Sr., pastor and president. The Convention opened with the acknowledgement that God had moved among the ranks and called to his reward Reverend Y. A. Roberts, D.D., one of the founders of the Progressive Convention and pastor of Calvary Baptist Church, Palatka, from 1896–1922 (Union St. James Association and General Baptist State Convention), and the Galilee Baptist Church, Fort Meade, 1915–1922 (First South Florida Missionary Baptist Association, Progressive Baptist South Convention). Reverend Roberts died March 19, and his funeral was held Friday, March 23, 1922, at 1:30 p.m. at Calvary Baptist Church.[30]

Reverend Anderson presided at the funeral and Dr. W. C. Brown, Pastor of the Tabernacle Baptist Church, Jacksonville, and President of the General Baptist State Convention delivered the eulogy. Many pastors, ministers, and messengers traveled to Sanford on Saturday to attend a final tribute held at the St. Paul Baptist Church, Rev. C. Brewer, Pastor (First South Florida

Missionary Baptist Association, General Baptist State Convention). Rev. Brewer delivered the Gospel Message and committed the remains to its earthly place of rest, March 24, 1922.[31]

The Convention reconvened on Friday night to continue its work. Rev. Anderson was succeeded at the close of the session by C. J. Smith, Pastor Mt. Gilboa Baptist Church, Bartow. Anderson remained in fellowship with the Progressive Baptist State Convention through 1930 when he left his second pastorage with the St. Matthew Baptist Church in Clearwater to accept a call from the Mt. Moriah Baptist Church, Ocala. From 1971–1975 Anderson served as pastor of the Mt. Bethel Baptist Church in Hawthorne. He died in 1975.[32]

Reverend Charles Johnson ("Cap") Smith

1922–1951

The name "Cap" followed Smith throughout his life. He was referred to affectionately by family and peers as Cap. Cap was not a nickname. The seventh of nine children, his parents Fred, Sr., and Lucy named him Captain John Smith at birth. When young Smith decided to change his name has never been revealed by family members nor very close friends who knew him during his early years in Greenwood, Jackson County, Florida. The 1910 U.S. Census listed him as Charles Johnson Smith, Head of Household, 612 E. 9th Street, Sanford, Florida. This was his permanent address from December 1900, until his death, February 1952.[33]

Smith's mother was left a widow when the children were very young. The family situation was so critical, stated Dr. Richard I. McKinney, "My grandfather, Rev. Richard Ellis of Greenwood moved the entire family to his farm to help with their support." Here the family was under the watchful care of the Ellis family. This relationship lasted throughout the life time of Rev. Ellis' daughter, Sallie R. Ellis, later Mrs. George P. McKinney, Sr.[34]

Reverend Smith was converted and baptized in 1889 by Reverend George W. Martin. The Reverends Martin and Ellis, and his mother, who had no formal education, combined to find for the boy the best possible school situation. Reverend J. N. Stokes, Sr., of Live oak, serving as a missionary as far as Greenwood, brought "Cap" back to Live Oak to live with his family and attend the Live Oak Institute. This should clear up the myth that "Cap" Smith and John N. Stokes, Jr. were half-brothers with the same mother, and that strife was so great between these men that they would not occupy a platform if both were to be seated.

Smith grew up with the Stokes' two sons, John, Jr. and Fred as a foster brother. He remained with the family until the end of the school year, May 1892, when a section of the Baptist Institute moved to Jacksonville, forming the Baptist Academy.[35]

Smith graduated from the Florida Baptist Academy and continued his studies at Atlanta Baptist College. He moved to Central Florida in 1892, and joined the Providence Missionary Baptist Church, Bartow. On May 9, 1897, he was ordained by the First Missionary Baptist Church in Mandarin, and became its first pastor.[36]

His administrative ability was recognized early in his career. He was the first chairman of the Board of Trustees of the Florida Baptist Seminary, Lakeland; President of the District Sunday School Convention, Auxiliary of the First South Florida Missionary Baptist Association for ten years, and Moderator of the First South Florida Missionary Baptist Association for eleven years.[37] He left the office of moderator of the First South Florida Missionary Baptist Association, November 1919, and was elected to office as president, March 1922. In the interim he built the St. Paul Baptist Church, Dade City, and after accepting the pastorate at Mt. Gilboa, Bartow, November 1921, he launched a building program that came on the eve of the Great Depression. This did not alter the plans nor his faith to lead the people into a new sanctuary.[38]

Before becoming the fourth president of the Progressive Baptist State Convention, he had assisted small bands of believers in organizing places for worship. He was the founder and first pastor of: St. John First Baptist, 1898, Ft. Myers, and Bethel Baptist Church, 1911, Winter Park. He also served as the first pastor of the Mount Moriah Baptist Church, Winter Park.[39] Smith served as pastor during the construction of: St. John, Sanford; St. Paul, Dade City; and Mt. Gilboa, Bartow. Also, preceding his election as president, he pastored several congregations including, St. Luke, Kissimmee; Bethlehem, Winter Garden; St. Mark, Port Tampa; and Bethel, Plant City.[40]

He became president of the Progressive Baptist State Convention at a time when the growth of South Florida was being revitalized by the land boom. The upswing in the economy and increased numbers of migrant workers indicated the need for a new direction in evangelism. The construction of new lines by railroad companies opened up new jobs for black laborers, which also made travel more convenient for pastors and encouraged the Convention to seek new churches through newly formed Associations. The Atlantic Coast Line was extended to Lake Okeechobee, connecting Moore Haven and Clewiston. The Florida East Coast expanded its line to Canal Point and Belle Glade.[41]

Smith encouraged the planting of new churches and placed more emphasis on missions and education. As a pastor he helped fellow pastors to develop church training programs and encouraged them to continue their own training at a church-related school of their choice. In addition, he gave personal assistance to them through tutorial coaching and by sharing his books and experience.[42]

Rev. Smith's interest spanned the total church with personal commitment and involvement. His belief was as he often stated: "Ministers should prepare themselves to serve acceptabl[y] in their vocations. And through their training, members in the congregation w[ill] be inspired to raise their levels of aspirations." This concern was not limited to the ministers, but many lay persons were also brought into the work of the Convention. Smith sought out new workers through the recommendations from their pastors and churches. Many of these persons held offices in the auxiliaries of the Progressive Baptist State Convention and eventually achieved status in the National Sunday School and Baptist Young Peoples Training Congress, and the National Baptist Convention of America. One such person, Ms. Frankie Berry, Bethel Baptist Church, Tampa, was an instructor in the Congress.[43]

It should be noted that some laymen rose from that rank to a higher calling, accepted the "Great Commission," and became successful pastors within the Convention. These included the Reverends Leon Freeman, Bartow; and L. E. McGee, Brooksville; G. Robinson, J. H. Murphy, and E. Daniels all from the Galilee Baptist Church, Ft. Meade; and the Reverend Leo Jenkins, First Baptist, Ft. Myers.[44]

E. Franklin Frazier likens the Black Church to "Centers of information and reservoirs of power for people seeking identity and purpose."[45] Reverend Smith, much like the former presidents, committed himself to the mission of the organization. The Convention expanded its boundaries by adding new churches and associations. Upon invitation of the association Moderators, Smith visited areas previously considered off the beaten path to cement the relationship between associations and the Convention. He used these visits to acquaint moderators, pastors, and laypersons with the work of the National Convention's Boards and Auxiliaries. One result of these visits was the mobilization of Moderators to organize a group from their associations under the National Baptist's state appointed Chairman of Transportation. This concerted effort was under the office of the State President who coordinated this service. The Railroad Regional office, recognizing the potential business, worked with Reverend Smith to offer Convention rates, extra coaches, and a dining car. These accommodations were much improved compared to the separated facilities.[46]

Several Associations became members of the Progressive Baptist State Convention during Reverend Smith's tenure: South Florida Progressive, Kissimmee Valley, Greater South Florida, Middle Florida and Clay

County, New Central, Gulf Coast Progressive, Greater Union, and North Florida Progressive.[47]

Smith's administration was longer than the first three presidents, but, it was not without specific and distinct problems. His tenure was interrupted twice by periods of severe illness. Smith accepted his illness as a reality and resolved to perform his required duties. His problem was compounded by an active group of contenders for the office of president. Smith did not view this as anti-administration, but as procedures within the guidelines of Baptist principles and polity.[48]

Reverend Smith met his opposition with faith and prayer. He never reversed his stand nor lost his spirit of militancy. When able, he attended sessions and, given the podium, he proclaimed God's word with force and conviction. His peers and laity did not always share his views, but they respected both him and his opinions. Smith was a planner, organizer, and skilled parliamentarian. With his unique style of leadership, elegant manner as a pulpiteer, keen wit, sound philosophy, and God's guidance, he remained in office until 1951.[49]

Records show that Smith's responsibilities were extremely heavy. Although Rev. Smith was unable to sit in sessions, he was present at the 37th Annual Session held with the Mt. Carmel Missionary Baptist Church, Clearwater, March 20–25, 1951. He held a vigil from his bed with his officers in preparation to passing the gavel on to a young man who had walked with him in his hours of deepest despair—an Elijah and Elisha experience. "I pray thee, let a double portion of thy spirit be upon me" (II Kings 2:9). One of Rev. Smith's greatest contributions was the time he gave to developing a father-son relationship with his successor, Dr. James Carl Sams.[50]

SUMMARY OF THE ELECTION

Friday Afternoon Session

The following persons were nominated from the floor after the Nominating Committee Report was rejected.

The order of names and tally of count are as follows:

Dr. K. D. Brett	8 votes
Dr. J. C. Sams	180 votes
Dr. H. H. Robinson	27 votes

Other Officers:

Rev. E. L. Hamilton, First Vice President
Rev. L. J. Jenkins, Second Vice President
Rev. F. G. Hilton, Third Vice President
Rev. G. J. Martin, Treasurer
Rev. J. A. Smart, Recording Secretary
Rev. G. H. Peterson, Assistant Secretary
Rev. O. D. Williams, Corresponding Secretary
Rev. S. Siplin, Jr., Editorial Secretary
Rev. I. Anderson, Chairman, Educational Board
Rev. W. A. Harrison, Financial Secretary

Dr. Cyrus Weaver, Pastor, Day Spring Baptist Church, Jacksonville, presided at this election. Dr. J. R. Shaver, Observer and Enumerator.[51]

James Carl Sams

1951–1985

A new reign was ushered in with the election of Reverend James Carl Sams. He accepted office with a strong commitment to the Convention and a desire to translate goals of the organization into workable ministries. Serving as President, fulfilling his duties as Pastor, and establishing a program of continuing education proved to be an ambitious task. Nevertheless, his faith, courage, and leadership suggested that he was, indeed, the man for this time.

James Carl Sams was born in humble surroundings, one of five children of Charlotte and Lonnie Sams, in Cochran, Georgia, February 19, 1909. His early schooling started in the Blakely County Public Schools in Cochran and continued as a young man at Jacksonville's Stanton

High School. Sams' early education was limited and his efforts to equip himself for service were taken after he had assumed responsibilities of a family, had been ordained for the ministry and had been pastor of his first church. Reverend Sams often related the following story. As a young pastor he enthusiastically extended invitations to persons whom he considered to be outstanding leaders to visit his congregation, First Baptist, Oakland, Jacksonville. One such person, Dr. N. W. Collier, President of Florida Normal, St. Augustine, was invited to speak at a service. After the service, "which went very well," Reverend Sams said to Dr. Collier, "I am so very glad that you came to visit my church." Dr. Collier replied, "And I want you to come and enroll in my school."[52]

This contact motivated Sams to enroll in the High School Department of Florida Normal. He completed the Normal course of study and remained through four years of college to earn a B.S. degree in 1945. His was the first class to graduate from the newly accredited four-year college. He additionally studied at Garret Theological Seminary in Evanston, Illinois, and Columbia University.[53]

Spiritual guidance from parents can give a child a base for building a personal identity with Jesus Christ. The place the guidance is given may be a one-horse farm as in the case of young Sams, or any other surroundings. Sams' major influence was his mother. The bond between the youth and his mother was so strong that the other four siblings noticed it, but from this nurtured relationship came more than a "mama's boy." Sams' was a potential leader, destined to become an innovator, counted among high-ranking African Americans, and recognized as a world personality in the Christian Community. Undergirding these unforeseen achievements was the simple trust and faith of a nine-year-old youth who stepped forward and accepted Jesus Christ as the Lord of his life. He was baptized into the fellowship of the Long Street Baptist Church in 1918.[54] "The child grew and became strong, filled with wisdom; and the favor of God was upon him" (Luke 2:40).

From his early experience Sams began to gain insight into the real meaning of the value of involvement. He sang in the choir and taught a class in the Sunday School. His continuing growth in the faith and Christian qualities led him to serve as a deacon and eventually as an ordained minister.[55] James Carl was blessed in that he had a brother-in-law, the late Reverend G. W. Jenkins, Little Rock Baptist Church, Jacksonville, who gave direction to his acquiring the basic doctrine of the church. At age twenty, Sams acknowledged his call to the ministry and was ordained. After preaching a trial sermon, he accepted a call to the First Baptist Church, Oakland, Jacksonville, in February 1935. Reverend Sams led this congregation for more than twenty-three years.[56]

Reverend Sams was not a newcomer to leadership in the Progressive Baptist State Convention of Florida when he became President. He had served as First Vice President since 1948, sharing many of the duties of the President , whose term of office had spanned twenty-nine years. Reverend Sams gained experience in this office which prepared him to deal later with Convention problems.

In his Annual Address as First Vice President he stated:

> Time, this week, has placed your humble servant in a very peculiar place, for since we were together, our Chieftain called your humble servant to his bedside, and said, "I have gone as far as I can, and by my request, I want you elected the man of the Convention to take over and carry on." Without any weight of compulsion on my part, your servant said, "Brother President, I will."
>
> A committee was summoned. One week later we met, and, in writing, we accepted the President's wishes. Your First Vice President has been sitting in the cab with the driver for these years. It was not mine to say to the driver, "move over." I dare not be the type to try and take the wheel out of his hands. But, I was always ready to drive, and kept

> an open ear to hear the driver say, "Come around and drive." And he did from time to time.[57]

Upon becoming President, Reverend Sams started a program adapted to a changing society rather than being bound by the trappings of religious traditions. He centered attention on people (programs) and structure (organization). He fervently worked to expand the work of Foreign Mission, not forgetting the immediate cause of Home Mission and the Educational Institutions supported by the State Convention.

President Sams led the Progressive Missionary Baptist State Convention to many achievements, and also established an international reputation as a forward-looking leader with a high visibility for Kingdom building and a concern for the church and its place in the arena of civil and human rights. Among other innovations Reverend Sams appointed a Committee on Social Justice that was to help the convention define the church's role or ministry in politics; hopefully, to remove such barriers as "the church is too political," or "we need to keep politics out of the church," and to alter negative feelings in regard to the church's involvement with political affairs. The committee was charged with attacking such broad issues as: education, social and political problems, and holding forums to present candidates and to promote voter registration.[58] During Dr. Sams' administration, the Committee on Social Justice expanded its role and activities. Each year outstanding African American activists, clergy, educators, and representatives of local, state, and national governments appeared. The black church played a prominent role in the Civil Rights Movement.[59]

In his thirty-four years as president, Dr. Sams received many honors for his leadership, reflecting credit upon Baptists throughout the nation. He espoused a vision of unifying the Baptists in the Convention and State and of bringing about a greater return for the enrichment of the believers. Two positive efforts in this direction were the merger of the Progressive and the Missionary and Educational Convention of West Florida, and the move of

Florida Memorial College from St. Augustine to Miami. The merger of the two Conventions united their resources to expand the ministries in missions and education, and gave more vibrancy to the field of evangelism.[60]

Merger

In 1905, churches from as far north as Pensacola, south to Quincy, west to Apalachicola, met at the Mount Moriah Baptist Church, Caryville, Reverend John W. Mitchell, Pastor, to organize a Convention. This was the beginning of the Missionary and Educational Baptist Convention. The name was chosen because of its main objectives: to promote mission, education, and evangelism. The Presidents who served the Missionary and Educational Convention were Reverend J. B. Lake, Reverend K. D. Britt, Reverend M. D. Dodonia, Reverend F. Byrd, Reverend L. C. Herring, Reverend W. J. Johnson, and Reverend A. H. Parker.[61]

The Missionary and Educational Baptist State Convention was organized with one Association: The West Florida Association. Later the Association divided into the First West and Second West, and these two organizations further divided and formed other associations. Equal Rights Association became the new name for the First West Association. Other Associations were the New Gulf Coast, Progressive Association of West Florida, Union Baptist, and Pine Bloome.[62]

In 1971, officers of the Progressive Baptist State Convention and the Missionary and Educational Convention met in DeFuniak Springs to plan a merger of the two conventions. The merger appeared imminent, based upon the fact-finding committee's report that both conventions supported the same objectives, including the National Baptist Convention of America and Florida Memorial College. Reverends A. H. Parker and Reverend J. C. Sams led this historic move. In a session held at the Galilee Missionary Baptist Church, St. Petersburg, Reverend Frank Cubby, Pastor, March 1973, the merger was effected and

Dr. J. C. Sams elected President. The late Reverend J. F. Hargrett, Orlando, Corresponding Secretary of the Progressive Baptist State Convention, is credited with naming the merged Conventions: The Progressive Missionary and Educational Baptist State Convention of Florida.[63]

The need to relocate Florida Normal and Industrial Memorial to Miami had garnered support with a united purpose to resolve a number of problems that were primary to the restoration of the school. To begin this process, a nine-member Joint Committee on Education was formed and was made up of three members from the Progressive Baptist State Convention, General Baptist State Convention, and the Missionary and Educational Baptist Convention. The president of each Convention served as Ex-Officio.[64]

A resolution adopted at the 1961 session of the General Baptist State Convention, in Jacksonville, and subsequently accepted by the other two cooperating conventions, authorized the Commission to plan and administer a unified budget for the college. The resolution also proposed that an office and an Executive Secretary, paid by the college, be provided to carry out the program.[65]

In 1961 a Resolution to Consider the Relocation of Florida Normal and Industrial Memorial College was presented:

> Florida Normal and Industrial Memorial College located at St. Augustine, Florida, having been founded primarily to serve the needs of the Baptist constituency of this state and owned and operated by the three Baptist State Conventions through an elected Board of Trustees, has passed through many stages of development and growth.
>
> Standing today on the threshold of the necessity for either growing with the demands of new trends in the educational accreditation or being forced to accept second-class status among the colleges of the nation and regions, which classification would disgrace the heritage received from the Fathers and deny the birthright of the generations

unborn, and should be totally unacceptable to the pride of Baptists today.

The leadership of the Board of Trustees in cooperation with the administration of the College, through surveys carefully conducted have determined certain significant facts, among these facts that the center of the State's Negro population is in the southern counties; that the majority of the students attending F.N.I.M.C. come from urban, rather than rural, communities; that the hope of present-day small colleges is to be located in larger cities able to afford increased numbers of day students and more liberal financial supports that certain indications suggest that the Miami Community may afford a liberal financial backing for a new physical plant.

Be it further resolved that the General Baptist Conventions do endorse and give full approval to any necessary action on the part of the Board of Trustees to effect such a relocation of the college for its best interest and good.

Be it further resolved that this Convention do[es] give an approval for the rewording of this resolution to comply with any legal requirements as may be hereafter determined.

Respectfully submitted and moved for adoption.

S. R. Bright
(Approved by voice vote)

Coordinating Committee:

Rev. J. A. Clausell—First Bethlehem and West Florida, Spring Hill-Truevine
Rev. F. W. Williams—First Central Suwannee River; New Light, Middle Central
Rev. A. H. Howell—Jerusalem, Second Bethlehem, Bethel and Mt. Sinai

Rev. J. W. Cole, Jr.—Northeast Coast, Peaceful and St. John River
Rev. I. H. Mickens—Atlantic Coast and Seaboard
Rev. A. H. Lockett—Florida Eastcoast, First Macedonia and Macedonia (N)
Rev. B. L. Wynn-Emmanuel Progressive, St. Joseph, Gateway, Union Progressive, and Union St. Joseph
Rev. W. J. Isaac—First South Florida

The Executive Boards of the three conventions were to meet following the Convention to act on the recommendations of the Joint Commission. The final outcome of this proposal does not appear in the available records.[66]

Other Reasons Given for Relocation

In addition to the reasons given above for relocating the school, others stated by the College administration may be summarized as follows:

1. There had been a shift of large numbers of the black population to the counties in South Florida and the large majority of students at St. Augustine were from Dade and Broward Counties, with Miami and Ft. Lauderdale the principle cities in the area. Thus, there was a large pool of black high school graduates in the area. Moreover, there was no black institution of higher education in that section of the state.
2. In an urban area such as Miami, the availability of financial assistance from corporations and individuals was much greater than at St. Augustine. The city of Miami attracted a large number of tourists and was a rapidly developing industrial area. As stated in the dedication brochure, "Miami was chosen because the metropolitan area offered greater opportunities in industry, government, business, and community relations. Its earning power was higher . . . "

3. Racial unrest created by Ku Klux Klan and similar groups was increasingly exacerbated by local black involvement in the civil rights struggle.[67]

A firm decision was made to move to Miami. In 1965 the College purchased a forty-eight acre air strip in the Opa Locka community for $32,500. The property was dedicated on November 4, 1966. In September 1967, a ground-breaking ceremony was held. Grants from the federal government and construction loans from the Fidelity Bank of Philadelphia, enabled the initiation of an extensive building program.[68]

The Miami business community and private donors also assisted the college, which employed a professional fund raiser, Harold Dunsky, to launch a $9 million goal. Dunsky conducted a successful campaign raising more than $10 million. Plans for the college moved progressively through each phase of development. Nine buildings, including classrooms, an auditorium, and science, music, and physical education buildings were built.[69]

Prior to the relocation to Miami, the Board of Trustees dropped the word "Industrial" from the school's name and it became "Florida Memorial."[70] The Progressive Missionary and Educational Baptist State Convention, under Dr. Sams' leadership, supported Florida Memorial in all phases of change and development.

The Convention produced several persons as National officers of the National Baptist Convention of America. They were Dr. James Carl Sams, President (1967-1986); Mrs. Gladys Vaught, First Vice President, Senior Women's Auxiliary; Reverend J. B. Adams, Chairman of the National Educational Board; Reverend J. W. Toomer, Vice Chairman, Foreign Mission Board; Reverend T. E. Ganious, Assistant Recording Secretary; Reverend N. S. Sanders, Co-Director, Young Men for Christ; and Reverend J. F. Hargrett, Secretary to the National President.[71] Other persons who had national offices were: Mrs. Barbara Kight, President of the National Junior Women's

Convention; Reverend Willie C. Barnes, President of the Youth Convention; and Reverend Harry Rucker, President of the Young Men for Christ.[72] The Convention also acquired extensive amounts of land under the administration of Dr. Sams, including twenty-one acres in DeFuniak Springs, twelve acres in Jacksonville, and two acres in Oviedo, Florida.[73]

The labor of a faithful steward is rewarded and Dr. Sams was not lacking in such honors. *Ebony* magazine selected him as one of the 100 most outstanding Black Americans, and a building on Florida Memorial's campus is named for him. In addition, he received an Honorable Mention in "Who's Who" and was awarded several honorary D.D. and L.D.D. degrees.[74]

Dr. Sams' health began to decline in 1984. This state in his life brought him into a full view of his career as a "professional soldier" for the Lord. He responded to deteriorating health with a resolve to leave the Convention with a plan for an effective and orderly transition. The July 24, 1985, Home Going Celebration for Dr. James Carl Sams brought together, at Second Missionary Baptist Church, Jacksonville, a great gathering to pay tribute to a Servant who had fought "the good fight." High points of Dr. Sams' life included 18 years as President of the National Baptist Convention of America, 34 years as President of the Progressive Missionary and Educational State Convention of Florida, 27 years as pastor of the Secondary Missionary Baptist Church, and 56 years of marriage to the lovely, beautiful-in-spirit, strong-in-character Cornelia who supported his efforts and took pleasure in his achievements.[75]

Rev. Flagger George Hilton

INTERIM PRESIDENT
1985–1986

The Reverend Flagger George Hilton became Interim President of the Progressive Missionary and

Educational State Convention of Florida at the convened session of the State Sunday School and Baptist Training Union Congress (Reverend A. H. Parker, President and Host Pastor, Marianna, Florida, July 20, 1985). Reverend Hilton's ministerial career spans fifty-five years of productive service to the Church: pastor; moderator; advisor to ministers' wives; one of the founders of the Baptist Fellowship, Tampa; twenty-two years as President of the Tampa Ministers Conference; President of the Sunday School Convention of the West Coast and Mt. Pilgrim Association for four years as Moderator and later as Moderator Emeritus. Reverend Hilton was a pastor of churches in the First South Florida Missionary Baptist Association before moving to the St. John Progressive Baptist Church. His first churches were Antioch, Bealsville, Florida; Mt. Moriah, Plant City, Florida; and St. John, Sanford, Florida. He left Plant City in 1944 to become the pastor of First Baptist Church of West Tampa. In 1948 he accepted the call to the St. John Progressive, and continued in this ministry for 37 years.[76]

Dr. Hilton often related the story of the deep, passionate desire he had for learning. His drive and motivation were so great that at an early age he left home to satisfy his aspirations. He said, "The hard manual labor I had to do did not give me the time to attend school. I ran away from home for the purpose of pursuing an education."[77] His early labor, however, provided young Hilton with the skills to perform in a competitive society. He worked in service occupations in the hotel industry and in the building trade as a carpenter and brick mason. He continued his education as he worked and graduated from the Florida Seminary, Lakeland. He later earned a Bachelor of Divinity, and was awarded the Honorary Doctor of Divinity from Easonian Baptist Seminary, Birmingham, Alabama. Dr. Hilton did further studies at The Morehouse School of Religion, Atlanta, Georgia.[78]

Dr. Hilton had served in the cabinets of two former Presidents of the Progressive State Convention in the office of Second Vice and moved to the position of First Vice President. The interim Presidency came to a servant who had earned every honor associated with the office. From the moment of his call and license to preach under his pastor, Reverend G. W. Jones, First Baptist Church of Clermont, Dr. Hilton kept his eyes focused on his goal. His struggle through the ranks equipped him for this special assignment, which required him to guide the organization through a period of adjustment and to sustain its mission and set goals for the convention year.[79]

Much of his spirit was reflected in the Annual Session of the Parent Body, March 1985, at the St. John Progressive, Tampa, Florida, on a Friday afternoon when Rev. Hilton, First Vice President, gave the Annual Message, "Lord Let Me Give Just a Little While Longer."

Dr. Hilton held forth with courage, confidence, and faithfully carried out his duties. A leader gets his power from God through divine guidance of the Holy Spirit. This is highly predicated upon working in His will. A leader's work is prescribed by God, and it is God who recognizes his abilities and limitations. And within this scope, if he will accept the assignment, however overwhelming, success is assured.

Dr. Hilton was named President Emeritus in Panama City, Florida, March, 1986. He remained loyal to the cause of the mission of the convention. Even though the years of toil and labor lay heavily upon him, he "endured hardness as a good soldier of Jesus Christ." He made his last visit to the Progressive Missionary and Educational Baptist State Convention of Florida, March, 1992 at Pensacola, Florida. Dr. Flagger George Hilton fulfilled his dream of becoming an educated man and gave as he received. He left a legacy of service to his community. He served actively on the Bi-Racial Committee for desegregation of Public Schools in Hillsborough County, Florida, was one of the outstanding pastors of America, and is well known in the ecumenical community. He was a teacher, organizer, builder, and humanitarian. On July 10, 1992, Dr. Hilton was called to join "so great a cloud of witnesses . . . " (Heb. 12:1). The Service of Celebration was held Saturday, July 18, 1992, at St. John Progressive

Missionary Baptist Church, Tampa, Florida, where he had served for forty-two years.[80]

Rev. H. T. Rhim

MARCH, 1986–

"A New Direction Through Communication"

The dreams of men are not always timed to bring immediate results. Joseph (Gen. 37:6–36) told his dreams to his brothers and father. He met with rejection and sibling jealousy. A long chain of events over a span of time brought about a surprising outcome. Joseph's brothers placed him in a pit to keep a vigil with destiny. He was rescued from one form of bondage to become entwined with another. This placed him into a stream of circumstances which were divinely guided. Joseph came from the bottom of a pit to the status of the "second chariot," and Food Administrator of Egypt.[81] God places the man with the dream (vision) where he can be the most productive—not always at home, but sometimes in an unrelated or remote area. However delayed the unfolding of the dream, there is a place for its fulfillment.

Reverend H. T. Rhim, Pastor of St. Joseph Missionary Baptist Church, Jacksonville, Florida, was elected President of the Progressive Missionary and Educational Baptist State Convention of Florida, in March 1986 at the Annual Session in Panama City. Before his election, Reverend Rhim had been appointed by the former president, the late Dr. J. C. Sams to the Finance Committee of the Convention, and was an instructor in the Progressive Missionary and Educational Baptist State Sunday School and Baptist Training Union Congress. In March 1983 he was appointed Second Vice President of the Progressive Missionary and Educational Convention.[82]

Based on these experiences and those gained from his involvement as a pastor and officer of the East Florida and Bethany Baptist Conference of Christian Education and the Chieftain of the Youth Department, Reverend Rhim made an assessment of the communication process and found that:

> In our Christian pilgrimage, the aliveness and spiritual awareness we experience is largely determined by our relationships with those who care about us or who refuse to care about us, and with those that we care about, or with those that we simply do not bother to reach out to in a significant way. Those relationships, their varied levels and the lack of them, have a great deal to do with the spiritual satisfaction of our Christian life.[83]

The foundation upon which to build is the common bond of "Love Thy Neighbour as Thyself," and this gives us the Christian principle for developing human relations.

Reverend Rhim was educated in Jacksonville's public schools and the Luther Rice Theological Seminary. He also had been deeply involved in ministerial seminars, conferences, and workshops. Reverend Rhim brought to the office many job-related skills gained by his years of service and training in personnel and administration as an employee of the United States Postal Services.[84]

In an organization as large as the Progressive Convention the need for good communication skills was of great importance. Sharing oneself with others in an open and trusting manner was necessary for desired unity. President Rhim may be styled a "People's Person." He played an active role in the National Association for the Advancement of Colored People (NAACP), Southern Christian Leadership Conference (SCLC), Civil Defence, and as an appointee in 1986 to the Florida Governor's Task Force on the Black Family. He further served on the task force on Education for Minorities at the Florida Community College of Jacksonville, and the Urban League's task force on the Blodgett Homes (Minority Housing). Reverend Rhim also helped to launch the organization and program for the Help Center for Drug Abuse, and served on its first Board of Directors.[85]

The key to human relations is deeply rooted in one's concerns for people, and the ability effectively to address needs and work toward resolution of problems. As president of the Progressive Missionary and Educational Convention, Rhim's perception was that communication was essential for a successful redirection of an organization. He had learned from his past work experience in his working relationships that the levels of stress and frustration may be lowered and sometimes avoided through open communication.

> Human relationships are based primarily on communication, and communication is the avenue to sharing and communion with others. The goal of our communication may at times be purely the transmission of ideas, and at other times it may be communicating a feeling and an atmosphere. Total communication is the encounter of one person with another.[86]

One form of communication that should not be overlooked, however unacceptable, is that of the "grapevine," a major informal communicating network. "It is a rapid form of communication. All types of information are transmitted via the grapevine. The flow of information follows no distinct pattern. Finally, the grapevine is notorious for distorting information. The point to recognize is that, based on the grapevine, vastly distorted messages can be developed."[87] Thus an organization with a dynamic approach will provide for a two-way flow of information, not always downward, but also upward. The upward flow policy can divert the efforts of subgroups to hold sessions to discuss personal agendas.[88]

Reverend Rhim sought to change the direction of the Progressive Missionary and Educational Baptist State Convention, and lead it to new standards. This course called for courage, commitment, and surrounding himself with persons with varied and special skills to act upon "probabilities instead of certainties, and put their whole energy into making them come true."[89]

> Thoughtful men choose persons to work with them, and particularly men who will be close to

> them, for special qualities. Their assistants should be different from them, capable of doing things the leader cannot do for himself. No leader in government, business, or any other sphere of activity will surround himself with rubber stamps if he wishes to be relieved of some of today's work, to be given time to plan for tomorrow and the more distant future. The leader must originate. He must be an innovator. But he needs to do more: he must push plans through to successful completion, coping with the unexpected and unpredictable through originality and ingenuity applied with courage.[90]

Set It Free

The President outlined his new direction for the Progressive Missionary and Educational Baptist State Convention of Florida in his First Annual Address, given at the 7th Session, Shiloh Baptist Church, Rev. J. H. Toomer, Pastor, Orlando, in March 1987. President Rhim appealed to the assembled body to come into full compliance with the mission and purpose for which they gathered, to do the work of the kingdom. He stated,

> We have been given the task of being God's people without having to make a choice. There is no doubt that we have not chosen God, and that God has chosen us. There are a number of things that we must do in order to be the Convention of God's people. The only way to do this is to acknowledge our faults, differences, and short comings. Once we acknowledge them, we must immediately "Set Them Free."
>
> For too long, the conventions have been a rendezvous point for immorality and abuse of Church money. It is time that we come to these meetings sanctified to do God's work and take all of our vices and "Set Them Free."
>
> With the many things that need to be done, we can no longer afford to put pleasure in the place of business. It is no small wonder that many of our churches are becoming disenchanted with our various meetings. Those of us who come to these

meetings have established a reputation of happy-go-lucky fun days . . . "We need to Set It Free."

This Convention is now computerized and restricted. The Progressive State Convention can and will be a model for others to follow. The need for more training and teaching will be reflected in our State Congress. Your support of these activities and your input are necessary if we are to be successful.

The priorities of this convention reflect a "New Direction" . . . "former things are passed away . . . ," they have been set free. We cannot sit back and let discord or indifference keep us from working together. We must take every limitation and each hindrance and "Set It Free." There is only one way to be free and that is to be free in Christ. The need to be set free is the need to do God's will. There is no way we can expect God to bless us with so many weights and sins on us. "We Must . . . We Will . . . Set Them Free!"[91]

Initiatives:

The State Convention will implement a Ministerial Conference on the Tuesday which will initiate the Annual Session of the Conference. March, 1988, at the State Convention in Lakeland, plans were introduced to us regarding the establishing of a permanent State Headquarters and Training Facility. The property is located in the City of Lakeland in a prime area. Dr. Lewis Lampley and Dr. Alex Harper have researched the project and made recommendations to the State Staff.

Regional Conferences to be organized to more effectively meet the needs of local churches.

Minister's Wives' Ministry to be formed.[92]

"Meeting of the Minds" (Conventional Leaders). The meeting of: General Staff Officers, Presidents of Auxiliaries, Ministerial Advisors to Auxiliaries, Regional Directors and Moderators.

To be held in Ormond Beach, Florida, August 19–20, 1988, at the Holiday Inn, Surfside on Atlantic Boulevard.[93]

Conference Center

Dr. Ned Saunders has followed the day-to-day operations of the James Carl Sams Conference Center as Second Vice-President and Chief Executive Officer. He brought to this position a wealth of experiences as pastor-administrator of several ventures in the Social Ministries at Greater St. Paul. To accept this managerial position, Dr. Sanders had to redefine his goals and reorder his priorities.

He was asked about the added responsibilities and the short fall of responses from unkept commitments. He said, "I thought about all of it, but I never gave up. One of the options that is not being used," Dr. Sanders said, " . . . is the availability of grants from non-profit organizations." He also stated that, "The property is zoned commercial/residential. We can operate a bookstore under the present code because of the pre-existing bookstore without going to the Planning and Zoning Board."[94]

Dr. Alex Harper, Sr. was appointed to survey and give an assessment of the site located near Lake Beulah, one of the beautiful lakes of the city and common to the county. Aware of the problems of keeping the Florida Baptist Seminary in operation, the author interviewed Dr. Harper and asked why he felt so strongly about a Conference Center being located in Lakeland.

Dr. Harper said, "Lakeland is centrally located and easily accessible to many towns smaller than Winter Haven, Haines City, Bartow, and Lake Wales." He referred to the county as "Imperial Polk, rich in natural and human resources." It is also near the Tampa Bay area and Orlando which attracts students. Dr. Harper envisioned the Conference Center being developed into a private Christian school with a good teaching program. What is needed most, he said, " . . . are leaders with more vision and commitment." The seventeen Associations, he believed, were obligated to provide more support for the Center. Dr. Harper has a background in education and has been involved part-time with the educational system of Florida in various teaching positions.[95]

When an idea is perceived by a person, the medium through which it will travel or even its final form can be uncertain. The painter with an array of colors can depict the beauty of his surroundings. The architect through designs, structure, and models can build or restore towns and cities. The engineer spanning chasms can suspend a bridge. Also, tunneling through the impenetrable rocks makes way for progress, contributing to a process that changes the present course of action.

Lewis C. Lampley drew from his long association with other Baptist agencies his own extensive academic background in church planning and administration. He combined them in his efforts to facilitate the move to acquire the site for establishing the James Carl Sams Convention and Training Center. This led to developing a series of strategies, upon which the principles of the Mission Action Program (MAP) were based.

"1988–1990, was the birth of a vision," said Pastor Lampley as he reflected upon the assignment given by President Rhim. "I saw a decline in 1990–91, but 1992 gave the fulfillment. We were able to meet the budget," he said. The Core Committee, under the leadership of Second Vice President N. S. Sanders, Dr. Alex Harper, Sr., and Reverend Lewis C. Lampley, brought new commitment and support for the Convention.[96]

The Progressive Missionary and Educational Baptist State Convention appears to have an untapped reservoir of skills and abilities among its fellowship, Reverend Richard L. Wilson, Moderator of the East Florida and Bethany Baptist Association, and pastor of West Friendship Missionary Baptist Church, brought experiences and technology as a builder and construction engineer to the project.[97]

The site of the James Carl Sams Convention Center had fallen prey to a series of break-ins and acts of vandalism, and had to be closed for an interval. At the annual session in Pensacola, Florida, March 1992, the Convention contributed more than $11,000 for the renovations of the property. Reverend N. S. Sanders, Project Director, and Reverend R. L. Wilson, Coordinator, started the restoration in June 1992.[98]

Reverend Wilson brought workers from Jacksonville who lived on the premises. The skilled craftsmen refurbished the classrooms and spear-headed the beautification project by having a fence built. The fence provides enhancements to the property and also security to deter intrusions. Future plans are to restore another building on the property.[99]

Messengers and pastors attending the State School of Christian Education, under the leadership of Dr. Alex Harper, Sr., witnessed the day-to-day operations of the restoration and viewed what cooperative efforts can produce. Continued restoration of the several units need not be an end, but the beginning to provide space for a collection of our Convention records, such collections as document the lives, culture, and experiences of the Church. The need for such a resource is becoming increasingly important as researchers are raising public interest in the history of the African American church. The Historian's Report, March 20, 1991, stated that: "understanding our history, past, present, and future is greatly dependent upon what is considered as traditional history, such as found in libraries, museums, archives, or historical and genealogical societies."[100]

Endnotes

CHAPTER 6

1. History of the St. John's First Baptist Church of Fort Myers, Florida: Altermese S. Bentley, *History of the First South Florida Missionary Baptist Association, 1888–1988,* pp. 135–136.

2. C. J. Smith, *1943 Report on the History of the Progressive Baptist State Convention.*

3. *Crisis* 98 (February 1990), p. 4.

4. Fitts, *A History of Black Baptists*, p. 90.

5. Fitts, *A History of Black Baptists*, p. 92.

6. Baptist Training Union, *The Baptist Leader Adult Quarterly*, V (Fourth Quarter, 1986), p. 12.

7. Fitts, *A History of Black Baptists*, p. 93.

8. Interview with Ms. Lula Owens of Elizabeth Baptist Church, Arcadia, Florida, November 1988.

9. Baptist Church Associations Florida Writers Project, 1938–1939, Florida State Archives, Tallahassee, Florida.

10. Personal Recollection of Altermese Smith Bentley.

11. Personal Recollection of Altermese Smith Bentley.

12. Personal Recollection of Altermese Smith Bentley.

13. McKinney and McKinney, *History of the Black Baptists of Florida,* p. 161.

14. McKinney and McKinney, *History of the Black Baptists of Florida,* p. 159, 163.

15. McKinney and McKinney, *History of the Black Baptists of Florida,* p. 163.

16. Baptist Church Associations, Florida Writers Project, 1938–1939, Florida State Archives, Tallahassee, Florida.

17. McKinney and McKinney, *History of the Black Baptists of Florida,* pp. 183–185, 256.

18. The Florida Normal and Industrial Institute Bulletin, 1943–44.

19. Personal Recollection of Altermese Smith Bentley.

20. Personal Recollection of Altermese Smith Bentley.

21. Interview with Ms. Hazel Hall, November 1988.

22. Personal Recollection of Mrs. Eunice Smith Whitehead.

23. Interview with Reverend L. E. McGee, May 1988, District Sunday School and Baptist Training Union Congress, Dade City, Florida.

24. Isadore Edwards, Jr., Executive Secretary Foreign Mission Board, National Baptist Convention of America, to Mrs. Altermese Bentley, September 30, 1992.

25. Isadore Edwards, Jr., Executive Secretary Foreign Mission Board, National Baptist Convention of America, to Mrs. Altermese Bentley September 30, 1992.

26. Fitts, *A History of Black Baptists,* p. 118.

27. Fitts, *A History of Black Baptists,* p. 127–28.

28. Constitution of the Progressive Missionary and Educational Baptist State Convention, Article VII, Section 2.

29. Isadore Edwards, Jr., Executive Secretary "Foreign Mission Board's Doctrinal Statement," National Baptist Convention of America.

30. Personal Recollection of Mrs. Eunice Smith Whitehead.

31. Funeral Program for the Reverend Y. A. Robers, March 23, 1922.

32. Church History of the St. Matthew First Missionary Baptist Church, Clearwater, Florida; A letter from Fay Counts of the First Baptist Church, Ocala, to Altermese Bentley March 13, 1986 documents the history of the Mt. Moriah Baptist Church.

33. U.S. Census, 1910; Personal recollections of Altermese Smith Bentley.

34. Interview with Dr. Richard McKinney, Florida Baptist Historical Society, Stetson University, DeLand, Florida, 1986.

35. Obituary for Reverend Smith written by G. T. Martin; Personal Recollections of Altermese Smith Bentley.

36. Personal Recollections of Altermese Smith Bentley; Ordination Certificate of C. J. Smith.

37. Records of the Florida Baptist Academy; Bentley, *History of First South Florida Baptist Association,* pp. 112–113.

38. Bentley, *History of the First South Florida Baptist Association,* pp. 112–13; "The History of St. Paul Missionary Baptist Church, Dade City, November 12, 1985"; "A Historical Sketch of Mt. Gilboa Baptist Church," Bartow in *Souvenir Program of the 92nd Anniversary of Mt. Gilboa Missionary Baptist Church, 1985.*

39. Church History of St. John First Baptist, Fort Myers; Church History of Bethel Baptist, Winter Park; Church History of Mount Moriah Baptist Church, Winter Park.

40. Church History of St. Paul Baptist, Dade City; Church History of Mt. Gilboa, Bartow; Church histories of St. Luke, Kissimmee, Bethlehem Baptist, Winter Garden, St. Mark, Port Tampa and Bethel Baptist in Plant City.

41. Charlton W. Tebeau, *A History of Florida* (Coral Gables: University of Miami Press, 1971), p. 351.

42. Personal Recollections of Altermese Smith Bentley.

43. Personal Recollections of Altermese Smith Bentley.

44. Personal Recollections of Altermese Smith Bentley.

45. Kessel, "The Fighting Black Clergy," p. 52.

46. Personal Recollections of Mrs. Altermese Smith Bentley.

47. Historian's Annual Report. The Progressive Missionary and Educational Baptist Convention of Florida, March 1990, Tampa, Florida.

48. Personal Recollections of Altermese Smith Bentley.

49. Minutes of the 37th Annual Session of the Progressive Baptist State Convention, March20–25, 1951, Clearwater.

50. Minutes of the 37th Annual Session of the Progressive Baptist State Convention, March 20–25, 1951, Clearwater.

51. Minutes of the 37th Annual Session of the Progressive Baptist State Convention, March 20–25, 1951, Clearwater.

52. *The National Baptist Union Review* (August 1985); obituary for The Reverend Dr. James Carl Sams, July 24, 1985; Personal Recollections of Altermese Smith Bentley.

53. School Records, Florida Normal; *The National Baptist Union Review* (August 1985).

54. *The National Baptist Union Review;* Obituary for The Reverend Dr. James Carl Sams, July 24, 1985.

55. *The National Baptist Union Review* (August 1985); Obituary for The Reverend Dr. James Carl Sams, July 24, 1985.

56. *The National Baptist Union Review* (August 1985); Obituary for The Reverend Dr. James Carl Sams, July 24, 1985.

57. Minutes of the 37th Annual Session of the Progressive Baptist State Convention, March 20–25, 1951.

58. Combined Minutes of the Sixty-Second Annual Session of the Progressive Baptist Missionary and Educational Baptist Convention of Florida, 1976.

59. Combined Minutes of the Seventieth Annual Session of the Progressive Baptist Missionary and Educational Baptist State Convention of Florida, 1984.

60. Joseph G. Hargrett, "Brief History of the Progressive Missionary and Educational Baptist State Convention"; McKinney and McKinney, *History of the Black Baptists of Florida,* pp. 282–284.

61. Joseph G. Hargrett, "Brief History of the Progressive Missionary and Educational Baptist State Convention".

62. Joseph G. Hargrett, "Brief History of the Progressive Missionary and Educational Baptist State Convention".

63. Joseph G. Hargrett, "Brief History of the Progressive Missionary and Educational Baptist State Convention".

64. McKinney and McKinney, *History of Black Baptists of Florida,* pp. 206–207.

65. McKinney and McKinney, *History of Black Baptists of Florida,* pp. 206–208.

66. McKinney and McKinney, *History of Black Baptists of Florida,* pp. 207–208.

67. McKinney and McKinney, *History of Black Baptists of Florida,* pp. 282–283.

68. McKinney and McKinney, *History of Black Baptists of Florida,* pp. 282–284.

69. McKinney and McKinney, *History of Black Baptists in Florida,* p. 284.

70. McKinney and McKinney, *History of Black Baptists in Florida,* p. 281.

71. Official Journal of the National Baptist Convention of America and Auxillaries, 1985, pp. 21–38.

72. Official Journal of the National Baptist Convention of America and Auxillaries, 1985, pp. 21–38.

73. Personal Recollections of Altermese Smith Bentley; Warranty deed, Seminole County Florida, Official Records Book.

74. *The National Baptist Union Review* (August 1985); Obituary for the Reverend Dr. James Carl Sams, July 24, 1985.

75. *The National Baptist Union Review* (August 1985); Obituary for the Reverend Dr. James Carl Sams, July 24, 1985.

76. Minutes of the Seventy-Second Annual Session of the Progressive Missionary and Educational Baptist State Convention, Panama City, 1986; Funeral Program for Dr. Flagger G. Hilton, July 18, 1992; *The Weekly Challenger* (St. Petersburg, Florida), May 14, 1988, p. 16.

77. *The Weekly Challenger,* May 14, 1988, p. 16.

78. *The Weekly Challenger,* May 14, 1988, p. 16; Funeral Program for Dr. Flagger G. Hilton, July 18, 1992.

79. Funeral Program for Dr. Flagger G. Hilton, July 18, 1992.

80. Funeral Program for Dr. Flagger G. Hilton, July 18, 1992.

81. Genesis 37:6–36.

82. Minutes of the Seventy-Second Annual Session of the Progressive Missionary and Educational Baptist State Convention, Panama City, 1986; Minutes of the Sixty-Ninth Annual Session of the Progressive Missionary and Educational Baptist State Convention, Ft. Lauderdale, 1983; Minutes of the Seventieth Annual Session of the Progressive Missionary and Educational Baptist State Convention, Jacksonville; McKinney and McKinney, *History of the Black Baptists of Florida, 1850–1985,* pp. 258–59.

83. Cecil E. Marsh, *Developing Skills in Human Relations* (Nashville: Convention Press, 1971), p. 6.

84. McKinney and McKinney, *History of the Black Baptists of Florida,* p. 258.

85. McKinney and McKinney, *History of the Black Baptists of Florida,* p. 259; Biographical Profile of Reverend H. T. Rhim.

86. Marsh, *Developing Skills in Human Relations,* p. 15.

87. James L. Gibson, John Ivavcevich and James H. Donnelly, Jr., *Organizations: Structure—Process and Behavior* (Dallas: Business Publications, Inc., 1973), pp. 181–182.

88. Gibson, Ivavcevich and Donnelly, *Organizations: Structure—Process and Behavior,* p. 175.

89. *Leadership, the Art of Developing People Training in Human Relations,* p. 44.

90. Ibid., p. 46.

91. "Set It Free," in *The Liberator,* 1 (July 1987).

92. *The Liberator,* 1 (July 1988).

93. Joseph F. Hargrett, Corresponding Secretary, Open letter, July 18, 1988.

94. Altermese S. Bentley Interview with Dr. Ned Saunders, July 1992.

95. Altermese S. Bentley Interview with Dr. Alex Harper, Sr., July 1992.

96. Altermese S. Bentley Interview with Reverend Lewis Lampley, July 1992.

97. "Renewing—Rebirth," in *The Liberator,* 6 (Winter 1993); p. 4.

98. Minutes of the Seventy-Eighth Annual Session of the Progressive Missionary and Educational Baptist State Convention of Florida, 1992.

99. "Renewing—Rebirth," in *The Liberator,* 6 (Winter 1993), p. 4.

100. Historian's Annual Report of The Progressive Missionary and Education Convention of Florida, March 20, 1991, p. 1.

Chapter 7

The Mission Action Plan

In an attempt to organize the Convention's goals, the M.A.P. was initiated. In a meeting held at Greater St. Paul, Lakeland, Dr. Rhim and the Core Committee developed the plan and made the following presentations:

> When Jesus told His eleven disciples to "go into all the world and make disciples," He was not merely suggesting radical action, He was mandating their Modus Operandi. The agenda was "MAKE DISCIPLES." Making disciples is the GREAT COMMISSION, for every local church. But in many instances, the Great Commission has become the GREAT OMISSION. Why? Because the most of our churches are suffering and coming short of the mandate for the lack of information. The Progressive Missionary and Educational Baptist State Convention of Florida is preparing to change that. Your response to the President's special report is one key that will open many doors for our convention and churches. M.A.P. is our Action Plan.
>
> M Missions at home and abroad
> A Actions with eternity in view
> P Plans for effective growth
>
> MISSIONS: God had only one Son, that is His only begotten Son, and He sent Him to planet Earth on a mission. Concerning the mission, Jesus said, "Behold, I have come to do thy will, O God"

(Heb. 10:7). Therefore, the will of God is critical in our every endeavor. Missions, then, must take on new emphasis in the M & E State Convention and our recent giving to our Foreign Board is proof positive that a new day had arrived. Watch for new directions in the areas of Home, State, and Foreign Missions, because the mandate is both LOCAL AND GLOBAL.

ACTIONS: It has been said that "actions speak louder than words." For seventy-five years our Convention has been active in the State of Florida and throughout the nation. Many of the giants in other states had their beginnings in the Progressive Convention and they are still influential for the Kingdom. When we take note of what is happening even now, we should exclaim with much jubilation, "TO GOD BE THE GLORY, GREAT THINGS HE HAS DONE." He is truly faithful, let us commit ourselves to missions at home and abroad and make sure that our collective actions be embarked upon the eternity in view. The MAP program is an acknowledgment that "actions are ours but the results are God's."

PLANS: Planning is the process of predetermining a course of action. Why should the convention adopt and implement the Mission Action Plan? The convention should adopt the plan because God advocates thinking ahead and we should be excited about moving toward objectives, not just meeting, greeting, eating, and enjoying the great fellowship and the preaching. MAP is a plan of clear directions into the twenty-first and twenty-second centuries. The unified budget is the MAJOR KEY. The projected income for the conventional year April 1, 1989, through March 31, 1990, is $201,300. The budget can be met easily [if] each church, association, and other convention affiliates commit themselves to support the MAP program on a monthly basis. After MAP has been approved by you, the convention, every church will receive the unified budget and monthly contribution forms.

The other keys to the success of MAP are the various commissions and ministries which are specifically designed to develop and equip our leaders. Thus, the 1989/1990 conventional year is critical to the lasting effect of the Mission Action Program. Much work has to be done. The President will need the cooperation of every pastor, association, moderator, and congressional leader as well as an elected conventional leader. The Core Committee has attempted to faithfully carry out all the assignments given it since the last Annual Session met. We want to thank you, our constituency for your past and continued support for your convention.

Sincerely yours,
The Core Committee[1]

In order for the MAP to realize its fullest potential, it was noted that all leaders must be informed of its objectives, goals, and plans. It was, therefore, proposed that Convention leaders attend three symposiums.

Symposium 1

The objective of this Symposium is to: "analyze and properly organize the administrative and organizational structure of the Progressive M&E state convention through the process of a SWOTS Analysis."

Goals:

1. To come to a collective understanding of what our Convention should be doing through its Boards, Commissions, Committees, and Departments.
2. To help every Convention head to be his/her best for the Lord as a leader in the Convention (1 Cor. 10:31)
3. To agree on job assignments and job descriptions.

Symposium 2

The second symposium has as its objective "to examine the present educational process of the State Congress and design more effective Christian Educational Methods by using the lens of a SWOTS Analysis."

Goals:

1. To evaluate our present process, strengthen it and design other educational ministries to be administered through our district Congresses.
2. To sharpen our focus on the State Congress' responsibility for equipping our district congress workers. The District Congress can then equip the fifth week Congress workers so that they can do a better job in our local churches.

Symposium 3

Goals:

1. The objective of this symposium is "to equip the Benevolent, Educational, Evangelical, Home Mission, State Mission, and Foreign Mission Boards in order that they may better assist the Associations and churches affiliated.
2. To strengthen the present ministries of these boards and plan to be more effective in areas of education, evangelism and in all phases of missions.[2]

Endnotes

CHAPTER 7

1. "Putting the MAP Program in Focus," *The Liberator Magazine,* Vol. 1, No. 1, p. 8.

2. *Ibid.,* pp. 9–10.

Chapter 8

The Role of Women in the Church

Any approach to the chapter on the Role of Women in the Church should not be done in a subjective manner. Such could create a forum for debates, controversy, and foster biased opinions. Rather, an approach of objectivity, could open channels of research and acceptance of history as written, without personal interpretation in light of doctrine and polity. This chapter is not an apology, giving the contents a pursuit in futility. Neither is it a feminist movement to create furor within a fellowship. The concern is not centered around crossing a line of tradition, but to look at the position given women at creation. "It is not good that man should be alone; I will make a help meet for him" (Genesis 2:18).

The connotation of help meet in this context is partnership. The treatment of the material, surpasses any desire, or effort to advocate, or solicit a conciliatory placement for women in the church.

> For as many of you as have been baptised into Christ have put on Christ. There is neither bond nor free, there is neither male or female; for ye are all one in Christ Jesus. (Galatians 3:27–28)

The growing numbers among women to announce their call, and seek ordination can best be resolved at the local level, and by denominational boards, whether evangelical, liturgical or others, that may not fit under such broad heading. Those women who feel the unction to follow the call will do so, even if they are denied the right to belong and the bond of fellowship. The strongest opposition and fear of reprisal will not threaten their cause.

Women are a part of God's creation. The entire Old Testament speaks most favorably of women under the rule of the patriarchs; women as Sarah and Rebecca are named, and mentioned as being endeared by Abraham and Isaac (Gen. 23:2, 24:67). Women, such as Miriam, sister of Moses, Hannah, Deborah, the prophetess, who delivered Israel from the enemy Sisera (Judges 4) and Queen Esther are mentioned. Others, including Huldah, who was consulted by the high priest Helkiah (2 Kings 22:14).

When David returned from his defeat of the Philistines, there was singing and dancing in the towns and cities by the women (1 Samuel 18). There was freedom and interaction between the males and females.

The ministry of Jesus is noted by the frequent encounters he had with women. Some appeared to have been closer and more intimate than others, however, treated with equity and respect. The contact with the woman of Samaria broke two cultural barriers—a woman, and a Samaritan (John 4). The principle to note is how each was approached and what solution used. The woman at Jacob's well was not from the Jewish community as the sisters from Bethany, Peter's mother-in-law, Jairus' daughter and the woman who pressed through the crowd to touch the master's robe. But, the Samaritan woman found total acceptance. A special tribute was given to the woman with the alabaster box of ointment. Her critics viewed the act as wasteful and without purpose. Jesus gave a high priority and endorsement: "She hath done what she could. . . . " (John 14:1–8).[1]

> Woman took an active and even prominent part in the history of the Early Church, from the very time of our Lord's ascension. They were present at

> the first meeting of the disciples after that occurrence, for the writer of the Acts of the Apostles says that the disciples "continued in prayer and supplication with the women and Mary the mother of Jesus. . . . " (Acts 1:14)
>
> Women also were quick to receive the Gospel news and were among the first converts of the Apostles' preaching: "multitudes of both men and women" being added to the Lord (Acts 5:14; and the deacon, Philip baptized many in Samaria, Acts 8:12).

These Christian women were supportive and showed unusual strength under the persecution by Saul. Saul followed the early believers throughout Jerusalem, going into homes arresting and putting them into prison.

Saul followed this course of tyranny until his conversion, which gave him a new direction. Where he had given chase and wrought havoc, now he had a declaration of deliverance and salvation. He went about gathering converts rather than convicts.

Lydia was Paul's first convert, after he moved on to Macedonia. She first heard him at Philippi. Lydia was a charitable and benevolent woman, with a profession. Also, she can be characterized as a "Business Woman," a seller of purple. These women in the early church were uniquely skilled and gifted. Dorcas with her dedicated needle and crafts served in her community visiting and ministering to the poor,

> Upon her death all her neighbors held up her name to praise, bringing forth practical evidence of her good works; and so much Peter impressed with her Christian character and example that he prayed she might be raised up again, which prayer God answered (Acts 9).[2]

The ministries of these women were not just confined to the sick and other charitable deeds, but carried over into the ministry of teaching. Priscilla, who labored with her husband Aquila, was cited for her instruction, and contrasted with Apollos' eloquence (Acts 18:24–26).

Other resourceful women are mentioned by name as helpers in spreading the gospel. Phebe took letters for St. Paul from Corinth to Rome, and Persis "labored" much in the Lord (Romans 16).

The services of Christian women have spanned centuries. Biblical and secular history has given them a place of honor and distinction. Their profiles may not have been highly mirrored during these times, due to changes in the development of the Church. Nevertheless, their position endured the rough and rugged terrains with faith. But the burning zeal for God's service kept the flame aglow, igniting a spark among women transcending many faiths, cultures and ethnic origins. The Church symbolizes a fortress and is able to stand in the face of adversities. The only authority that women have for freedom within the Church is found in God's will as given in His Word. God's will, "Will" be done on earth, and surely, the thing we can do is to prayerfully await the working out of His purpose in His own time.

Black women have been an integral and essential part of church life from the earliest days of the religious experience in this country. They have given unreservedly of their time, energy, skills, talents and intelligence to the creating of the Black Church,

> The Negro Church was a multi-purpose agency, serving not only as a temple of worship, but as a social center, a meeting place for reformist groups, a sanctuary for escaped slaves, and a school house.[3]

We must consider that their role in the Church has varied through the unfolding of its history, but remained constant. Too often their contributions have gone unrecorded and unrecognized. These persons, if listed, would reflect a gem studded mosaic of deeds, with dedication and commitment.

The role of Black women in the Church vividly portrays some of the distinguishing features of women in past centuries. Where comparisons are cited they are not set to measure validity or rank. Rather they unleash the dynamics of ones own resources to work within the bonds of fellowship. Moving beyond this thrust, and accepting as non-theological interpretations of a term, taken from John's Second Letter—"to the Elect Lady—"[4]

The role of Black women is uniquely diverse, because of the span of backgrounds and cultures. There is unity in these diversities, giving place for aspirations and putting into place a visionary productivity with fulfillment and hope. It is not surprising that in Puritan New England the only Negro who attracted wide attention was the deeply religious Phillis Wheatley, born in Senegal, West Africa:

> Phillis had been brought as a young girl to Boston, where she was purchased by John Wheatley and quickly won the affection of his family. Phillis learned easily how to read and write, and showed marked aptitude for study and reflection.[5]

Phillis was an internationally known poet by twenty years old. She wrote on various subjects, as Religious and Moral. She advocated the cause of her people and put all efforts to win their freedom. She did not know the hardship and ravages of slavery and felt a burning zeal for the deliverance of all people. Despite poor health at a very early age, and a failed marriage, her contributions were outstanding and received with acclaim by General George Washington, for a poem she wrote in his honor, "*The Father of His Country*" and "*Liberty and Peace*."[6]

These poems illustrate her devout character and how early Christian teachings influenced her life.

"On Being Brought from Africa to America"

"Twas mercy brought me from my pagan land,
Taught my benighted soul to understand
That there's a God, and there's a Saviour too;
Once I Redemption neither sought or knew
Some view our sable race with scornful eye,

> "Their color is a diabolic die."
> Remember, Christians, Negroes, be black as Cain.
> May be refined, and join the angelic train.[7]

The Black Church, born in protest, was given militant support by zealous women abolitionists as Harriet Tubman and Sojourner Truth. These women were born slaves, and desired that the yoke of bondage be broken and human rights and dignity be given to mankind. Both women were deeply spiritual and religious.

> Harriet Tubman, was a woman of action, but in the times of stress her favorite prayer was, 'Lord you have been with me through six troubles. Be with me in the seventh.'[8]

Tubman and Truth were divinely inspired, neither were considered literate, but their "mother wit" led them through opened doors, and upon a road of fame. Their names are recorded among great Americans. The paths they led were overshadowed with perils and dangerous threats were often made upon their lives. However unsafe their travels, the faith and belief in the mission they were upon led them through the darkest of despair into a safe haven to a better day.

These earlier heroines reflect the true spirit of the Negro women who have shared in building the bulwark of the Black Church. Toiling the fields, the drudgery of domestic services, blended with their own responsibilities of family and community. The status of these women differs very little from that of today—widowed, single parents (does not always suggest unwedded), or broken families. The sociological implication is not to define or analyze, but to acknowledge that the Church community has confronted such problems since the genesis of the church, as we perceive it to be an organization that emerged as a fortress. This protective fellowship became the channel for socioeconomic, educational, political and religious identification.

These efforts found support among the advocates for social justice and human rights. Educational opportunities for women were not as plentiful as for men. The early schools founded were to train men for the ministry and as teachers. However, young women, not at the same rate and more often not at the same schools, were able to find opportunities for schooling. These barriers did not stifle their desire to learn.

> With the rise of independent churches, the intellectual development of the race progressed slowly. Most churches served as weekday schools and houses of worship on Sunday. Hence, early blacks experienced the oneness of their churches and schools.
>
> Moreover, the progress of independent black Baptist churches gave new momentum to other emerging institutions of intellectual and cultural development. As noted, the denominational schools, primary through college, grew up in direct relations to local churches. This was especially true of the primary and secondary schools.[9]

One of the first black Baptist women to venture into the mission field of Africa was Miss Nora A. Gordon. Born in Columbus, Georgia, in 1866, Nora attended the public schools in La Grange, Georgia and entered Spelman School for Girls in the fall term of 1882. While attending the seminary she was converted and joined a Baptist church in Atlanta. Nora Gordon became very active in the mission of the church and community. She taught Sunday School and organized a variety of programs for her students and their families. While involved at home, Miss Gordon, "experienced a call or inspiration to work on the foreign fields of Africa." She obeyed the call and set sail to Africa where she labored until 1893.[10]

The Baptist Women of Florida sent Emma B. Delaney, First African Baptist Church, Fernandina, Florida, to Spelman College to be trained for mission work. Sponsored by the Foreign Mission Board of the National Baptist Convention, Miss Delaney left the United States in 1901 for British East Central Africa. She founded several schools in Central and West Africa including the Providence Industrial School. Miss Delaney, one of Florida's distinguished daughters, labored in the foreign fields until her death in 1920.[11]

The list of women is both illuminating and inspiring. It pictures Christian women from many occupations and professions. Mothers, educators, celebrated artists, and business entrepreneurs, each bringing something different and special to affirm their dedication and commitment to the service and mission of the church. S. Willie Layton, V. M. Broughton and Dr. M. A. B. Fuller each brought something special to the church.

S. Willie Layton, lived in Philadelphia, Pennsylvania. She was elected in 1900 as the first president of the Women's Department of the National Baptist Convention, U.S.A. Layton was involved with the social, civic and religious movements in our country. Ms. V. M. Broughton was one of the first graduates of Fisk University. A distinguished teacher of the Bible, and writer, Broughton was one of the Founders of Howe Institute.[12] Dr. M. A. B. Fuller was born in Texas. She has been associated with many profitable business enterprises. Dr. Fuller will be remembered for her witnessing to her "experience of God's Saving Grace and her acceptance of Jesus as the Lord of her Life." She was a musician, elementary school teacher, principal and business woman. Dr. Fuller was elected in 1923 at Shreveport, Louisiana, in an annual session of the National Baptist Women's Convention of America. She held this office for over forty years. "Dr. Fuller was a reservoir of good will."[13]

Mrs. Mattie J. Shaw Cohen, founder of the *Florida Watchman,* the Sun Light Pall Bearers Charitable Society. With her husband, Reverend Nathan Shaw, she pioneered Negro education in rural sections of Florida and "established the Ocala Theological Seminary and Kindergarten and Grammar School." Mattie Cohen taught in the public schools at Yulee, Citronell, Dunnellon and Ocala, Florida. She pursued higher education at Florida Normal Industrial, St. Augustine and Florida A&M College in Tallahassee. The school system did not overshadow her services in the area of Christian and Missionary Education. She will be remembered as a positive force in the several departments in her church. She served as Superintendent of the Church School, and conducted Bible Studies at the Seminary under the Second Bethlehem Baptist Association.[14]

Agnes Lewter Dean, a Baptist minister's daughter, found a model from within her family. Two of her three brothers accepted calls to the ministry, and pastored churches in the Progressive Baptist Convention of Florida. Agnes took on another form of leadership. Serving in the local church began early in her childhood after affirming her faith and belief in Jesus. Mrs. Dean performed many duties in the Youth and Junior Women's Convention with credit and success. The year of 1945 was a breakthrough for her when she was elected to the office of President of the Junior Women's Convention. Mrs. Dean's ministry extended beyond her native state. She was appointed in September 1949, by the President of the Junior Women's and Young Women's Auxiliary as Regional Director of the National Baptist Convention of America. The area included Alabama, Florida, Georgia and Mississippi. Combined with this office for nineteen years, she also served as Secretary-Treasurer for the Junior Women.[15]

Agnes moved from the Junior Department in the State Convention in 1963 to the Senior Women's where she was elected Fourth Vice President. She filled this position for nine years. These years were more than the capacity to carry out a job description or a perfunctory task. Her leadership style appeared to flow from her deepest inner self, reflecting her relationship with a risen and ascended Saviour. The effectiveness of her ministry found expression through opportunities she used to give of herself. Agnes found fulfillment when she was recommended by the retiring President, and elected in Belle Glade, Florida, in 1971, to the office of President of the Progressive Baptist State Senior Women's Convention of Florida. Even though her tenure was the second shortest in the history of the Women's Convention, Mrs. Dean set a standard of excellence. This quality of leadership impacted the lives of many women who are still actively involved.[16]

Women in the local church have many orientations for witnessing, and sharing their creative ideas and skills. We never know how one will be directed. In November 19, 1927, Mrs. R. C. Robinson, a member of the Harmony Baptist Church, Lakeland, Florida, translated a vision into one of the first, an organization of ushers of all churches in Polk County. A spirit of unity prevailed. Support came from pastors in recognition of the concerns of a Christian woman, bringing together an Inter Faith group, often called "Door Keepers." It is not where we serve, but how. Mrs. Robinson found relevancy in her gift, and from this, she found opportunity to bring into the mainstream an auxiliary whose members may not have gone beyond the local church in isolated areas.[17]

The organizational plan presented a shared management concept. The President of the host Usher Board would preside at the session. This would give each President a chance to experience and interact with larger groups.

> This unusual church organization has had a very distinguished record in its existence. In tracing its activities from its beginning, there has been outstanding work in the field of religious performance by this organization.
>
> Through untiring efforts, Mrs. Robinson, was successful in doing so, until today they have reached their eleventh year of service to the churches. The dignity that they have exemplified in performing their duties is well displayed where ever they are on duty.[18]

One of the unique characteristics of this organization is that wherever the Convention is held every three months, the proceeds raised are left to the church which entertains the Conventions. All expenses are underwritten by the Ushers Union.[19]

Johnnie Jean Davis Barnes, lived in a community that was termed a model for building a strong family structure. The community was a plan of the American

Agricultural Chemical Company. The principle upon which the company was designed was to provide the environment with the basic needs: regular employment, homes, school and church. Families working for the company would find in place a base for building a strong value system to help shape the destiny of their children. The church was the center of life in Pierce, Florida, where Johnnie Jean was born and lived through adulthood.[20]

John and Emmaline Davis gave their daughter every advantage to grow spiritually. And they sought every available opportunity for her educational and physical maturity as well. The family did not send the child to Church School and worship services. She was taken, along with another daughter, who preceded Johnnie in death. Johnnie's earliest recall of the local church's contributing to the support of the District and State work was by accompanying her mother to these meetings. The influence of the family chartered a course which led into paths of rewarding services for Johnnie. She followed closely in her mother's steps by becoming active with the District Sunday School and Baptist Young Peoples Union Convention, District Association, State and National Conventions. These involvements, did not preclude her leadership at the St. Paul Baptist Church, where she gave a life of dedicated and committed services.

Johnnie Jean Davis Barnes merits many credits. The E. Armster Memorial Scholarship was a direct beneficiary of her total self. Her training and experiences in the field of education, civic and social organizations were of value in planning this project as was her Christian Education philosophy.[21]

Mary H. Whitehurst, wife of the late Reverend Harold B. Whitehurst, counts among her greatest accomplishments and honors that "she is a child of the King." Mary's love for music started as early as when she made her own piano by using a chair, and another chair for her seat. This aspiration was a motivational drive until she was accepted by her first music teacher, the late Mrs. Irene H. Davis. At the age of fourteen Mary made her first appearance in a musical program.[22]

Mrs. Whitehurst joined Shiloh Baptist Church, Orlando, Florida, as a child. There she embarked upon an uninterrupted vocation in church music, serving choirs at all age levels. She also has represented the Youth Department at District Sunday School and Baptist Young Peoples Union, before its present reorganization, (Baptist Training Union). Mary's music ministry at Shiloh covered a period of more than fifty years. Mary's faith has been a testimony to her unwavering resolve to stand fast in the Lord. During her years as a parent she filled her role, growing with her children as they advanced from one school level to another. To combine a bi-vocational career was not an easy feat, Mary continued to give of her time to the ministry of music as she taught music in the Orange County School District. These years were marked several times with serious periods of illnesses, but Mary kept her mind set on her goal. Mrs. Whitehurst's record is unheralded. Her performance was not a "juggling" act, but one of love and dedication. With artistry, brilliancy and efficiency much of this discipline was reflected in the various groups under her directorship. Presently at Shiloh she is musician for Choir Number Three, Director of the Mass Choir and Chairman of the Music Department. Mrs. Whitehurst is a past Dean of Music of Congress Number One, Auxiliary to the First South Florida Association, Musician/Director of the Brotherhood Jubilee Singers, State Music Director of the State Sunday School and Baptist Training Convention and The State Music Director for the Progressive Baptist Convention for seventeen years.[23]

Linda Carol Lewis uses the "market place" to share her faith. Linda's occupation as an Accounts Payable Auditor with the Agri-Chemicals Corporation brings her in contact with many people. The interaction on the job with other employees is counted a blessing. Linda said, "I introduce the wonders of Jesus the Christ." Linda Lewis is an active member of the Galilee Missionary Baptist Church, Fort Meade, Florida. She teaches a Sunday School Class for Adult Ladies, Directs Choir Number 2, is Director of the Vacation Bible School, and serves as

Church Reporter, and Vice-President of the Junior Women's Ministry.[24]

Her activities are from local to national:

> President of Congress #5 Junior Women's Auxiliary of the First South Florida Missionary Baptist Association
>
> Dean of the Workshop of the First South Florida Missionary Baptist Association, Junior Women's Auxiliary
>
> Past President Junior Women's Auxiliary of the Progressive Missionary and Education State Convention of Florida[25]

Linda presently is President of the Junior Women's Auxiliary of the National Baptist Convention of America, Inc. Linda's ministry is an example of the vitality that young women bring to the church when they attune their lives to the call to service.

Gladys C. Vaught's image is reflective of many wife, husband and family bonds, associated with the ministries of the Progressive Convention. To trace her movements through the several auxiliaries, and define the bonding, without mentioning the name of her late husband, Charles Sr., would be a very difficult task. Here, again, we started with a basic principle and that is: "woman as given to be a 'help meet'." The relationship then can be complementary and supportive. This partnership is not isolated, but evidenced by Biblical examples. Brother Charles, Sr., was always there sharing with Gladys in joint efforts.

Gladys' Christian life is built around her church, Second Missionary Baptist Church, Jacksonville, Florida. Much of her Christian Education training has its roots deeply embedded in the history of Second Missionary. Gladys often has been heard to say: "I have been working with the Senior Women in mission since a child. The Senior Women's group was all we had so the children met with the adults. I did not move from one level to another. I was taught the mission program of the church. Her on the job training was through performing tasks that were related. Along with the training was the Bible class, and sewing circle."[26]

This source of nurturing prepared Gladys Vaught for a fruitful and productive life at Second Missionary. It also widened her horizon and extended the boundaries of her spiritual outreach. Investing in a youth will return manifold. Gladys was a moving force in the early days of the Sunday School and Baptist Young Peoples Union State Convention. She was in East Florida and Bethany District Association. Inadequate facilities, little, if any, equipment or materials, whatever was at hand, Gladys used the available supplies to instruct those who came seeking better methods to design educational programs within the local church. Mrs. Vaught's quest for knowledge led to her involvement in Study Courses in the National Congress. There she earned credits toward certification in several disciplines in the Department of Christian Education. She found time for continuing education through Florida Normal Industrial Institute, and later established a Real Estate Office for sales and rentals.[27]

Her services gave her the distinction of holding many key positions in the East Bethany District Association, the State Sunday School and Baptist Training Union, the National Baptist Congress, the Senior Women's Department of the Progressive Missionary and Educational Baptist State Convention of Florida, Inc., and with honor, the Vice President of the National Baptist Convention of America, Inc.[28]

Christian Women's potentials can not be estimated merely by citing contributions made through their involvement in any one area of the total ministries of the church or entities in a Convention. The real source of becoming involved is through the enabling power of God. The fellowship of the believers provides a reservoir of gifts that can be drawn upon for the enrichment of their ministries. Sometimes the absence of this force can create an impersonal climate that is so powerful that one can become lost. At this point the fellowship ceases to be effective in providing the needed support for continued growth as a Christian.

Sister Lillie Mae Bogan may have had encounters in her years of endeavors in this "warfare," but she has remained true to her commitment. She found that change or reordering one's priorities was not a loss of one's real self, neither an assignment to a lower rank. The marks of a Christian are so stratified within the personality of the believer, that they will come through. So it was when Sister Bogan became a member of the Progressive Baptist State Convention, at the merger of the Missionary and Education Convention of West Florida. Her leadership skills at Emmanuel Missionary Baptist Church, Pensacola, Florida, had preceded her. It was quickly seen, that there was a spirit of caring, and sharing. She affirmed her faith through a positive witness and assumed as well responsibilities shared by those making up the fellowship. Sister Bogan leads the Deaconess Council, a group of dedicated women within the convention. The services of the women, like those of the President, are not limited to this one ministry. Many are enrolled in the Senior Women's Workshop in the District Associations, the State Congress of Christian Education and are regular attenders of the National Baptist Congress of Christian Workers and the National Baptist Convention of America, Inc.[29]

"God is working His purposes out through a long history and has generously allowed us a part." The Deaconess Council is leaving a legacy in training and teaching, sharing with the local church a plan of action to help reenforce its ministry. "Finally, we have the privilege of the Spirit of God living permanently in each of us. We can cooperate with Him and discover truth and ultimate reality (1 John 2:27). We can ask Him for guidance in all the decisions of life. We can draw upon His unlimited power to live victoriously. We can yield ourselves to Him and discover gifts and callings beyond our human expectations."[30]

Aquilla Mae Jackson Morgan was likely to be an achiever when she was admitted to the Public Schools in Palmetto, Florida. She advanced from elementary through high school, graduating from Lincoln Memorial. At this level, she had shown great potential, and continued her education at the University of South Florida, earning a Bachelor of Arts degree, graduating with honors. Mrs. Morgan's teaching career has been a successful one in the Hillsborough County School District. She is a teacher at Wimauma Elementary School. Since her employment she has added a Master of Arts in education and presently is in a Doctoral program at the University of Tampa. These accomplishments have meaning for Aquilla and her family. Because of the early guidance and encouragement that her parents and friends gave her, she moves forward with persistence.[31]

But at the age of nine, this child came into an awareness from the same family's guidance, that Jesus' love was extended to her, if she would open her heart to Him. Aquilla said: "I was taken to Sunday School, taught at home, and I made the decision to accept Jesus as my Savior. I was converted and baptized by Reverend G. W. Jones at the St. Mary Missionary Baptist Church, Parrish, Florida." Parrish was Aquilla's place of birth. Her parents were the late Charlie and Carrie Bell Jackson. It was at St. Mary that she began her work as a child. Her first office was president of a Children's Choir followed by President of the Children's Department of the Mt. Pilgrim District Association.[32]

Aquilla had several role models, "Mothers in the Lord." "I give thanks for the motivators in my early life: the late Nina Covington McNeil, my grandmother, and Rachael Jackson, my aunt who reared me. She taught me how to pray, took me to church, and instructed me in the doctrine and discipline of the church. The others were the late Rebecca Williamson, Maudie Fowler, and the late Ola Mae Sims, who took me places that I had to go to attend meetings. And the entire St. Mary Missionary Baptist Church."[33]

The years of maturity brought Sister Aquilla into positions of responsibility within the church. She served as church clerk, President of the Junior Women's Mission, Sunday School Teacher, Church Reporter, President of Ushers Board No. 1, Church Program Coordinator, and President of the Pastor's Aid Board. After Sister Aquilla's election to President of the Junior Women's Department of the Mt. Pilgrim District Association, she gave leadership that inspired these first time ventures; A Queens Contest for Educational Funds, a campsite for the Mt. Pilgrim District Association, Workshops, Fellowship Hour, Visitation Program for nursing homes, preparing fruit baskets, organizing a choir to sing at President's Hour at the Mt. Pilgrim District Association Women's Department, the Junior Women's Project to promote Souvenir Booklets, and a Calendar of Events.[34]

After coming into the Senior Women's Convention, Mrs. Morgan continued to give her creative leadership to the Youth and Children of Congress No. 3, an Auxiliary of Mt. Pilgrim District Association. In addition, she served as Corresponding Secretary and Third Vice President. Mrs. Aquilla Mae Morgan presently is President of the Senior Women's Mission Society of St. Mary Baptist Church, Teacher of the Adult Sunday School Class, Church Reporter, Member of Usher Board No. 1. She also prepares the Church's Bulletin Board Monthly. Mrs. Morgan is District President of the Senior Women's Department of the Mt. Pilgrim District Baptist Association, Bible Teacher for Congress No. 3, third Vice President of the Progressive Missionary and Educational Baptist State Convention of Florida, Inc., and the Secretary for the Youth and Children Camp at Florida Memorial College. Her philosophy is: "to work while it is day and only what you do for Christ will last. I believe in giving my time, talents and tithes. Let me help somebody as I pass along this way. My favorite saying is: To God Be The Glory."[35]

This is reminiscent of the faithful workers who have gone on to receive their rewards. Not just from one church or area, but like hosts of unnamed believers who saw the beginning of the Progressive Baptist State Convention evolve from a concept. Many of the women whose names are chronologically in this historical representation have followed in the "footsteps" of family.

Doris Catherine English-Copeland has found her ministry similar to that of her late mother, Angelenia Hardy. Doris accepted Christ at a young age and was baptized at Shiloh Missionary Baptist Church of Dunedin,

Florida, under the leadership of the late Reverend W. A. Harrison. In a very unusual employment situation, the New Hope Missionary Baptist Church employs her as Secretary. She has been a member for twenty-three years. With her duties as secretary, she is committed to her stewardship as a believer. A Sunday School teacher, instructor of Baptist Training Union, Chorister, Vice President of Usher Board No. 2, and a member of the Budget, Education, and Pastor's Aid Committees, Deacons and Ministers Wives Ministry, President of Senior Women's Missionary Society and Past President of Young Women's Auxiliary and Junior Women's Society, Doris Copeland gives unselfishly of her time. Even though her involvement in the internal affairs are many and varied, she actively attends prayer meetings, teacher's meetings and Bible Study.[36]

She is President of the Senior Women, Past Youth Counselor of the Local Congress, and an Instructor in the Graduate-Evangelical Training Association. In addition, Mrs. Copeland is an Administrative Assistant to the Mt. Pilgrim Missionary Baptist Association and Past President of Young Women's Auxiliary and Junior Women's Society. She also has served in the Progressive Missionary and Educational Baptist State Convention as Financial Secretary and Treasurer to the Senior Women's Ministry. Mrs. Copeland's training in Business Secretary School in Newark, New Jersey, and the H. R. Block Tax School and Continued Education at Hillsborough Community College has made her ministry in Financial Departments of our Conventions of value. Such training has also given her many opportunities to perform in "key positions." These services have been extended to the National Baptist Convention of America.[37]

The minutes of the Women's Conventions, State and National, reflect the years of service that Ruby F. Herndon has given to spreading the good news of God's Salvation to mankind. Mrs. Herndon is not a "rolling stone." She settles in and attacks her tasks with force, vigor, and determination. This trait has been the source of her strength, and as a compass for her direction.

Ruby was off to the city, Jacksonville, Florida, in 1941 to attend Walker Business College, graduating in 1943. Motivated at an early age to prepare herself for a career in communications, she did not find it hard to adjust, study and seize every opportunity.

Leaving a family of eleven siblings, and facing a larger environment as compared to the hometown, Haines City, Florida, appeared not to deter Ruby from her goal. After completing her training, she immediately found employment in an office as a secretary, one block from her college. The job lasted for 49 years.

She was hired for the position by the Most Worshipful Union Grand Lodge of the Free and Accepted Masons, Jurisdiction of Florida, Prince Hall Affiliation—The Masonic Temple.

Her quality of character, devotion and commitment has its highest visibility when viewed from the equal years that Ruby has given to her church and its ministries. Her secretarial and organizational skills have been dedicated to God. Her labor started at home, Mount Sinai Baptist Church, Jacksonville. She has been secretary to the board of trustees for over 30 years. Since 1949, she has published weekly the church bulletins, is a member of the choir, led the mission women of the East Florida & Bethany Association for more than 18 years, and filled several offices in the Progressive Baptist State Convention Women's Department before being elected president in Pensacola, Florida, March 1992.

Mrs. Herndon is nationally known. She is active in the Congress of Christian Workers and Treasurer, Senior Women of the National Baptist Convention of America, Inc. She is also involved in several women's Masonic organizations, National Council of Negro Women, and serves as trustee of Florida Memorial College, Miami.

The Women's Convention of the Progressive Missionary and Educational Baptist State Convention has as its president a woman of vision and spiritual fortitude. We are looking toward soaring to a higher level of service under her leadership.[38]

Mrs. Maudie Mae Anderson Fowler was the third child born to Simon and Tina Jones Anderson on June 30, 1911, in Dothan, Alabama. During her early childhood her parents moved to Cairo, Georgia, where she attended school in Grady County. She was converted in Grady County and united with the Macedonia Missionary Baptist Church.

Sister Fowler moved to Tampa from Polk County in 1951 and united with the St. Matthew Missionary Baptist Church under the leadership of the late Reverend R. D. Dawson. She was united in matrimony to the late Deacon Carranza W. Fowler and lived happily with him until his death in December 1989.

Sister Fowler gave of her life to the work of the Kingdom of God as she gave of herself to the women's missionary involvement at her local church, the St. Matthew Missionary Baptist Church. There, she served as President of the Missionary Society, a Sunday School teacher and organizer of the Pearl Stokes Circle. She also served as president of the Senior Women's Auxiliary of the Mt. Pilgrim District Association for forty-two years. Other offices held by Sister Fowler were financial secretary, Vice President and President of the Senior Women's Auxiliary of the Progressive Missionary and Educational Baptist State Convention of Florida, Inc., a member of the executive committee of the Senior Women's Missionary Union of the National Baptist Convention of America, Inc., a trustee of Florida Memorial College, Miami, Florida. Sister Fowler traveled extensively representing her district and state conventions throughout these United States and several other continents. She attended the World Baptist Alliance in Miami, Florida, Seoul, Korea and Stockholm, Sweden. She was a District Deputy of the Lily Grand Lodge. Early on the morning of Monday, August 15, 1994, at 3:30 she moved from this life unto eternal rest.[39]

Dorothy E. Borroughs, accepted a call to leadership, when she was named the first President of the M. A. B. Fuller Mission Group—Senior Mission No. 2. She served in this capacity from March 1969 to 1990. The growth of this auxiliary was nurtured in prayer, dedication and commitment.

The motivation to become involved appeared to have been a personal resolve by the newly formed group to set attainable goals, and draw from them experiences that would be meaningful in planning programs.

Dorothy did not set sail without being fully equipped for the voyage. Her zeal sparked a flame, and the group reflected a glow of readiness to move. "Most women are discontented with limited opportunities; they desire to bring glory to God in a wider sphere. The ministries of Evangelism, Christian Education, Home and Foreign Missions gives that opportunity for women great or small to exercise their God given talents in the church, community and around the world."[40]

Sister Borroughs envisioned the breadth of her leadership and service as the scope of missions is global. However, the urgency to serve, started at home. This was evidenced by her participation in her home church, Bethel Baptist Institutional, Jacksonville and the East Florida and Bethany Association.

The leadership and support of the women of Senior Mission No. 2, were recognized several times by the National Baptist Convention of America, Senior Women's No. 2., Dr. Hattie L. E. Williams. The credits were: Outstanding Contributions to the Auxiliary.[41]

Dorothy Borroughs has made a place for herself among the loyal devoted women in the Christian arena. Her present position as Advisor to the Matrons, substantiates her spiritual and emotional maturity. It is also a role by which she can share the richness of her experiences.

Amelia E. Houston, was elected the sixth president of the Women's Convention in April 1973. Mrs. Houston's rich background in business and management was an asset, in that she was credited with an appeal to the district association, that increased the financial contributions to Donation Day. More local churches became involved. Mrs. Houston also brought an awareness of the share each should take in support of our church related school.

This type of leadership was effective, and led to the participation of more women. As a result, several new areas were explored and some problems were resolved. Some of the operations were:

Pre-planning sessions (January before the annual Session in March)
Retreat (Cooperative Program with Florida Baptist Women's Mission Union)
Reorganization of the Senior Women's Mission Workshops
Two Sessions a year: a. March—at the Annual Meeting; b. July—at the State Sunday and Baptist Training Congress of Christian Education.
The appointment of Field Coordinators.
Expanded the Camp Program at Florida Memorial (a joint project between the General Baptist State Convention and the Progressive Baptist.
Revised the plans for recruiting youths for Summer Camp
Instituted a referral plan by which tuition and transportation could be given to families in need of help, within the local church.
Accepted responsibility to provide an equal share of Camp Staff.
Supervised equitably the overall operations of day to day camp activities
Shared in the planning and building of the Susie B. Holly Religious Center for Worship
The Women of the Progressive Baptist State Convention contributed in excess of over $800,000 to Florida Memorial College for Donation Day from 1972–1986.

Sister Houston's leadership mobilized women into a bond of fellowship that brought them into a relationship with their sisters of different ethnic backgrounds. Their travels extended beyond the district, state and national meeting. In August 1975, the Women of the Progressive

Baptist joined with others en route to Stockholm, Sweden to attend the Baptist World Alliance.

Her forceful impact was positive and direct. She gave freely of herself and time. She returned much of her material blessing to help carry out her ministry of service. Mrs. Amelia Houston will be remembered for her long years of dedicated services to the growth and development of the women's mission endeavors within our church.[42]

We usually think of the corporate boardroom, high-tech fields and related areas as having the brightest and most articulated minds. Rarely do we give thought to the diversities of talents and skills that are found within the Christian Fellowship for the edification of the Body of Christ. It is only when these gifts are given over, too, and set into motion under the empowerment of divine guidance that they are recognizable.

They are many examples that could be used to shed light on this specific case in point. But, here, we want to cite an individual who, over a long period of years, has represented the Progressive Missionary and Educational Baptist State Convention from her youth.

> When I call to remembrance the unfeigned faith that is in thee, which dwelt first in thy grandmother Lois, and thy mother Eunice; and I am persuaded that in thee also. 2nd Timothy 1:5

Barbara Wright has been an invaluable asset. Her services have been performed with precision and dignity. To characterize and personify her place, we may think of her as Ruth's Loyalty; Deborah's Leadership; Sarah's Faithfulness; Esther's Diplomacy; Lydia's Business Skills; Priscilla's Teacher of the word; Phebe's Dedication; Mary of Bethany's Hospitality; Queen of Sheba's Beauty and Charm.

The successful coordination and day to day operations of the several ministries of our Convention's projects and involvements at large have gone forth because of Barbara's administrative ability and excellent human relations and personnel skills.

The potentials of women in the Black Church have not come into its fullest view. A nurturing community can do much to help the church develop an educational program, dealing with issues and problems. This resource could become a base to draw persons who are committed to larger goals in the Body of Christ. This curriculum would not exclude the young male. But opportunities for young women are traditionally more likely to be fewer. However, the door should be open for whomever would accept.

The role of women is changing in the field of Christian Education. This parallels other careers and professions. Women are excelling in the area of higher education, serving as presidents of church-related colleges, as engineers, doctors, judges, astronauts, presidents of banks and other financial firms. Should we not, then, see that young women, such as Barbara Wright, with their many talents and abilities, are encouraged and equipped to fill church offices and ministries. For example, we are without a Ministry for Social and Supportive Services for the Black child within our fellowship.

> The highway to the slightest measurable change of any kind travels by many blocks that can deter and lead away from the goals desired. Indeed the highway may run into the stumbling blocks. But the voice of education within the church must ever sound the clarion command: "Forward!" Past failures and frustrations must not lead to defeatism. Defeatism and ignorance are the greatest of the blocks that can deter the Black Church in its mission toward helping its sons and daughters in their search for identity.[43]

The women noted above are but a few of the thousands who have played a role in building and sustaining the Black Church and the Progressive Missionary and Educational Baptist Association. It is time that their contributions are recognized.

Endnotes

CHAPTER 8

1. F. D. Bacon, *Women In The Church,* (Lutterworth Press, London and Redhill, 1946), p. 15.

2. Bacon, *Women In The Church,* p. 16.

3. Leslie H. Fishel, Jr., *The Negro American: A Documentary History* (Glenview, Illinois: Scott Foresman, 1967), p. 36; Benjamin Quarles, *The Negro American,* (Baltimore: Morgan State College, 1967), p. 130.

4. "The Lady Elect" in *Women of the Bible* (Gastonia, North Carolina: Goodwill Publishers, 1969).

5. Hughes and Milton, *A Pictorial History of the Negro in America,* pp. 128–129.

6. *Ibid.*

7. *Ibid.*

8. *Ibid.*

9. Fitts, *A History of Black Baptists,* pp. 165–65.

10. Fitts, *A History of Black Baptists,* p. 123.

11. Fitts, *A History of Black Baptists,* pp. 124–25.

12. Smith and O'Neal, *Baptists and Our Nation's Story,* pp. 26, 27, 28; Woman's Missionary and Educational State Convention of Florida, 1890–1941, Historical Facts.

13. Foreign Mission Board National Baptist Convention of America, Inc.,; M. A. B. Fuller's Christmas Offering, Pamphlet.

14. Bruce Ergood, "The Female Protection and The Sun Light: Two Contemporary Negro Mutual Aid Societies," 50 *Florida Historical Quarterly* (July 1971), pp. 25–38; Mattie J. Shaw Cohen, How to Lead: Brief History of Mrs. Mattie J. Shaw Cohen in the *Florida Watchman.*

15. Bentley, *History of the First South Florida Missionary Baptist Association,* pp. 227, 231; Eulogistic Service Program for Agnes L. Dean, Kerney-Wilson Funeral Home, April 14, 1973, Sebring, Florida.

16. Bentley, *History of the First South Florida Missionary Baptist Association,* pp. 227, 231; Eulogistic Service Pro-

gram for Agnes L. Dean, Kerney-Wilson Funeral Home, April 14, 1973, Sebring, Florida.

17. Paul Diggs, "Polk County Ushers Union," Florida Writers' Project, Lakeland, Florida, November 25, 1938.

18. *Ibid.*

19. *Ibid.*

20. Paul Diggs, "A Negro Community—Pierce, Florida," Florida Writers' Project, Lakeland, Florida, December 2, 1938.

21. *Ibid.*

22. Combined Minutes of the Seventy-Third Annual Session of the Progressive Missionary and Educational State Convention of Florida, March 17–22, 1987, p. 82; Combined Minutes of The Golden Jubilee Session of The Progressive Baptist State Convention of Florida, March 18–22, 1964, pp. 7, 8, 11, 130, 132; Autobiography of Mrs. Mary H. Whitehurst, St. John Metropolitan Missionary Baptist Church, Sanford, Florida.

23. Combined Minutes of the Seventy-Third Annual Session of the Progressive Missionary and Educational State Convention of Florida, March 17–22, 1987, p. 82; Combined Minutes of The Golden Jubilee Session of The Progressive Baptist State Convention of Florida, March 18–22, 1964, pp. 7, 8, 11, 130, 132; Autobiography of Mrs. Mary H. Whitehurst, St. John Metropolitan Missionary Baptist Church, Sanford, Florida.

24. Combined Minutes of the Seventy-Fifth Annual Session of the Progressive Missionary and Educational State Convention of Florida, March 22–25, 1989, p. 75; Official Journal National Baptist Convention of America and its Auxiliaries, 1986, p. 261; Official Journal National Baptist Convention of America and its Auxiliaries, 1987, p. 284.

25. Combined Minutes of the Seventy-Fifth Annual Session of the Progressive Missionary and Educational State Convention of Florida, March 22–25, 1989, p. 75; Official Journal National Baptist Convention of America and its Auxiliaries, 1986, p. 261; Official Journal National Baptist Convention of America and its Auxiliaries, 1987, p. 284.

26. Unpublished History of the East Florida and Bethany Missionary Baptist Association; Combined Minutes of The Golden Jubilee Session of The Progressive Baptist State

Convention of Florida, March 18–22, 1964, pp. 63, 65, 68; Combined Minutes of the Seventy-Third Annual Session of the Progressive Missionary and Educational State Convention of Florida, March 17–22, 1987, p. 47.

27. Unpublished History of the East Florida and Bethany Missionary Baptist Association; Combined Minutes of The Golden Jubilee Session of The Progressive Baptist State Convention of Florida, March 18–22, 1964, pp. 63, 65, 68; Combined Minutes of the Seventy-Third Annual Session of the Progressive Missionary and Educational State Convention of Florida, March 17–22, 1987, p. 47.

28. Unpublished History of the East Florida and Bethany Missionary Baptist Association; Combined Minutes of The Golden Jubilee Session of The Progressive Baptist State Convention of Florida, March 18–22, 1964, pp. 63, 65, 68; Combined Minutes of the Seventy-Third Annual Session of the Progressive Missionary and Educational State Convention of Florida, March 17–22, 1987, p. 47.

29. Progressive Missionary and Educational Baptist Convention of Florida, Inc., School of Christian Education 21st Annual Session, Lakeland, Florida, July 19, 1994, Banquet Awards Program; Official Journal of the Seventy-Sixth Annual Session of the Progressive Missionary and Educational Baptist State Convention of Florida, Inc. and Its Auxiliaries, 1990, pp. 104–108.

30. Progressive Missionary and Educational Baptist Convention of Florida, Inc., School of Christian Education 21st Annual Session, Lakeland, Florida, July 19, 1994, Banquet Awards Program; Official Journal of the Seventy-Sixth Annual Session of the Progressive Missionary and Educational Baptist State Convention of Florida, Inc. and Its Auxiliaries, 1990, pp. 104–108.

31. Combined Minutes of the Mt. Pilgrim Missionary Baptist Association, November 9–13, 1977, pp. 44–45; Biographical Profile.

32. Combined Minutes of the Mt. Pilgrim Missionary Baptist Association, November 9–13, 1977, pp. 44–45; Biographical Profile.

33. Combined Minutes of the Mt. Pilgrim Missionary Baptist Association, November 9–13, 1977, pp. 44–45; Biographical Profile.

34. Combined Minutes of the Mt. Pilgrim Missionary Baptist Association, November 9–13, 1977, pp. 44–45; Biographical Profile.

35. Combined Minutes of the Mt. Pilgrim Missionary Baptist Association, November 9–13, 1977, pp. 44–45; Biographical Profile.

36. Official Journal of the Seventy-Sixth Annual Session of the Progressive Missionary and Educational Baptist State Convention of Florida, Inc. and Its Auxiliaries, 1990, p. 64; Biographical Profile.

37. Biographical Profile.

38. Jacksonville Florida Times Union, 1993.

39. This biographical sketch was taken from the "Home Going Celebration for Maudie Mae Anderson Fowler, Saturday, August 20, 1994."

40. Dr. Fannie C. Thompson, *The 1984 Guide and Program Woman's Home and Foreign Mission Societies,* (Nashville: National Baptist Publishing Board, 1984), p. 5.

41. Tenth Year History Book of Mission No. 2. Auxiliary To The Progressive Missionary and Educational Convention. March 1979. Compiled by the Staff—Dorothy E. Borroughs, President, p. 2.

42. From the Director's of the Workshop, Annual Report, July 1985, Marianna, Florida; The School of Christian Education, Progressive Baptist State Convention, Altermese S. Bentley.

43. Vivenna H. Salley, "Blocks That Deter" in Earl R. Riggins. *To You Who Teach In The Black Church: Essays on Christian Education In the Black Church* (Nashville: National Baptist Publishing Board, 1972), p. 21.

PHOTO SECTION

Progressive Missionary and Educational Baptist State Convention of Florida, Inc.

Rev. Robert H. Pittman
1913–1915

PRESIDENTS

Dr. John E. Ford
1915–1920

Rev. Laurence N. Anderson
1920–1922

Rev. C. J. Smith
1922–1951

Rev. James Carl Sams
1951–1985

PRESIDENTS

Rev. F. G. Hilton, Interim
1985–1986

Rev. Henry T. Rhim
1986–

Rev. E. B. Williams
First Vice President

Rev. N. S. Sanders
Second Vice President

VICE PRESIDENTS

Rev. W. M. Davis
Third Vice President

Rev. H. H. Wynn
Fourth Vice President

Recording Secretary
Rev. H. C. McCray, Panama City

Second Recording Secretary
Rev. K. Tyrone Turner, Bartow

OFFICERS

Treasurer
Rev. Price Wilson
Chipley

Financial Secretary
Rev. L. Norris, Jr.
Lakeland

Corresponding Secretary
Rev. J. L. Jones, Lake Wales

Parliamentarian
Rev. S. L. Thigpen, Fort Walton Beach

OFFICERS

Vice President
Senior Women
Ida M. Spires, Bonifay

Director of Music
Mrs. Betty Sanders, Lakeland

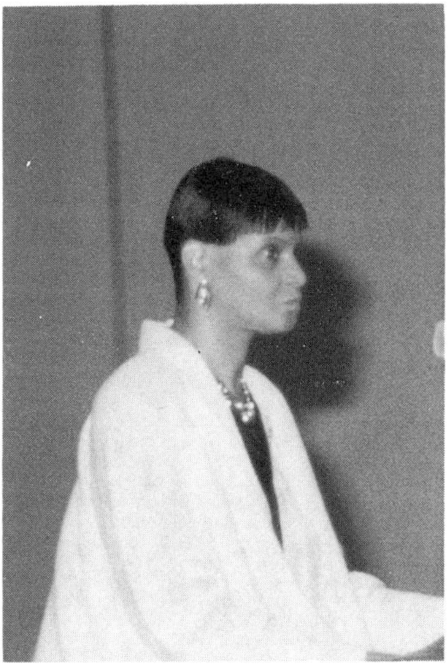

Assistant Director of Music
Mrs. Mamie E. Taylor
Ft. Lauderdale

President
Congress of Christian Education
Rev. Alex Harper, Palmetto

OFFICERS

Executive Director
of Youth Convention
Rev. T. G. Bess, Indiantown

Chairman of Foreign Mission
Rev. J. E. Atkins
WinterHaven

Property Development Officer
Rev. R. L. Wilson, Jacksonville

Chairman of State Mission
Rev. S. D. Hicks (deceased), Tampa

OFFICERS

Chairman of Education
Rev. J. B. Adams
Belle Glade

President-Emeritus
Congress of Christian Education
Rev. A. H. Parker, Marianna

Administrative Assistant
Liaison Officer
Miss Barbara Wright, Tampa

Pastors Conference Sr. Chairman
Rev. Harry D. Rucker, Sanford

OFFICERS

Chairman of Social Justice
Rev. Charles B. Dailey
Jacksonville

Band Director, State Congress
of Christian Education
Mr. Charles Maxwell, Jacksonville

President Senior Women's Auxiliary
Mrs. Ruby F. Herndon
March 1992–

SENIOR WOMEN'S AUXILIARY PRESIDENTS

Mrs. Theresa Moore

Mrs. Hannah B. Miller

Senior Womens Auxiliary President
Mrs. Amelia E. Houston

Senior Womens Auxiliary President
Mrs. Maudie M. Fowler

James Carl Sams Convention Center
and State Convention Headquarters
Lakeland, Florida
Named for the First President of the P.M. & E.

Second Vice President
Mrs. Mary Miller

Third Vice President
Mrs. Aquilla Morgan

First President of Senior Mission No. 2
Mrs. Dorothy Burroughs

President
Womens Intermediate Auxiliary
Mrs. Meriam Ruth Newsome

Youth Convention
Mrs. Jeresa C. Austin

Former Director of
Youth Department
Mrs. Elizabeth Jenkins

Counselor Summer Camp
Mrs. Hattie Alexander

Former Recording Secretary
Senior Women (Deceased)
Mrs. C. J. Smith

Women in the Cabinet

YWA and Junior Women's Ministry
Mrs. Patricia Lott (President)
Rev. Samuel L. Maxwell—Advisor

State Deaconess Council Emeritus
Mrs. Lillian Mae Bogan

State Deaconess Council
Mrs. Hazel N. Jones

PRESIDENTS

State Ushers Convention
Mrs. Mary K. Heard

Ministers Wives Widows
Aux.
Mrs. Gloria Murray

President
Nurses Corps.
Mrs. Daisy Washington

President
YWA and Junior Women's Ministry
Mrs. Willean T. Hadley

Counselor
Youth Convention
Mrs. Elizabeth Rosier

Historian
Altermese Smith Bentley

National Representative
Assistant Secretary
Rev. T. G. Gainous

Former Vice President
Rev. Samuel Fields

OFFICERS

Moderator
Union Foreign Association
Rev. H. M. Dillard

Recording Secretary Emeritus
Rev. C. W. Dawson (deceased)

Statistician
Rev. J. W. Daughtery (deceased)

Mt. Pilgrim
Rev. C. H. Bolden (deceased)

OFFICERS

Moderator
First South Florida
Rev. P. H. Jackson (deceased)

Former Trustee for the Progressive
Baptist Conference Center
Rev. Leon King (deceased)

Former Vice President
Rev. Eddie Burroughs (deceased)

Moderator First South Florida
Baptist Association
Rev. M.C. Johnson

OFFICERS

Speaker, Pastors Conference
Jacksonville
Rev. Rudolph McKissick

Junior Women Auxiliary
Rev. Samuel L. Maxwell–Advisor
(At Podium)

Moderator
Progressive of West Florida
Rev. Rufus Woods

Moderator
Equal Rights Association
Rev. Ceaser Smith

OFFICERS

Moderator
Progressive M.E. Association
(Before Merger)
Rev. Jordan

President
Brotherhood Union
Rev. Leroy Williams

Secretary to the President
Rev. Rollie Murray, Jr.

Mt. Pilgrim Association
Rev. L.W. Williams

OFFICERS

Former Correspondence Secretary
Rev. Joseph F. Hargrett

Mission Action Plan
(MAP) Coordinator
Rev. Lewis Lampley

Appendix I

President's Job Description

I. **PURPOSE:** To give overall leadership and lead the Convention in carrying out its objectives: To facilitate the union and cooperation of Baptists of Florida in the work of upbuilding the Kingdom of Christ in the State and throughout the world. Its more specific objectives will be to promote spiritual relationships of all scriptural means; to foster the spirit of worldwide missions; to support Christian and theological education; to direct all contributed funds according to the wishes of the individual and organization making the contribution, if such wish is expressed. The President's primary responsibilities are to preside in the annual, semi-annual, and special-call meetings of the Convention, Board of Control, and to make sure that the Mission Action Plan is implemented according to the Constitution and bylaws.

II. **AREAS OF RESPONSIBILITY AND AUTHORITY**

A. Life style as a Conventional Christian leader
   1. An example (Titus 2:7–15; I Cor. 11:1)
   2. Qualifications (1 Tim. 3:1–7; Ex. 18:17–27)

B. Prayer Ministry (1 Thess. 5:16–18; James 5:13–18)—Pray for:

1. Yourself (James 1:5; Phil. 4:4–7)
2. All of the Conventional Leaders (Eph. 6:18; Col. 1:9–14)
3. Ministry of all the Conventional Churches (Matt. 9:35–38)
4. All men everywhere (1 Tim. 2:1–16)

C. Equipping the Leaders of the Convention Through Designated Conference and Workshops
   1. For the work of service (Eph. 4:1–11)
   2. To building up the conventional churches (Eph. 4:1–16)

D. Proclamation During the Annual Sessions and in the State
   1. With consistency (1 Tim. 4:1–6)
   2. With urgency (1 Cor. 9:1–27)
   3. With conviction (Rem. 1–16)
   4. With clarity (1 Tim. 4:6–16)

E. Counsel and Advisory when Requested by Churches/Pastors
   1. On personal matters (Gal. 6:1)
   2. On family concerns (Cor. 3:18–21)
   3. On marital problems (Eph. 5:18–32; Col. 3:13–21; 1 Pet. 3:1–7)
   4. On conflicts between church and pastor (Matt. 18:15–17; Matt. 6:4–14; Eph. 4:32)

F. Discipline in Conventional Churches that Violate the Spirit of the Convention's Constitution
   1. Recommend it when there is a need
   2. Instruct the "How to" for the discipline of the
      a. Unchristian conduct (1 Cor. 5:1–13)—Disfellowship from the Convention
      b. Unrepentant offenders (Matt. 18:15–18)—Disfellowship from the Convention
   3. Recommend restoration of the disciplined church /pastor when correction is evidenced (2 Cor. 2:6–11) (This is Paul's recommendation concerning the man in 1 Cor. 5)

G. Administration of Conventional Affairs (taking the oversight)
   1. Leading by example (1 Peter 5:1–4)
   2. Encouraging unity (Eph. 4:1–7)
   3. Encourage every auxiliary to operate in a budget
H. Representative for the Convention
   1. In the State and Nation: National Convention et al
   2. In the world: The Baptist World Alliance et al
I. Expansion and Growth
   1. Lead in setting Convention objectives (Eph. 3:20)
      a. Evangelism
      b. Educational
   2. Plan (with other leaders) programs/ministries to reach established objectives and goals (Prov. 3:3–6; Prov. 16:3)
   3. Lead the Convention to greater challenges (Matt. 28:16–20)

III: WORKING RELATIONSHIPS

   1. The president reports to the Board of Control and the Convention
   2. Reporting to the President; Vice Presidents; President of Congress on Christian Education; Secretary to the President; Corresponding Secretary; Recording Secretary; Financial Secretary; Treasurer. The President must work in cooperation with the sixteen Associations, the State Congress on Christian Education and the Convention.

Progressive Missionary and Educational Baptist State Convention of Florida

JOB DESCRIPTION FOR THE VICE PRESIDENT

I. **PURPOSE:** To be responsible to the president for providing additional leadership in the auxiliary work, committees, boards and presiding when requested by the President.

II. **AREAS OF RESPONSIBILITIES AND AUTHORITY**

   A. Life Style as a Christian leader
      1. An example (Titus 2:7–15; I Cor. 11:1)
      2. Qualification (I Tim. 3:1–7)

   B. Prayer Life as a Christian leader—Pray for:
      1. Yourself (James 1:5; Phil. 4:4–7)
      2. All of the Conventional leaders (Eph. 6:18; Col. 1:9–14)
      3. The churches and their ministry (Matt. 9:35–38)
      4. All men everywhere (I Tim. 2:1–6)

   C. Sharing the Leadership Load
      1. The First Vice President shall oversee:
         a. Budget Committee
         b. Finance Committee
         c. Education Board
         d. Evangelical Board
         e. Home, State, and Foreign Mission Boards
         f. Benevolent Board
      2. The Second Vice President shall oversee:
         a. Place Committee
         b. Church Development Commission (Regional Conferences)
         c. Pastoral Development (Pastors' Conference) Commission
         d. Publicity Commission
         e. Social Justice Commission

f. Family Life Commission

3. The Third Vice President shall oversee the advisories and auxiliary heads for the:
   a. Senior Women Mission
   b. Mission #2, Minister's Wives
   c. YWA and Junior Women
   d. Brotherhood
   e. Ushers
   f. Nurses
   g. Youth
   h. Children
4. The Vice President's leadership to the various auxiliaries, advisors, boards, commissions, and committees is one of encouragement and support.

III. WORKING RELATIONS

A. The Vice President reports to the President, reporting to the:

B. First Vice President: Budget and Finance committees, Education and Benevolent, Evangelical Boards, Home Mission, State Mission, and Foreign Mission Boards.

C. Second Vice President: Place Committee, Church Development, Pastoral Development, Publicity, Social Justice, and Family Life Commissions

D. Third Vice President: Senior Women Mission, Mission #2, Ministers' Wives, YWA and Junior Women's Brotherhood, Ushers, Nurses, Youth, Children, and the Advisors to the above auxiliaries.

Trustees for the Progressive M&E Baptist Conference Center from the sixteen associations to be elected by the Convention for two two-year terms, not to exceed four years.

First South Florida Asso.

Dr. J. E. Atkins
P.O. Box 1842
Winter Haven, FL 33888
Rev. Rollie Murray
654 W. Anderson Street
Orlando, FL 32805

Mt. Pilgrim Association

Ms. Eleanor Ball
Sarasota, FL 33580
Rev. Samuel Maxwell
8616 Progress Blvd
Tampa, FL 33580

South Florida Progressive Asso.

Rev. Alex Harper
102 17th Street, NE
Bradenton, FL 33508
Rev. Lewis Lampley
3619 18th Avenue, South
St. Petersburg, FL 33711

Kissimmee Valley Association

Rev. Leon King
400 Della Tobias Avenue
Clewiston, FL 33440
Rev. F. L. Carter
2007 Staples Avenue
Key West, FL 32805

Greater S. Florida Asso.

Rev. J. D. Johnson
1905 First Avenue
Palmetto, FL 33561
Rev. Leon Campbell
P.O. Box 1178
Okeechobee, FL 33472

Second West Association

407 North Blount
Chipley, FL 32428
Rev. D. W. Waddell
Route 1, Box 115
Campbellton, FL 33525

Equal Rights Association

Rev. R. J. Miller
1808 North Sixth Avenue
Pensacola, FL 32503
Rev. Fred Wright
10 East Pearl Street
Pensacola, FL 32501

Middle FL & Clay Co. Asso.

Rev. J. C. Finney
1435 West State Street
Jacksonville, FL 32209
Rev. Bruce Phillip
96 Ines Street
Jacksonville, FL 32209

Union Foreign Association

Rev. J. L. Overstreet
2716 North 34th Street
Tampa, FL 33605
Mrs. F. Brinson
2104 East Beal Road
Plant City, FL 33566

New Gulf Coast Association

Rev. James Bush
1942 East Seventh
Panama City, FL

East FL & Bethany Asso.

Mrs. Dorothy E. Borroughs
5711 Breve Road
Jacksonville, FL
Rev. W. H. Mack
916 Ionia Street
Jacksonville, FL 32206

Gulf Coast Association

Rev. Joseph Reed
503 S. Tampania Avenue
Tampa, FL 33609
Rev. D. Glover
New Macedonia
Tampa, FL 33610

New Central Association

Rev. Jessie Ivory
1110 Drew Avenue
Orlando, FL 32805
Mrs. Joyce Leonard
4957 Minosa Street
Orlando, FL

Union Baptist Association

Rev. N. L. Sumpter
P.O. Box 418
Gretna, FL 32332
Rev. N. Bowers
Corner of Clark & Clay
Quincy, FL 32351

Progressive Asso. of West FL

Mrs. Ruth Newsome
4000 E. 7th Circle
Panama City, FL 32401
Rev. L. Randall
1912 West Strong Street
Pensacola, FL 32501

Greater Union Association

Rev. Jessie Ferguson
1360 NW 61st Street
Miami, FL 33142
Rev. C. Drane
8080 NW 22nd Avenue
Miami, FL 33147

Greater St. Paul Baptist Church, Lakeland, FL

MAY 2, 1989, 10:00 A.M.
THE CORE COMMITTEE OF THE PMEC

The meeting opened with Project Chairman 2nd Vice President Ned Sanders presiding. The first matter discussed was the work to be done on the parking lot. Ned indicated that he had received a bid to resurface the lot for $9,600, and a possibility of a reduced price with some terms.

The second matter discussed was the repairing of the old dormitory's roof. Ned gave two bids of $2,240 and $3,150.

The third matter discussed was the demolition of the old chapel building, and the bid to do that work was $8,975, and a possibility to get this reduced.

The fourth matter discussed was the replacing of the external doors at the price of $1,150.

The fifth matter discussed was purchasing $200 of metal roofing paint, and Pastor Rentz will do the work.

Special Noted: The building that is being used by the Blessed Hope Baptist Church is to be labeled as a mission effort of the Convention.

The chairman was given the task of convening a committee to formulate an educational calendar from August 1989 to July 1990.

The activities to be recommended during the congress in July are the following:

Monday 17th, the dedication service; Tuesday 18th, opening program; and Wednesday 19th, banquet, tickets $25.

Notices are to be sent out to all board members of the center around the first of July in regard to the board meeting.

Forms are to be made up and sent to organizations in regard to use of these facilities in order to set up calendar dates.

Finally, signs are to be printed: 1. The Convention Headquarters and Baptist Conference Center, 2. Board Chairman, 3. The President and Vice Presidents, 4. Executive Director, 5. Receptionist, 6. Office of Moderators, 7. Congress President and Staff, 8. Music and Band Room, 9. Conference Room.

Committee Members

Vice President	N. S. Sanders, Cmn.
Secretary,	Alex Harper
	Lewis Lampley

Important Dates Following the Initial Presentation of the Proposal to Purchase the Lakeland Property

MAY 3, 1988—Chairman Sanders called a meeting of the Core Committee and the Moderators. The meeting was held at New Mt. Zion, Rev. L. Norris, Pastor. In this meeting, the proposed plan was read in full and adjusted. The real money was collected toward the project.

AUGUST 12, 1988—The convention entered into a contract to purchase the property. Present were President Rhim, Vice Presidents E. B. Williams, N. S. Sanders, and Rev. Richard Wilson.

DECEMBER 20, 1988—A special meeting was held at Greater St. Paul, Lakeland, FL. In that meeting Dr. Rhim added Rev. E. B. Williams and Rev. Joseph Gordon to the Core Committee and instructed them as to what to include in the plan—MAP was born. This is our Mission Action Plan. The committee worked hard to put the plan in the present booklet form.

JANUARY 20, 1989—The Core Committee met in Altamonte Springs. This was the first full briefing on the MAP Program.

JANUARY 21, 1989—The MAP Program received its first full reading before the convention. Rev. Harper was the reader.

MARCH 22, 1989—During the convention meeting in Sanford, the MAP Program was read the second time in full by Rev. Harper.

MARCH 25, 1989—In the Convention's business session, the MAP Program received its third and final reading, read by Rev. Lampley. It was approved and adopted without any opposers.

JUNE 6, 1989—The Core Committee held its meeting on the campus as it conducted Symposium I.
JUNE 29, 1989—The Convention hired its first full-time staff person, Mrs. Barbara Gary, as the Administrative Assistant.
JULY 17, 1989—The property was dedicated on the 21st. The Convention named the center The James Carl Sams Conference Center.

Dear Fellow Laborers:

This letter comes to express the Core Committee and President Rhim's deep appreciation for your attendance and participation in our very first symposium on the beautiful campus of our Headquarters and Conference Center in Lakeland, Fl.

This first symposium was vitally important in that it brought to our attention some of our strengths, weaknesses, opportunities, and tensions. This valuable information will facilitate our efforts to mobilize and rally our resources to execute our Christ's kingdom mandate.

You will find enclosed the record of the first symposium. More importantly, what can we do to correct these problems? The Core Committee believes correcting the problem will require many different approaches. One vital approach is that of offering a symposium for all elected officers to acquaint them with the convention's goals and their job description before they assume their positions.

We suggest that the Convention's strengths are warm fellowship, enthusiastic preaching, and exciting worship.

WEAKNESSES

1. Duration of leadership
2. Narrow involvement of laymen
3. Discouragement of creativity
4. Undefined or unclear objectives and goals
5. Poor methodology
6. Inconsistency and poor planning
7. Narrow input
8. Inadequate program to plant new churches
9. Poor evangelistic program
10. Poor influence on the local churches
11. Lack of leadership in education for districts and local churches

OPPORTUNITIES

1. Initiate biblically sound evangelistic and outreach programs
2. Expository preaching and theologically sound music
3. Bible-centered educational center for workshops, seminars, and conferences on this campus for pastors/ministers, leaders, businessmen, laity, youths and children across this state and nation.
4. Commence a program to plant new churches
5. Publish, sell, and handle religious books and material for the State and nation

Lastly, the next symposium will be announced soon by our President.

Respectfully yours,
Project Director,
2nd Vice President Sanders
Core Committee

SYMPOSIUM

June 6, 1989

Place: State Convention Headquarters and Conference Center, Lakeland, FL
Time: 10:45
Devotion: Pastor Flemming Tarver
Presider: Pastor Alex Harper
Presentation of President Rhim by Pastor Harper
Lunch Break

AFTERNOON SESSION

Time: 1:45
Presiding: President Rhim
Land Developer's Report presented by Rev. Wilson
President Rhim presented Pastor Lampley to conduct the SWOTS analysis and he was assisted by Pastor Harper.
Greetings: President Rhim

STRENGTHS

Dedication, unity, strong teaching program, dedicated leadership.

WEAKNESSES

Insincerity, pride, self-gratification, inconsistency, poor organization, power struggle, destructive criticism, ignorance, lack of discipline.

OPPORTUNITIES

Serve people, strong educational program, motivation, self-contained, role models.

TENSIONS

Tradition (structure), over-extended, allocations, disrespect.

PERSONS PRESENT

Ass't. Corresponding Secretary J. L. Jones

President H. T. Rhim
Moderator H. H. Wynn
Pastor F. Tarver
Treasurer Price Wilson
Vice President E. B. Williams
Pastor Lewis Lampley
Pastor Alex Harper
Congress President Parker
Home Mission Chairman Hicks
Pastor R. L. Wilson

Pastor J. D. Johnson
Pastor Richard Wilson
Vice Moderator T. Brown
Sister Susie Bowens
Sister M. M. Fowler
Sister Jeresa Austin
Pastor S. L. Thigpen
Sister Dovin
Sister Elizabeth Rosier
Pastor Lovelace

General Staff Officers,
Presidents of Auxiliaries,
Ministerial Advisor to Auxiliaries,
Regional Directors,
and Moderators

Dear Sirs:

Please be informed that President Rhim has called for a "Meeting of the Minds" (Conventional Leaders). The meeting will be held in Ormond Beach, FL on August 19–20, 1988, at the Holiday Inn, Surfside on Atlantic Boulevard.

The Friday afternoon session will begin at 2:00 p.m. allowing those coming from afar time to travel and yet be on time. Saturday morning session will begin at 8:30 a.m. with breakfast together. A Florida Buffet breakfast will be served at the cost of $6.75 per person with no tax.

Listed below are names of persons for whom reservations have been made. If you are not able to arrive before 6:00 p.m. on Friday, August 19, please inform the hotel or call the corresponding secretary. The room rate is $45.00 per night—Holiday Inn, Surfside.

Each auxiliary head, with the cooperation of the ministerial advisor, is to bring a Plan of Work for that auxiliary for the year 1988–89. Please use forms provided. This will be an agenda item. Make several copies of the Plan of Work for working purposes.

RESERVATION LIST:

H. T. Rhim
N. S. Sanders
C. W. Dawson
J. D. Johnson
K. T. Turner
J. F. Hargrett
J. E. Atkins
H. D. Rucker
T. G. Bess
J. B. Adams
J. J. Miller
Rollie Murray, Jr.
C. T. Kirkland
Dorothy Borroughs
G. I. Bradley
W. H. Mack
Henderson Powell
Marilyn Reed
E. B. Williams
W. M. Davis
H. C. McCray, Jr
J. E. Jones
P. H. Jackson
W. O. Granger
Altermese Bentley
S. D. Hicks
L. P. Davis
Frederick Haynes
Rudolph McKissick
H. M. Lewis
M. M. Fowler
Linda Lewis
Daisy Henderson
Veronica Fung
I. M. Jones
H. L. Alexander

N. F. Sumpter
H. H. Wynn
T. E. Gainous
L. H. King
Joseph Gordon
T. J. Reed
G. Washington
R. B. Brooks
S. M. Maxwell, Sr.
(And six additional rooms available)

A. H. Parker
L. Norris, Jr.
Elizabeth Rosier
H. E. Harmond
Price Wilson
C. Smith
B. J. Lane
Rev. McIntyre
Annie Amos

Please make every plan to attend this most important meeting.

Respectfully,
Joseph F. Hargrett,
Corresponding Secretary

Toward Being a More Effective Trustee

I. **BACKGROUND:** The history in connection with the James Carl Sams Conference Center and the Progressive M & E Baptist State Convention's Headquarters can be tersely tabulated as follows:

February 19, 1988—President Rhim, Vice President Williams, Alex Harper, and Lewis Lampley visited the property for observation. On that same date, President Rhim delegated the following responsibilities: plans for purchase to Alex Harper and proposed use plans to Lewis Lampley. In early March of '88, with the help of Rev. L. Norris, Jr., Rev. Harper met with a real estate agent and received the necessary information for the first draft of the proposed plan.

March 26, 1988—The moderators visited the property and recommended that the president pursue the purchase . . . on that same date during the Convention's business sessions, President Rhim called on Rev. Lampley to present the first proposed plan. The Convention gave President Rhim the authority to pursue the purchase of the property. He appointed Second Vice President N. S. Sanders as the chairman in charge of the project . . . appointed Alex Harper and Lewis Lampley to work with him and named the group "The Core Committee."

II. DEFINITION: A person to whom another's property, or the management of another's property, is entrusted . . . any of a group or board of persons appointed or elected to manage the affairs of an institution, convention etc.

III. PURPOSE: The purpose of the trustees (of the James Carl Sams Conference Center and Headquarters of the Progressive Missionary and Educational Baptist State Convention of Florida, Inc.), is to manage the affairs of the said Conference Center by action of the majority in attendance of the regular and special-call meetings of the Board of Trustees, and support and promote the MAP program.

IV. DUTIES:

1. To be thoroughly familiar with the purpose and objectives of the J. C. Sams Conference Center and the Convention's Headquarters (see Constitution - Articles II and III).
2. To have a thorough working knowledge of the Constitution and by-laws of the Conference Center as well as understanding the functions of each committee.
3. To be committed to the purpose and objectives of the J. C. Sams Conference Center and the Convention's Headquarters; this commitment includes regular attendance at board meetings and committee meetings; that is, the one you have been placed on.
4. To be a full supporter of the adopted actions and directions mandated by the Board of Trustees. The support must be financial, moral, spiritual, and promotional. None of the supporters could be recommended for

removal by the Executive Committee before his/her term expires.

5. To live exemplary lives which is required by those who represent the Lord, His church, the J. C. Sams Conference Center and the Convention's Headquarters.
6. To see the dream of churches, associations, and individuals.

DUTIES OF THE STAFF

1. Executive Director:

   PURPOSE: To give over-all leadership to the James Carl Sams Conference Center and the Convention's Headquarters. The executive director reports to the Board of Trustees and the convention's Board of Control Executive Committee.

   Entities: the J. C. Sams Conference Center and the Convention's Headquarters

V. THE MOTIVATION:

Whatever you do, do your work heartily, as for the Lord rather than for men; knowing that from the Lord you will receive the reward of the inheritance. It is the Lord Christ whom you serve. For he who does wrong will receive the consequences of the wrong which he has done, and that without partiality. (Col. 3:23–25)

VI. DETECTING AND AVOIDING THE SEEDS OF DISINTEGRATION

In order to avoid the seeds of disintegration, *each* Trustee must understand:

A. The Danger of Loving the World (1 John 2:15–17)
   1. " . . . all that is in the world, the lust of the flesh"—sinful passions
   2. " . . . all that is in the world, the lust of the eyes"—sinful possessions
   3. " . . . all that is in the world, the pride of life"—position

B. The Danger of Building in Vain (Ps. 127:1)

1. Building in vain is leaving the Lord out of every detail, "except the Lord builds the house (organization), we will labor in vain."
2. Laboring in vain is when we serve ourselves, rather than the Lord in blamelessness and harmless . . . without rebuke. (Phil. 2:15)

C. The Blessings of Being Godly in both a Negative and Positive Way (Ps. 1:1–3)

D. The Privilege of Serving as a Trustee is a Sacred Trust/Stewardship (Luke 16:10–13)

Appendix II

Auxiliaries

In a March 1914 meeting at the Mt. Gilboa Baptist Church the Progressive Baptist State Convention organized the first two Auxiliaries, the Women's Convention and the Sunday School and Baptist Young People Union.

The concept that every believer is called to minister was not new, but formalizing it was a recognition of its value and importance. Also, it emphasized the Ministry of the Laity as stated by Norman H. Maring. The application to such terms as "full-time Christian service" to pastors, Maring claimed, tended to create the impression that other people serve God only when they are doing "church work" as such. False distinctions can be removed by returning to the biblical understanding that every Christian is "called to be a full-time witness of Jesus Christ."[1]

Laymen shared the responsibility to witness in the marketplaces, work sites, homes and schools. This gives the whole church an involvement in the active fulfillment of the Christian concept of Ministries.

The acknowledgment that the laity had a shared ministry in shaping policies and in decision-making, resulted in other Auxiliaries (ministries) being organized. The Sunday School and Baptist Young People Union remained an active and vibrant auxiliary until the merger of the West Florida Baptist. (The merger has been referred to earlier.)

Records, including published Annual Minutes in chronological order, giving dates and listings of elected officers and the years they served before 1974 have not been available. However, some copies have been acquired through contacts with churches and individuals. From them, the following list of persons who have served as president of the Sunday School and Baptist Young People Union (BTU) State Convention has been reconstructed. The list is not necessarily in the order in which they served.

PRESIDENTS

J. W. Moore
Fred Marshall
W. E. Dancer
J. W. Canady
J. M. Bing
W. M. Smith
Harry Taylor
S. W. White
H. G. Dayes
Molly J. Walker Thomas
L. T. Sutherland

THE 36TH ANNUAL SESSION OF THE PROGRESSIVE BAPTIST STATE SUNDAY SCHOOL AND B.Y.P.U. CONVENTION.

Sebring, Florida
July 19, 1951

Sunday School State Convention

President:	Mr. G. W. Scott, Jacksonville
Recording Secretary:	Mrs. C. M. Graham, Orlando
Vice President:	Mr. W. J. Butler, Okeechobee
Financial Secretary:	Mrs. L. C. B. Thomas, Bartow
Treasurer:	Mrs. Elizabeth Jenkins, Sebring
Chorister:	Mrs. E. Dickson, Avon Park
Pianist:	Mrs. Agnes Dean, Sebring
Corresponding Secretary:	Mrs. C. J. Smith, Sanford

B.Y.P.U.

President:	Rev. S. M. Daniels

First Vice President:	Mr. Harry Taylor
Second Vice President:	Mr. J. W. Boks
Recording Secretary:	Mr. W. J. Patterson
Corresponding Secretary:	Mrs. Jerusa Austin
Financial Secretary:	Mrs. H. B. Miller
Treasurer:	Mrs. Lucy White[2]

43RD ANNUAL SESSION

Progressive Baptist State Sunday School
& B.Y.P.U. Convention
July 23–27, 1958

President:	Bro. G. W. Scott, Jacksonville
Vice President:	Rev. G. W. Mitchell, Tampa
Recording Secretary:	Mrs. Claudia M. Graham, Orlando
Financial Secretary:	Mrs. L. C. B. Thomas, Bartow
Treasurer:	Mrs. Elizabeth Jenkins, Sebring
Dean of Workshop:	Rev. R. H. Wilson, Jacksonville
Assistant Dean of Workshop:	Rev. J. L. Stephens, Arcadia
Dean of Music:	Dr. W. Don Pelham, Arcadia
Corresponding Secretary:	Mrs. Agnes Dean, Sebring

B.Y.P.U. CONVENTION

President:	Bro. Leon T. Freeman, Bartow
First Vice President:	Rev. O. D. Williams, Pahokee
Second Vice President:	Bro. Freddie Floyd, Sarasota
Recording Secretary:	Mrs. M. L. D. Stephens, Arcadia
Corresponding Secretary:	Mrs. Lillie M. Birts, Okeechobee
Financial Secretary:	Mrs. Estella C. Dickson, Avon Park
Treasurer:	Mrs. Lucy White, Lakeland
B.Y.P.U. Director:	Bro. Alexander Heard, Jacksonville[3]

49TH ANNUAL SESSION

Progressive Baptist State Baptist Training Union &
Sunday School Convention

President:	Rev. L. T. Freeman, Bartow
First Vice President:	Rev. O. D. Williams, Belle Glade
Second Vice President:	Rev. M. J. Williams, Tampa
Recording Secretary:	Mrs. Lula Campbell, Sebring
Corresponding Secretary:	Mrs. L. A. Bullard, Winter Park
Financial Secretary:	Mrs. Estella C. Dickson, Avon Park
Treasurer:	Mrs. M. M. Jones, Tampa
State BTU Director:	Bro. Alexander Heard, Jacksonville

Sunday School

President:	Deacon G. W. Scott
First Vice President:	Rev. G. W. Mitchell
Second Vice President:	Rev. W. R. Lovelace
Recording Secretary:	Mrs. Bettye C. Battle
Financial Secretary:	Mrs. H. L. Floyd
Corresponding Secretary:	Mrs. Agnes L. Dean
Dean of Workshop:	Rev. J. L. Stephens
Assistant Dean of Workshop:	Rev. M. J. Williams
Director of Music:	Rev. A. J. Hughes
Organist:	Mrs. Mary Whitehurst
Treasurer:	Rev. J. C. Burney[4]

GOLDEN JUBILEE 50TH ANNUAL SESSION

Progressive Baptist State Sunday School & B.T.U.
Convention of Florida
July 20, 1965

St. Paul Missionary Baptist Church, Rev. H. H. Robinson, Minister, Bradenton, Florida[5]

President of Sunday School	Bro. G. W. Scott
President of BTU:	Rev. L. I. Freeman

51ST ANNUAL SESSION

Progressive Baptist State Sunday School &
B.T.U. Convention
July 19–24, 1966

St. John Missionary Baptist Church, Rev. H. B. Whitehurst, Pastor, Sanford, Florida

SUNDAY SCHOOL CONVENTION

President	Bro. G. W. Scott, Jacksonville
First Vice President:	G. W. Mitchell, Tampa
Second Vice President:	Rev. W. R. Lovelace, Lakeland
Recording Secretary:	Mrs. Bettye Battle, St. Petersburg
Financial Secretary:	Mrs. H. L. Floyd, Sarasota
Corresponding Secretary:	Mrs. Agnes Dean, Sebring
Treasurer:	Rev. J. D. Burney, Jacksonville
Dean of Workshop:	Rev. J. L. Stephens, Ft. Myers
Director of Music:	Rev. A H. Hughes, Jacksonville
Organist:	Mrs. Mary Whitehurst, Sanford

BAPTIST TRAINING UNION CONVENTION

President:	Rev. L. T. Freeman, Bartow
First Vice President:	Rev. O. D. Williams, Belle Glade
Second Vice President:	Rev. Isadore Edwards, Ft. Myers
Recording Secretary:	Mrs. Lula Campbell, Sebring
Financial Secretary:	Mrs. Estella Dickson, Avon Park
Corresponding Secretary:	Mrs. L. A. Bullard, Winter Park
Treasurer:	Mrs. M. M. Jones, Tampa
BTU Director:	Bro. Alexander Heard, Jacksonville[6]

58TH ANNUAL SESSION

Progressive Baptist Sunday School &
Baptist Training Union Convention

SUNDAY SCHOOL CONVENTION

President	Bro. G. W. Scott, Jacksonville
First Vice President:	Rev. G. W. Mitchell, Tampa
Second Vice President:	Rev. W. R. Lovelace, Ormond Beach
Recording Secretary:	Mrs. A. P. Boatman, Orlando
Financial Secretary:	Mrs. H. L. Floyd, Sarasota
Treasurer:	Rev. J. C. Burney, Jacksonville
Dean of Workshop:	Rev. J. L. Stephen, Ft. Myers
Assistant Dean of Workshop:	Rev. Mac J. Williams, Clearwater
Corresponding Secretary:	Mrs. Edith Ewings, Sebring

Director of Music:	Mrs. Mary Whitehurst, Sanford
Assistant Director of Music:	Mrs. A. K. Bridges, Clearwater
Assistant Director of Music:	Mrs. Annie L. Amos, Lakeland

Baptist Training Union

President:	Rev. L. T. Freeman, Bartow
First Vice President:	Rev. Alex Harper, Lakeland
Second Vice President:	Rev. A. Drayton, Moore Haven
Recording Secretary:	Mrs. Lula Campbell, Sebring
Financial Secretary:	Mrs. Estella C. Dickson, Avon Park
Treasurer:	Mrs. M. M. Fowler, Tampa
BTU Director:	Bro. Alexander Heard, Jacksonville[7]

History of Senior Mission #2 M.A.B.

MARCH 1969-WINTER HAVEN, FLORIDA

The constitution of the Progressive Baptist State Convention was changed to organize a new Auxiliary, The M. A. B. Fuller Mission Group, Sister Dorothy E. Borroughs of the Bethel Baptist Institutional Church, Jacksonville, Florida was named as President by the parent-body. It was stipulated that members would serve in this group for ten (10) years.

A committee consisting of Rev. Eddie Borroughs, Rev. J. L. Stevens, Sister Gladys Vaught, Sister Agnes Dean were named by President Sams to formulate the balance of the official roster for this group. The following names were offered and accepted by the parent-body:

President	Sister Dorothy E. Borroughs
1st Vice President	Sis. William M. Haynes
2nd Vice President	Sis. Grovenia Lafittee
Recording Secretary	Sis. Bernice McGhee
Financial Secretary	Sis. Altha Wilson
Corresponding Secretary	Sis. Aline Tarver
Treasurer	Sis. L. A. Bullard
Chorister	Sis. A. P. Boatman
Pianist	Sis. Alpha Ross
State Advisor	Rev. B. J. Lane

The first session found us in Fort Myers, Florida, where God blessed us mightily.

From here to Belle Glade, Florida, where Sister Annie M. Henderson replaced Sister Haynes and Sister Frankie Whitfield became corresponding secretary. In October of that year, God called our pianist Sister Ross home for reward.

In 1972, we moved to Orlando, Florida, where God blessed us with two replacements, Sister Evelyn Eads and Sister Josephine Kennedy who has since become organist for the parent-body. We also began our 1st Street Ministry, witnessing to the lost outside of the "Glass Stained Windows" for the next (3) years we continued to broaden our service's with workshops headed by Sister Marion Haywood, Queen Contest (our fundraising effort), visiting of the incarcerated and nursing homes, clothing of the naked and feeding the hungry.

In 1975, our President, Sister Borroughs was sponsored on a trip to the "Baptist World Alliance" in Stockholm, Sweden. God is still continuing to shower us with his blessing. We have shared fellowship with the Regional Conferences and the National Baptist Convention where our president holds the office of 2nd Assistant Secretary. Many of our members have been programmed and shared their talents, 3 of our Queens have gone on to become National Queens.

We have held the Sunday School banner for 5 years. We still strive to continue to be a light in darkness for lost mankind. Bible lessons—Themes—Sermons—Songs have bound us closer together as we shared fellowship one with the other.

In St. Petersburg, Florida, following the merger, with the Missionary and Educational Convention of West Florida, Sister Annie L. Walker, of Panama City became the 1st Vice President. Due to ill health she resigned the following year in Pensacola in favor of Sister Ida M. Spires of 2nd West District. The influx of the ladies of West Florida has added strength to our ranks. Sister Spires spearheaded our educational drive and enabled us to surpass all previous efforts.

We have continued to grow and now have (10) ten Districts participating:

1.	East Florida & Bethany	Sister Marinda Tennant
2.	1st South Florida	Sister L. C B. Thomas
3.	Union Foreign	Sister Mattie Smith
4.	Kissimmee Valley	Sister Annie M. Henderson
5.	2nd West	Sister Acile Spears
6.	Mt. Pilgrim	Sister Eva Herndon
7.	Gulf Coast	Sister Pauline Porter
8.	New Gulf	Sister Louise Brown
9.	Equal Rights	Sister Margaret Williams
10.	Progressive	Sister Flora McIntyre

In June 1978, God called our Historian, Sister Alberta Jackson, home from labor to reward. To her memory this history is dedicated.

In March 1979, as we came to the end our 10 year span, we prayed God would see our efforts, "In as much as ye have done it unto the least of these my Brethren, ye have done it unto me."

May we hear His welcome saying—

WELL DONE MISSION #2

President	Dorothy E. Borroughs
1st Vice President	Ida M. Spires
2nd Vice President	Annie M. Henderson
3rd Vice President	Doretha Waters
Recording Secretary	Bernice McGhee
Financial Secretary	Altha Wilson
Corresponding Secretary	Frankie S. Whitfield
Treasurer	L. A. Bullard
Pianist	Evelyn Eads
Chorister	A. P. Boatman
Assistant Chorister	Lucille Lowery
West Coast Secretary	Willie Dickens
Historian (deceased)	Alberta Jackson
Advisors	Rev. B. J. Lane, Rev. H. S. Covington

SEVENTH ANNUAL SESSION OF SENIOR MISSION NO. 2 AUXILIARY TO THE PROGRESSIVE MISSIONARY & EDUCATIONAL BAPTIST CONVENTION OF FLORIDA

March 23–28, 1976
Mt. Pleasant Missionary Baptist Church
Orlando, Florida
Rev. J. F. Hargrett, Pastor

Sister Dorothy E. Borroughs	State President
Sister Frankie S. Whitfield	Corresponding Secretary
Rev. B. J. Lane	State Advisor
Rev. H. S. Covington	State Advisor
Rev. James Carl Sams	General President

THEME

"Christ's Responsible Church In An Irresponsible World"
Matt: 5:13–16; 25:35–30; Micah 6:8
THEME SONG:
"Blessed Assurance"

OFFICERS

Dorothy E. Borroughs	President
Ida M. Spires	First Vice President
Annie M. Henderson	2nd Vice President
Doretha Waters	3rd Vice President
Bernice McGhee	Recording Secretary
Louise Brown	Assistant Recording Secretary
Altha Wilson	Financial Secretary
Frankie S. Whitfield	Corresponding Secretary
L. A. Bullard	Treasurer
A. P. Boatman	Chorister
Lucille Lowery	Chorister
Evelyn Eads	Musician
Alberta Jackson	Historian

COMMITTEES

Finance	Sister Ceola Hamilton, Chairman
Music	Sisters A. P. Boatman, Evelyn Eads, Lucille Lowery, Josephine Kennedy
Temperance	Sisters Hazel Hall, Verlee Suggs, Evelyn Howell, Sophronia Romeo, Noel Jackson

Evangelistic	Sisters Jessie Henderson, D. Gallington, Carrie Pope, Flossie Boyd
Education	Sisters Elton Riley, Charlie Mae Flowers, Beaty Baisden, Ida M. Spires
Deacon Wives	Sisters Blanche Raymond, Bertha Anderson, Ella Bibbs, A. M. Henderson
Local Presidents	Sisters Edith Jones, Edna Williams, Robbie Cooper, Linnie Myrick
District Presidents	Sisters L. C. B. Thomas, Chairman (All District Presidents)
Willing Workers	Sisters Elnora Small, Bertha Redden, Ossi Delaughta, Coral Walker
Business and Professional Women	Sisters Peaches Hamilton, Dallas Peacock, Josephine Jenkins, Jeanette Brewington, Edna P. McRoy
Field Workers	Sisters Mary Spann, Marva Hawkins, Gussie Grey, Talmadge Moody, Eva Hearn
Bible Teachers	Sisters Doretha Waters, Annie Porter, L. A. Bullard, Harriett Wilson, and Edna Jackson
Workshop	Sisters Marian Haywood, Aline Tarver
Dramatic Art Queens	Sisters Althea Wilson, Mary Williams
Ushers	Sisters Alberta Dixon, Mable Parker
Flowers	Sister Edna Mae Malloy
Badges	Sister Lucille Lowery

National Baptist Convention	Sister Sadie Payne
Arts and Crafts	Sisters Annie Massalena, Ruby Cleveland
Ministers' Wives	Sisters Price, Chairman, Donald, Wilson, Glover, Davis, Covington

FIRST SOUTH FLORIDA MISSION NUMBER TWO AUXILIARY

Greetings:

Since the birth of Mission Number Two Auxiliary in our State Convention, we the members of First South Florida's Mission #2, have found it indeed a blessing as well as a privilege to be a part of such a dynamic movement. For us it was merely a change of name (Junior Women to Mission #2). All officers and members remained the same.

Under the very capable leadership of our illustrious president, Sister L. C. B. Thomas, we have met all obligations to the State, Regional and National work, and have given full support to the causes with our time, talents and finances.

We are happy to report that we have had three Queen contestants from First South Florida to win the State title in the past nine years. They are Sisters Ideoa Reynolds, Meizola Bullard and Ruby Cleveland. Sister Cleveland also won the National title in 1975. This achievement encountered untiring work for all those involved.

There are over 30 local societies enrolled in First South Florida at this time. Sincere appreciation to the pastors and churches of these societies who found it not robbery to organize a Mission Number Two Society. Without your support, no accomplishment could have been made.

Allotted space hinders us from mentioning all achievements of our societies separately. Thus, they shall be listed under our five Congresses. All have contributed through Bible Study, Outreach, Witnessing and other phases of the Mission work. Remember that if any participating Society is not named, it is from the HEAD—not from the HEART!! Hats off to you, too!

CONGRESS #1

Marva Y. Hawkins, President

St. Paul - Sanford, Florida
Sister Mercedes Medlock, Pres.

Shiloh - Sanford, Florida
Sister Alfreda Wallace, Pres.

Snow Hill - Geneva, Florida

CONGRESS #2

Ocie DeLaughter, President

Bethel - Orlando, Florida	Sister A. M. Doctor, President
Bethlehem - Winter Garden, Florida	Sister Mary Johnson, President
Mt. Zion - Tildenville, Florida	Sister Amanda Booker, President
Mt. Moriah - Winter Park, Florida	Sister Lizzie Hawkins, President
New Hope - Winter Park, Florida	Sister Sadie Singleton, President
Greater Harmony - Groveland, Florida	Sister Daulah Wilson, President
Bethlehem - Orlando, Florida	Sister Cherry Crum, President
Bethel - Winter Park, Florida	Sister Naomi Hamm, President
St. John - Orlando, Florida	Sister Margaret Roby, President

CONGRESS #3

Peaches L. Hamilton, President

First Baptist - Winter Haven, FL.
Sister N. H. Jackson, Pres.

Harmony - Lakeland, FL
Sister G. Allen, Pres.

Mt. Olive - Medulla, FL.
Sister Lorraine Jones, Pres.

Buelah - Haines City, FL.
Sister Pearl Anderson, Pres.

Sand Hill - Lake Hamilton, FL.

Mt. Moriah -
Plant City, FL
Sister Sophronia Romeo, Pres.
New Mt. Zion -
Auburndale, FL.
Sister L. M. Gallington, Pres.
New Mt. Zion -
Haines City, FL
Sister Ruby Cleveland, Pres.
Sister C. Robinson, Pres.
First Baptist Institution
Lakeland
Sister P. H. Hamilton, Pres.
Mt. Calvary - Lakeland, FL
Sister A. Reynolds, Pres.

CONGRESS #4

Shiloh - Dunedin, FL
Sister Gussie Hadley, Pres.
New Mt. Zion - Tampa, FL.
Sister Doris Jacobs, Pres.
St. Mathew - Clearwater, FL.
Sister Hazel Hall, Pres.

CONGRESS #5
J. J. Barnes, President

St. John - Ft. Myers, FL.
Sister Marion Haywood, Pres.
First Providence -
Bartow, FL.
Sister Ella Bibbs, Pres.
St. Mark -
Punta Gorda, FL.
Sister Lorene Bailey, Pres.
Friendship - Ft. Myers, FL.
Sister Essie Dawkins, Pres.
Mt. Gilboa -
Bartow, FL.
Sister Bernice McGhee, Pres.
St. Paul - Pierce
Sister J. J. Barnes, Pres.

Christian friends on behalf of the 1979 Official Staff of First South Florida Mission #2 Auxiliary (named below), I, Sister Bernice McGhee, recorder, most solemnly and joyfully submit this report. We have by the grace of God overcome many obstacles in our missionary endeavors.

Some workers have ventured into other auxiliaries, some have fallen by the wayside, and others have answered the Master's Call; but their memories shall forever warm our hearts. We shall forever keep the faith. Let us be forever mindful that if we continue to trust in God, nothing will be impossible. (2nd Corinthians 2:19)

1979 OFFICIAL STAFF

President	Sister L. C. B. Thomas
1st Vice President	L. A. Bullard
2nd Vice President	C. L. Spikes
3rd Vice President	Coleen Baldwin
Recorder	Bernice McGhee
Assistant Recorder	Amanda Booker
Corresponding Secretary	Charlie M. Wilder
Financial Secretary	Ocie DeLaughter
Chairman of Finance	Sis. Sophrona Romeo
Treasurer	Sis. Lula Campbell
Editorial Secretary	Sis. Peachie L. Hamilton
Statistical Secretary	Sis. Johnnie J. Barnes
Historian	Sis. Nora Jackson
Mission Dean	Sis. Evelyn Howell
Assistant Mission Dean	Sis. Marion Hayword
Dean of General Workshop	Rev. J. L. Stephens
Assistant Dean	Rev. W. Goynes
Spiritual Advisor	Rev. T. L. Jenkins
Chairman of Music	Sis. A. P. Boatman
Pianist	Sis. Evelyn Eads
Chorister	Sis. Cleo Capers
Senior Counsellor	Sis. N. E. Pelham
Field Workers	Congressional Presidents

MISSION NUMBER TWO AUXILIARY OF THE EQUAL RIGHTS MISSIONARY BAPTIST ASSOCIATION

This Auxiliary was organized at our annual District Association held in July of 1968 under the leadership of Moderator E. L. Causey. The members of this group were actively involved in quarterly district meetings, annual district associations and some times the president and some members have been blessed to attend their state conventions. We have been able as a group to visit the hospital, nursing homes, sick persons, Ninety and Nine Boys Ranch and Youth Harbor, a detention home for young offenders. During these visits we were always able to share the Lord, express His great love and provide them with gifts and/or donations, Several instances we were even able to provide refreshments for a party for the young people. Our annual project is to render service to those confined to the nursing homes by regular church service and buying each a gift. We have also made liberal donations to education, local and state. We have five active groups in the district and we are pleased to say another mission has been organized at the Tabernacle Number II Baptist Church and will be installed on Sunday, February 18, 1979. Our groups at this time are Emmanuel, Mrs. Ethel Burnette, President; Englewood, Mrs. Mary Stallworth, President; Morning Star, Mrs. Cora Walker, President; New Hope, Mrs. Etta M. Gray, President; Tabernacle #2, and Union Baptist Oakfield, Mrs. Vera Brown, President.

Our present officers are: Mrs. Margaret L. Williams, President; Mrs. Jessie McCants, Vice President; Mrs. Nettie Jones, Secretary; Mrs. Mary L. Stallworth, Treasurer and Mrs. Laura Pugh, Counselor. As a group, we have managed down through the years to fulfill our obligations, spiritually and financially and thanks to an almighty God for the privilege to serve.

MT. PILGRIM MISSION #2 DISTRICT HISTORY

Sister Eva Hearn, President
Rev. C. H. Bolden, Moderator

Mission #2 was organized into Mt. Pilgrim District in Tampa, 1971 with Sister Grovenia Lafvette, President; Sister Laverne Morris, Vice President; Sister Beatrice

Zeigler, Recording Secretary; Sister Doretha Waters, Financial Secretary; Sister Tsora Daughty, Corresponding Secretary; Sister Mildred Gaither, Treasurer; Rev. F. G. Hilton, Rev. G. E. McCrary were elected Advisory, Rev. G. W. Deering, Dean.

Mission #2 was organized with the following churches participating:

New Bethel M.B. Church, Sarasota, Florida, Rev. W. C. Grimsley, Pastor and Sister Hattie Williams, President

St. John Progressive M.B. Church, Tampa, Florida, Rev. F. G. Hilton, Pastor and Sister Linnie Myrick, President

Truevine M. B. Church, Rev. G. E. McCrary, Pastor and Sister Mildred Gaither, President

Mt. Tabor M. B. Church, Tallavast, Florida, Rev. G. Hopkin, Pastor

President Lafvette worked hard to build and keep Mission #2 going. In 1973 Sister Doretha Waters was elected President. She began to work and pray and send letters to the different churches, very few responded, but she did not get discouraged. New Mt. Zion, Lakeland, Florida, and Mt. Olive, Plant City join hearts and hands with the Mt. Pilgrim District and began work. Mission #2 really had a struggle trying to grow in Mt. Pilgrim but President Waters kept the faith and kept trying. New Bethel, St. John, New Mt. Zion, St. Paul, Ft. Myers worked faithfully. In 1976, St. Matthew, Tampa, Florida, Mission #2 joined their hands, hearts, time and talent and began work.

Mission #2 History of St. John M. B. Church: Mission #2 was organized January 1972 under the leadership of Rev. F. G. Hilton, Pastor. The purposes of this mission are to get more Christians out in the field, working to carry out the Mission endeavors of Jesus Christ.

Officers elected by the church were: Sister Linnie Myrick, President; Sister Hannah Fatherly, Treasurer; Sister Mary Parker, Secretary. Later a meeting was set up to complete the election of officers. At this meeting Sister Eva Hearn was elected Vice President; Sister

Beatrice Lester, Chairman; with the five members we started on our way telling the unbelievers about Christ . . . By the month of May, six (6) persons joined the Society. With these we were very thankful to our Lord and Savior Jesus Christ, still realizing that God wants us to keep marching on that we may reach others. Later fifteen (15) more members joined this Mission which gave a total of twenty-six (26) members, both men and women. We thank God for these members that decided to give their time for God's program.

In 1976 Sister Eva Hearn was elected as president of Mission #2; Sister Gracie Houston, Vice President at the end of this 1976 session. These presidents' and offices join hearts and hands in prayer for the growth for Mission #2 in the session. Sister Charlotte Sim was elected as counselor, she has been and is a supporter and help to Mission #2. Mt. Pilgrim District is grateful to Rev. S. N. Sanders, Pastor and Sister Doretha Spenser, President of St. Paul in Lakeland.

On July, 1978, St. Paul, Lakeland, joined hearts and hands with Mt. Pilgrim District and began work July 28, 1978.

SECOND WEST FLORIDA MISSIONARY BAPTIST ASSOCIATION

Senior Women No. 2

The senior Women No. 2 Convention was organized November 19, 1969, at New Galilee Missionary Baptist Church, Marianna, Florida. Reverend A. H. Parker is Moderator, Sister Lelar Jones was elected President. Sister Lelar Jones was also our Junior President before we changed to Senior Women No. 2.

Sister Lelar Jones works diligently and prays each day to be a good leader for Senior Women No. 2, and with God being her Guide she was a good leader. The task never got too hard nor the journey too long for her. Sister Lelar Jones went many, many places trying to carry out the work. Some of the places she traveled so enthusiastically were as follows: The Morning Star Sunday School Convention, National Convention, State Convention.

Through her going, we added workshops for our leaders and workers. Councils, Foreign Mission, and plays were also organized to help our convention grow. Through her leadership we now have good conventions. We have 14 societies.

The following is a list of Officers who worked by her side:

Vice President	Sister Alice Spears
Recording Secretary	Sister Willie Dickens
Corresponding Secretary	Sister Andellia Blount
Pianist and Director	Sister Ida M. Spires
Chorister	Sister Mary G. Jones
Treasurer	Sister Angeline Bolds
Organizer (West)	Sister Myrtle Robinson
Organizer (East)	Sister Doris Lewis

Through the years we have shared our joys and sorrows together. In 1976 Sister Lelar Jones retired from the Presidency after 34 years of tremendous service. She was then elected President EMERITUS. Sister Alice Spears was then elected President. Since then Sister Spears has gone many places such as: The National Convention, and the Morning Star Sunday School Convention.

Sister Alice Spears is doing a great job with the Leadership. Sister Anna Granberry, our Vice President, is doing a great job and working very hard with the Foreign Mission. Sister Ida M. Spires has been our pianist and director for several years. After she was elected Vice President of our Progressive Convention, she became over loaded and had to give up being our Pianist and Director.

Listed below are officers who work very hard with Sister Alice Spears trying to carry the work on:

Sister Lelar Jones	President EMERITUS
Sister Alice Spears	President
Sister Anne Granberry	Vice President
Sister Willie Dickens	Recording Secretary
Sister Andellia Blount	Corresponding Secretary

Sister Lillian Parker	Pianist and Director
Sister Mary G. Jones	Chorister
Sister Angeline Bolds	Treasurer
Sister Myrtle Robinson	Organizer (West)
Sister Frances Hodges	Organizer (East)

Sister Alice Spears is blessed in many, many ways to be able to go and work and serve her convention as the Lord sees fit. So it takes a lot of praying in times like these. In our Association we have other committees namely: Letter Committee, Enrollment Committee, Mission Committee and Councils.

Our devotion is spiritual at all times. The President, Sister Alice Spears and her co-workers have done a good job. Our Moderator has been very helpful to Senior Women No. 2. Always willing to stop and listen and help straighten things out.

"Help others too, Oh Lord, I pray,
To work to right all wrong;
Guide our foot steps all the way,
Lord, Help us to be strong."

Sister Lelar Jones	President EMERITUS
Sister Alice Spears	President
Sister Anne Granberry	Vice President
Sister Willie Dickens	Secretary
Reverend A. H. Parker	Moderator

MISSION #2 OF UNION FOREIGN MISSIONARY BAPTIST ASSOCIATION

Reverend L. S. McCree, Moderator

Mission No. 2 of Union Foreign Missionary Association has served faithfully for the past ten years. We are facing a new year with faith and courage. When Mission No. 2 was first organized in the district, we had only five societies. Today we have fourteen. We thank God for his leadership in helping us to reach our goal.

We were organized in 1941, as Y.W.A.'s by Sister Irene Carleton. In later years, we became Junior Women. As in keeping with our state and national convention, ten years ago we were organized as Mission Number 2.

Most of the work accomplished by Mission Number 2 has been done for mission and education. We are dedicated in trying to help others.

We are very proud of our President, Sister Mattie Smith who has served us faithfully and well for the past ten years. We pray for her continued service to the cause.

Our society has worked faithfully down through the years in our district, state and national convention. For two years, State Mission No. 2 Queen was from Union Foreign and went on to represent Florida in the national Convention.

One of our mottoes is "Let your light so shine that men may see your good work and glorify our Father who is in Heaven." We have a great job to do and we know that the only way we can succeed is through prayers. The group that prays together, stays together. We pray that you will have much success with your booklet.

Sister Mattie Smith	President
Sister Ceola Hamilton	Vice President
Sister Nash	Second Vice President
Sister Flora Holland	Recording Secretary
Sister Mary Lee Spann	Financial Secretary
Sister Dorothy Mott	Corresponding Secretary
Sister Jeannette Brewington	Treasurer
Reverend L. Wardell	Advisor

FIRST ANNUAL SESSION OF THE PROGRESSIVE MISSIONARY & EDUCATIONAL BAPTIST STATE CONGRESS

Dr. James Carl Sams	General President
Dr. A. H. Parker	President of Congress

Convened with
GREATER BETHEL BAPTIST CHURCH
808 Short Emory, Tampa, Florida 33602
July 24–28, 1974

Theme: Training for Effective Witnessing

Roster of Officers

Dr. A. H. Parker	President
Rev. W. R. Lovelace	Vice President
Rev. J. L. Stephens	Dean
Mrs. L. A. Bullard	Recording Secretary
Rev. J. F. Hargrett	Corresponding Secretary
Rev. J. C. Burney	Treasurer
Mrs. Estella C. Dickson	Chairman of Finance

NINTH ANNUAL SESSION OF THE PROGRESSIVE MISSIONARY AND EDUCATIONAL BAPTIST STATE CONGRESS

The Reverend Dr. J. C. Sams, General President
The Reverend Dr. A. H. Parker, President of Congress
The Reverend J. F. Hargrett, Corresponding Secretary

To Convene With The
Little Rock Baptist Church
1418 Van Buren St.
Jacksonville, Florida 32206

July 20–24, 1982

THEME:
"Spiritual Growth and Development: The Commitment of Today's Church."
Luke 2:40; Matthew 28:20

ROSTER OF OFFICERS

First Vice President	The Reverend W. R. Lovelace

Second Vice President	The Reverend A. W. Hodge
Third Vice President	The Reverend Alex Harper
Recording Secretary	Mrs. L. A. Bullard
Assistant Recording Secretary	Mrs. B. C. Covington
Treasurer	The Reverend J. C. Burney
Secretary to the President	The Reverend Rollie Murray
Dean of Workshop	The Reverend J. L. Stephens
Asst. Dean of Workshop	The Reverend N. F. Sumpter
Chairman of Finance	Mrs. Estella Dickson
Director of Music	Mrs. Mary Whitehurst
Assistant Director of Music	Mrs. Edna S. Hargrett

STATE ORATORICAL CONTEST

On Thursday, July 25, 1985, at Marianna Middle School, Dean Stephen appointed a committee to draw up Guidelines for a State Oratorical Contest.

They were:

Reverend J. E. Atkins
Dr. T. G. Bess
Mrs. Reola M. Bryan
Mrs. Margie McGriff
Mrs. Lillian D. Parker
Mrs. Chris B. Gibson
Dean Stephen, Ex-officio Member

Reverend J. E. Atkins, Chairman
Chris Barnes Gibson, Secretary

GUIDELINES

I. It shall be an Oratorical Contest

II. Contestants selection shall be from:

1. Local Church
   A. 5th Sunday Congress and/or Ministers' and Deacons' Union
2. Association District Congresses
3. State

Organizational Chart

STATE

ASSOCIATION DISTRICT CONGRESSES

LOCAL CHURCHES

III. THEME

The Theme shall be the same as used in the National Congress.

IV. TIME LIMIT

The Time limit for each contestant shall be ten minutes

V. CONTESTANTS' ELIGIBILITY

Each contestant shall be a graduating Senior or a Junior.

VI. PRIZES

1.
2.
3.

A. Funds shall be used for scholarship purposes only. These funds shall be paid directly to the college that the recipient enrolls. It shall be the responsibility of the recipient to notify the dean of the choice and acceptance of college.

B. A scholarship committee shall be formed.

C. The contestant that chooses Florida Memorial College in Miami, Florida, or a Vocational College shall be given a BONUS.

VII. JUDGING

Judging of the Contestants shall be on:

a. speaking
b. reading
c. writing
d. content
e. pronunciation
f. enunciation
g. posture

VIII. Judges

There shall be from 5 to 7 judges for the contest.

a. Judges shall be non-members of the Progressive M. And E. State Congress

b. Qualifications of Judges
Judges shall have expertise in Com munication Skills.

PROGRAM OF THE NINETEENTH ANNUAL SESSION OF THE PROGRESSIVE MISSIONARY AND EDUCATIONAL BAPTIST STATE CONVENTION OF FLORIDA, INC.

July 21–24, 1992

CONVENING at the
DR. JAMES CARL SAMS CONFERENCE CENTER
And STATE CONVENTION HEADQUARTERS
1030 West Olive Street
LAKELAND, FLORIDA

THEME:
"Biblical Injunctions for Family Solidarity"
Acts 16:31–34; I Timothy 3:5; Mark 5:19

Dr. Alex Harper, Sr.
Congress President

Dr. Henry T. Rhim
Convention President

CONGRESS OFFICERS

Dr. A. H. Parker	President Emeritus
Dr. Alex Harper, Sr.	President
Reverend H. H. Wynn	First Vice President
Reverend S. L. Maxwell	Second Vice President
Dr. F. Lee Carter	Third Vice President
Sister Vivian Patten	Recording Secretary

Sister Joyce Williams	Assistant Recorder
Reverend R. Robinson, Jr.	Corresponding Secretary
Reverend B. B. Dinkins	Financial Secretary
Reverend J. C. Burney	Treasurer
Sister Yvonne Moore	Secretary to the President
Reverend N. F. Sumpter	Dean
Reverend Rollie Murray	Assistant Dean
Reverend W. J. Haynes	Administrative Assistant
Sister Estella Dickson	Chairman of Finance
Sister Mary Whitehurst	Director of Music
Dr. H. T. Rhim	Convention President

PROGRAM

TUESDAY, July 21, 1992

10:00 A.M. BREAKFAST/WORKSHOP for Congress Staff
Florida Seminary Dining Hall
214 West 5th Street, Lakeland

7:30 P.M. Musical and Program of Welcome
New Jerusalem Baptist Church
1124 North New York Avenue, Lakeland
The Reverend J. L. Downing, Pastor

WEDNESDAY, July 22, 1992

8:30 A.M. OFFICIAL OPENING of the 19th Annual Session
President Alex Harper, Presiding
General Greetings and Remarks
The Reverend H. T. Rhim, Convention President

9:15 A.M. Theme: "Biblical Injunctions for Family Solidarity"
The Reverend Robert L. Johnson
Jerusalem Baptist Church, Ft. Myers

9:45 A.M. Introduction of Congress Workers and Directions
Dean N. F. Sumpter

10:00 A.M. CLASS PERIOD
11:00 A.M. General Assembly
KEYNOTE MESSAGE: THE REVEREND
T. W. JENKINS, Pastor
Blackwood Grove Baptist Church
Nettleton, Mississippi
Noon LUNCH

WEDNESDAY Afternoon

1:20–2:55 P.M. AFTERNOON CLASSES
3:00 P.M. Afternoon Session Called to Order
Vice President H. H. Wynn, Presiding
"A MODEL SUNDAY SCHOOL"
The Reverend Rudolph McKissick
Bethel Baptist Church, Jacksonville
Registration Continued
4:20 P.M. Afternoon Break

WEDNESDAY Evening

7:30 P.M. Evening Session Called to Order
Vice President S. L. Maxwell, Presiding
Evening Worship Service
SERMON: The Reverend L. H. King
Mt. Calvary Baptist, Clewiston
ALTERNATE: The Reverand W. J. Haynes
Mt. Olive, Medulla
Choir and Ushers are asked to serve
Invitation to Discipleship, Offering
Information Flashes
8:45 P.M. EVANGELICAL BOARD SERVICE
The Reverend Thomas Brown, Chairman
The Reverend Carl Brooks, Vice Chairman
SERMON: The Reverend Fred L. Brown
St. John First Baptist, Palmetto

ALTERNATE: The Reverend A. L. Phillips
New Bethel, Sarasota
TERMINATION OF EVENING SESSION

THURSDAY, July 23, 1992

8:30–10:55 A.M.	MORNING CLASS INSTRUCTION
11:00 A.M.	GENERAL ASSEMBLY Session Called to Order Vice President F. Lee Carter, Presiding
NOON	LUNCH
1:20 P.M.	AFTERNOON CLASS INSTRUCTION
3:00 P.M.	GENERAL ASSEMBLY WORKSHOP: Business Entrepreneurs DR. MARVIN DAVIES Special Assistant to Senator Bob Graham
4:00 P.M.	Afternoon Break

THURSDAY Evening

7:30 P.M.	Evening Session Called to Order President Alex Harper, Presiding SERMON: The Reverend Raymond Rogers Mt. Moriah #2, Panama City ALTERNATE: The Reverend Z. S. Hudson New Mt. Zion, Tampa Choirs and Ushers are to serve Invitation, Offering, Information Flashes
8:45 P.M.	EVANGELICAL BOARD SERVICE The Reverend Thomas Brown, Chairman The Reverend C. Brooks, Vice Chairman Sermon: The Reverend N. S. Sanders Greater St. Paul, Lakeland

ALTERNATE: The Reverend L. Norris, Jr.
New Mt. Zion, Lakeland
TERMINATION OF EVENING SESSION

FRIDAY, July 24, 1992

8:30 A.M.	MORNING CLASS INSTRUCTION
10:30 A.M.	GENERAL ASSEMBLY New Bethel A.M.E. Church Martin Luther King Boulevard Session Called to Order First Vice President, H. H. Wynn THE PRESIDENT'S HOUR President H. T. Rhim, Presiding ANNUAL MESSAGE Congress President Alex Harper, Sr. Dismissal LUNCH
2:00 P.M.	ANNUAL BOARD MEETING of the PROGRESSIVE M&E BAPTIST STATE CONVENTION OF FLORIDA, INC. Dr. H. T. Rhim, President, Presiding
4:00 P.M.	ORATORICAL CONTEST Youth/Children Convention The Reverend T. G. Bess, Executive Director New Bethel A.M.E. Church

FRIDAY Evening

7:00 P.M.	AWARDS BANQUET HONOREES: Brother and Sister Alexander Heard Sister Mary Whitehurst

BANQUET SPEAKER:
The Reverend Odell Smith, Jr.
Second Baptist, Jacksonville
Banquet Location:
HIBISCUS
714 E. Orange Street, Lakeland

8:45 P.M. EVANGELICAL BOARD SERVICE
The Reverend Thomas Brown, Chairman
The Reverend C. Brooks, Vice Chairman
CLOSING SERMON:
The Reverend C. L. Johnson
First Baptist Church, Wauchula
ALTERNATE:
The Reverend C. C. Reeves, Dean of Workshop
State Evangelical Board
Invitation to Discipleship, Offering
FINAL REMARKS:
The Reverend Alex Harper, Jr., Congress President
The Reverend Henry T. Rhim, President, Progressive M&E
Baptist State Convention of Florida, Inc.
OFFICIAL CLOSING OF THE NINETEENTH ANNUAL SESSION OF THE SCHOOL OF CHRISTIAN EDUCATION
CHURCH ENROLLMENT: $110.00
INDIVIDUAL REGISTRATION: $10.00

THE BROTHERHOOD UNION
Organized March 1947

Officers: Bro. Sam Davis
Bro. I. M. Jones
Bro. Leroy Williams

PROGRAM OF THE BROTHERHOOD UNION CONVENTION AUXILIARY TO THE PROGRESSIVE MISSIONARY and EDUCATIONAL BAPTIST STATE CONVENTION OF FLORIDA

TO CONVENE with the MT. GILBOA MISSIONARY
BAPTIST CHURCH
BARTOW, FLORIDA
Rev. Eddie Burroughs, Pastor
March 18–23, 1975

Deacon I. M. Jones	President
Deacon P. J. Bryant	Vice President
Dr. J. C. Sams	General President

Theme: "The Gospel of Liberation for the Sin-Bound" St. John 8:32, 36.

PROGRAM OF THE BROTHERHOOD UNION CONVENTION AUXILIARY TO THE PROGRESSIVE MISSIONARY and EDUCATIONAL BAPTIST STATE CONVENTION OF FLORIDA

TO CONVENE with the MT. PLEASANT MISSIONARY
BAPTIST CHURCH
Orlando, Florida
The Reverend J. F. Hargrett, Pastor
March 23–28, 1976

Deacon I. M. Jones	President
Deacon P. J. Bryant	Vice President
The Reverend T. E. Gainous	Counselor
The Reverend Dr. J. C. Sams	General President

Theme
"Christ's Responsible Church In An Irresponsible World"
Matt: 5:13–16, 25:30–35; Micah 6:8

-PROGRAM-

Wednesday Afternoon

2:00 P.M. Deacon I. M. Jones, President, presiding
Brotherhood Fellowship Hour
Adoption of the Program, Announcements, and Adjournment

Wednesday Evening

7:30 P.M. First Vice President Bryant, presiding
Devotional Services led by appointees
Sermon: The Reverend John Willis, New Hope Baptist Church, Tampa, Florida
Alternate: The Reverend Tommie Bess, Indian Town, Florida
Offering, Announcements, and Adjournment

Thursday Morning

9:30 A.M. Go to Parent Body for Social Justice Hour

Thursday Afternoon

Third Vice President, presiding
Devotion Services led by appointee
Theme: Brother W. C. Taylor and Brother O. L. Merriet
Remarks: The Reverend T. E. Gainous, Counselor
Offering, Announcements, and Adjournment

Thursday Evening

7:30 P.M. Second Vice President, presiding
Devotional Services led by appointees
Sermon: The Reverend R. W. Wiggins, Daytona Beach, Florida
Alternate: The Reverend W. Crumbs
Offering, Announcements and Adjournment

Friday Morning

9:30 A.M. Fourth Vice President, presiding
Panel Discussion: Brothers Albert Phillips, O. L. Merrett, and Fred Evans
Theme: What Can I Do To Help Someone Who Is Lost? by Brother O. L. Merrett, "Why Are We Here?" by Brother Albert Phillips, "What Are the Aims of Brotherhood?" by Brother Fred Evans.

Friday Evening

7:30 P.M. Presiding, President I. M. Jones
Devotional Services by appointees
Sermon: The Reverend E. Gordon, Macedonia Baptist Church
Alternate: The Reverend O. Glover

Saturday Morning

9:00 A.M. Business Period

Saturday Evening

7:30 P.M. President's Night
The Reverend W. Tunstall, Mt. Moriah Baptist Church
Alternate: The Reverend C. Fletcher

SPECIAL NOTE: All choirs and Ushers are to serve with their pastor.

MARCH 1995
PROGRAM OF THE BROTHERHOOD UNION AUXILIARY of the PROGRESSIVE M&E BAPTIST STATE CONVENTION OF FLORIDA, Inc.

DEACON LEROY WILLIAMS, PRESIDENT

DR. H. T. RHIM CONVENTION PRESIDENT

Theme: "A New Look At An Old Mission"

BROTHERHOOD SESSION
Will Be Held At
Greater Peace Missionary
Baptist Church
102 4th Street
Fort Walton Beach, Florida

The Reverend Clanston Seymore, Pastor

STATE USHERS

The Ushers Auxiliary was organized July 1953 in a one-day session in Kissimmee, Florida. Reverend J. C. Sams, President, appointed Mrs. Idella Williams, Sarasota, as president. Reverend J. A. Shaver was appointed director. Before the adjournment of this session, Reverend Shaver met with the group for organization.

These officers were elected:

Vice President:	Mrs. Fannie Garner, Jacksonville
Recording Secretary:	Mrs. Viola Johnson, Jacksonville
Financial Secretary:	Mrs. Lula Campbell, Sebring
Treasurer:	Mrs. Conley, Lakeland
Captain:	Mr. Omie Sharper, Lakeland

PRESIDENTS OF THE USHERS AUXILIARY AND TERMS OF OFFICE

Mrs. Idella Williams	1953–1966
Mrs. Leanna Johnson	1967–1988
Mrs. Daisy Henderson	1988–

DIRECTORS

Reverend J. A. Shaver
Reverend L. W. Williams
Reverend Leon Freeman
Reverend J. J. Jones
Reverend A. J. Hughes
Reverend W. H. Mack

OFFICERS

President	Mrs. Daisy Henderson
First Vice President	Mrs. Christine Picett
Second Vice President	Mrs. Karen Hoover Brown
Financial Secretary:	Mrs. Flora Holland
Recording Secretary:	Mrs. Lucille Scott
Assistant Recording Secretary:	Mrs. Margaret Potter
Corresponding Secretary:	Mrs. Mable Dunbar
Asst. Corresponding Secretary:	Mrs. Mary K. Heard
Treasurer:	Mrs. Georgia Smith
Historian:	Mrs. Beatrice Lester
Director:	Reverend W. H. Mack

The history of the Ushers stated that "Mrs. Queen Williams, Jacksonville, was chorister in 1973." There are no further references to this office, neither is it listed with the officers serving at this time.

PROGRESSIVE M AND E BAPTIST STATE CONVENTION OF FLORIDA

Mt. Gilboa Missionary Baptist Church
Bartow, Florida

Rev. Eddie Burroughs, Pastor
March 18–23, 1975

OFFICIAL ROSTER OF THE USHERS' CONVENTION

Sis. Leanna C. Johnson	President
Sis. Daisy Henderson	1st Vice President
Sis. Josephine Eady	2nd Vice President
Sis. Viola F. Johnson	Recording Secretary
Sis. Flora M. Holland	Financial Secretary
Sis. Mable Dunbar	Corresponding Secretary
Sis. M. K. Heard	Assistant Secretary
Sis. Shirley Brooks	Secretary to President
Sis. Georgia M. Smith	Treasurer
Sis. Queen B. Williams	Chorister
Sis. Beatrice Lester	Historian
Rev. A. J. Hughes	Director

PROGRAM OF THE TWENTY-THIRD ANNUAL SESSION OF THE STATE USHERS CONVENTION

Auxiliary of the PROGRESSIVE MISSIONARY and EDUCATIONAL CONVENTION OF FLORIDA

Dr. James Carl Sams, President

To Convene with the
MT. PLEASANT BAPTIST CHURCH
Orlando, Florida
March 23–28, 1976

Reverend Joseph Hargrett, Pastor

OFFICIAL ROSTER

Sister Leanna C. Johnson	President
Sister Daisy Henderson	First Vice President
	Second Vice President
Sister Josephine Eady	Third Vice President
Sister Viola F. Johnson	Recording Secretary
Sister Flora M. Holland	Financial Secretary
Sister Georgia M. Smith	Treasurer
Sister Mable Dunbar	Corresponding Secretary
Sister Mary K. Heard	Assistant Corresponding Secretary
Sister Shirley Brooks	Secretary to the President
Sister Beatrice Lester	Historian
Sister Queen B. Williams	Chorister
Rev. A. J. Hughes	Director and Bible Instructor

PROGRAM
Wednesday Afternoon

3:00 P.M. Devotion, Sister Queen B. Williams
3:15 P.M. Remarks by the President, Sister Leanna C. Johnson
Adoption of Program, Enrollment,
Expressional Meeting
Announcements and Adjournment

Wednesday Evening

7:30 P.M. Devotional and Welcome Program by Entertaining Church
Enrollment Period
Sermon: Rev. C. J. Long
Alternate: Rev. James Scantling
Choirs and Ushers Serving
Enrollment and Offering
Respond to Program, Sister Fannie Garner
Remarks, Announcements and Adjournment

Thursday Morning

9:30 A.M. Go to Parent Body for Social Justice Hour

Thursday Afternoon

2:30 P.M. Theme: "Christ's Responsible Church in an Irresponsible World," by Sister Shirley Brooks
Devotion, Sister Queen B. Williams
Enrollment
Sermon: Rev. Clanston Seymore, Greater Peace Baptist Church
Alternate: Rev. Joseph Smith, New Bethel Baptist Church, Belle Glade

Thursday Evening

7:30 P.M. With Parent Body

Friday Morning

9:15 A.M. Instructional Workshop: Director & Bible Instructor, Rev. A. J. Hughes
President's Hour, 1st Vice President, Sister Daisy Henderson, Presiding

Friday Afternoon

2:30 P.M.	With Parent Body

Friday Evening

7:30 P.M.	Devotion and Enrollment Continued
8:00 P.M.	Sermon: Rev. L. I. James, Miami, Fla.
	Alternate: Rev. Leon Campbell, Belle Glade, Fla.
	Choirs and Ushers Serving
	Remarks, Offering
	Announcements and Adjournment

Saturday Morning

9:30 A.M.	Devotion
	Enrollment Continued

1995 Convention Program
Officers

Sister Mary K. Heard	President
Sister Christine Pickett	Vice President
Sister Mary Alexander	Recording Secretary
Sister Eloise Wells	Assistant Recording Secretary
Sister Flora Holland	Financial Secretary
Sister Wilhelmenia Carter	Asst. Financial Secretary
Sister Mable Dunbar	Corresponding Secretary
Sister Dorothy Gordon	Asst. Corresponding Secretary
Sister Edith Bigham	Historian
Brother Samuel Bryant	Devotional Leader
Brother Josh Hilliard	Assistant Devotional Leader
Reverend E. J. Walker	Ministerial Advisor

PROGRAM

Tuesday, March 21, 1995

11:00 A.M. Official Brunch with State President Dr. H. T. Rhim

	Congress Board Meeting
	Reverend Alex Harper, Sr. Congress President
2:00 P.M.	Pastor's Conference
	Reverend Harry D. Rucker, Sr. Chairman
7:30 P.M.	Pre-Convention Musical and Welcome Program

Wednesday, March 22, 1995

9:30 A.M.	Progressive Missionary & Educational Baptist State Convention 81st Annual Session Called To Order by President Dr. H. T. Rhim (All Auxiliaries in Session with the Parent Body)
2:30 P.M.	All Auxiliaries Report Back to the Parent Body for all Board Reports
6:00 P.M.	Official Opening of the Fortieth Annual Session of the State
	Ushers Session by President Sister Mary K. Heard
	Greetings and Remarks by the President
	Organization and Directions for Enrollment
	Remarks by our Minister/Advisor, Reverend E. J. Walker
7:00 P.M.	Welcome Program by Local Ushers
	Appointments of Committees
	Song by Audience
8:00 P.M.	Sermon: Reverend Levi White, Pastor Little Rock Baptist Church Jacksonville, Fl.
	Alternate: To be Named
	Choirs and Ushers Serving
	Invitation to Discipleship
	Offering, Announcements and Adjournment

THE SENIOR WOMEN'S MISSIONARY & EDUCATIONAL CONVENTION

Auxiliary of the Progressive Baptist
State Convention of Florida

The earliest record of a Black Baptist Women's Mission organization in Florida is February 7, 1890. A group of women met at the First Baptist Church, Fernandina, on the recommendation of the Reverends John N. Stokes, Sr., Live Oak, Peter R. Anderson, Belleview, James Jamison, Jacksonville, C. H. Hampton, Ocala, G. P. McKinney, Live Oak, R. Kemp, Fernandina, A. Anderson, Wiggins Brown, Washington Faclks and Professor Maddox, Lake City.

The following women were in the organization: Sisters R. M. Ross and E. M. Bailey, First Baptist Church, Fernandina, R. M. English, St. Mary's Church, St. Augustine, A. R. Seymore, Russel Church, Stage Pond, H. A. Miller, First African Baptist Church, Live Oak, M. Williams, Damascus Church, Madison, Julia A. Patterson, Tampa, Emma Edwards, H. Cook, Ella Hogan, St. Paul, Sanford, P. Morris and S. Williams.

The brethren who assisted in the organization were: the Reverends John N. Stokes, Sr., C. N. Hampton, George P. McKinney, Peter R. Anderson, James Jamison, and R. Kemp.

The officers elected were:

President:	E. M. Bailey, Fernandina
Vice President:	A. R. Seymore, Stage Pond
Recording Secretary:	H. A. Miller, Live Oak
Treasurer:	M. Williams, Madison

The first annual session was held simultaneously with the General State Convention, Ocala, Mt. Moriah Baptist Church, February 5, 1891.

There were five presidents who led the women in their missionary and educational tasks. They were:

Mrs. E. M. Bailey	1890–1891
Mrs. A. A. Johnson Scott	1891–1895
Mrs. Annie M. Holman	1895–1900
Mrs. Susie M. Mitchell	1900–1909
Mrs. P. A. James	1909–1919

This history would be remiss if the support that Baptist Women of Florida have given to their local churches, associations, and conventions was not recognized. They have made meaningful the concept of "Mission Action" as it relates to the foreign field.

RESOLUTION, 1899

That this convention keep in mind the missionary of Africa, Reverend Koti, and his plea for assistance. That once a year each society have a missionary rally, and money raised therefrom be sent to the State Treasurer who will report the same to the president of the General State Convention, who will forward the total amount to Reverend Koti, Queenstown, South Africa.[8]

Respectfully submitted,

Rebecca C. Murry, Des Verney Carr, Rachel Phillips, Fannie Summers, L. P. Lawrence (White), Ellen Green, Marion Jones (White) and Fannie Morris.

1900-RESOLUTION

Whereas, the Florida General Baptist State Convention at its last session held in April in Fernandina, passed a resolution endorsing Miss Emma B. Delaney of Fernandina as a missionary to Africa, and recommended her to the National Baptist Foreign Mission Board of Nashville, Tennessee, for appointment.

Resolved, that the Woman's Missionary and Educational Convention heartily endorse the action of the General State Convention and do pledge itself to cooperate with the General State Convention in her support on the Foreign Field.

Respectfully submitted,

Alice L. Mitchell[9]

Miss Emma B. Delaney with Doctors M. W. Gilbert and J. T. Brown, sailed as a missionary to British Central Africa, a distance of fourteen thousand miles, January 15, 1902[10]

We must move nearer home so that we can get a larger picture of our personal involvement and contributions to the overall support of the mission program.

In 1901 the Missionary Women of the Second Bethlehem Association founded an orphanage for children at Belleview, Florida. The first matron was Mrs. Louisa Allen. Mrs. Delia Blackshear Simmons was the second matron. This orphanage remained in operation until 1936 when the State Department of Health and Human Services ordered it closed because of problems with organization, management, the lack of modern equipment, and programming. Also, the need for a qualified director or social worker, staff, and support services was a contributing factor in its closing. Even though the General Convention did not own the Home, when a group withdrew in 1913 and formed the Progressive Baptist State Convention, there was consolidated support for the orphanage by both until it closed.

The Board of Trustees for the orphanage were the presidents of the General Baptist State and Progressive Baptist Conventions, moderators of the affiliated Associations and the Women's Societies. The orphanage was supported through annual sales of arts and crafts, and donations of food, clothing, bedding, and other items for a linen closet. The Conventions and related Associations annually budgeted for its support. Local pastors invited the matron to their churches to make a personal appeal for supplementary support. Occasionally the matron brought a group from the orphanage to present programs to demonstrate the kinds of activities and learning experiences provided for children.

A number of churches enrolled in the organization of the Women's Convention, February 5, 1891. Twenty-three years later, it became the Women's Auxiliary to the Progressive Missionary Baptist State Convention.

The churches were: Mt. Gilboa, Bartow; Mt. Hermon, Tarpon Springs; Shiloh, Orlando; St. Mark, Punta Gorda; St. James, Key West; St. John, Sanford; Bethel, Jacksonville; Mt. Moriah, Winter Park. Two of the first Secretaries of the Women's Convention were Mrs. Mary Lewter and Mrs. Rachel Boone both of Mt. Gilboa, Bartow. Board Members included: Mrs. S. V. Reese, Mt. Hermon, Tarpon Springs; Mrs. R. C. Boone, Mt. Gilboa, Bartow; and Mrs. Laura Arnette, Shiloh, Orlando. Mission Women were: Miss S. A. Blocker, Baptist Academy, Jacksonville; Mrs. Lucy Lancaster, Jacksonville; and Mrs. Lula Mills, Jacksonville. Pastors were: the Reverends Frank Lancaster, Jacksonville; L. A. Johnson, Arcadia, and W. B. Mills, Jacksonville.

SOCIETIES ENROLLED 1890–1891

Mt. Gilboa, Bartow
Mt. Hermon, Tarpon Springs
St. Mark, Punta Gorda
St. James, Key West
St. John, Sanford
Bethel, Jacksonville
Mt. Moriah, Winter Park
Baptist Academy, Jacksonville.

The Women's Convention, Auxiliary to the Progressive Baptist State Convention was organized March 1914 following the founding of the parent body. In addition to the women previously mentioned, the following were present at the organization meeting in Bartow: Sisters Idella Cason, Eliza Lewis, T. H. Moore, Mary Lewter, Lucy White, Hannah B. Miller, and C. B. Smith.

The group drafted and later presented a resolution which was read by Reverend Castle Daniel, pastor of the First African Baptist Church, Green Cove Springs. Thus, the Women's Missionary and Education Convention had its beginning.

The presidents who have served the organization since March 1914 are:

Ms. Idella Cason	1914–1918
Mrs. Eliza Lewis	1918–1920
Mrs. Theresa H. Moore	1920–1953
Mrs. Hannah B. Miller	1953–1971
Mrs. Agnes Dean	1971–1973
Mrs. Amelia Houston	1973–1987
Mrs. Maude M. Fowler	1987–1992
Mrs. Ruby F. Herndon	1992–

The presidents with the longer tenures are:

Theresa H. Moore	33 years
Hannah B. Miller	18 years
Amelia Houston	14 years

Leaders of the women's department have been drawn from a diversity of occupations, backgrounds, and community participation. The timing of their services appeared to have significantly affected the expansion of the missionary task. The first president, Miss Idella Cason, was a teacher at the Baptist Academy, Jacksonville, at the time of her election. She was known for her very special talent, skills, and methods for Bible Teaching. Miss Cason was a fluent and impressive speaker. Each succeeding president emerged as a distinct personality, giving of herself to make a contribution to pass on as a religious heritage and legacy. They have been businesswomen and professionals, leaders of fraternal organizations, and self-employed women. They commanded a position of respect and involvement in civic and community affairs. Most importantly, they were dedicated women. Not every president led in the same manner, but each served in her own particular way, sharing her gifts with others.

Reverend H. T. Rhim, president, recommended at the 76th Annual Session of the Progressive Missionary and Educational Baptist State Convention of Florida, Inc., Tampa, Florida, on March 23, 1990, that the Senior Women's Auxiliary and the Senior Mission No. Two Auxiliary be merged, thus having only one Senior Women's Auxiliary.

The merger of the Senior Women's Auxiliary, the Mission No. Two, and the organization of the Matrons Auxiliary is scheduled for Saturday, March 24, 1990, at 9:00 a.m. at the New Friendship Missionary Baptist Church, 3107 E. Lake Avenue, Tampa, the Reverend H. L. Daniels, pastor.

Persons 36 and older may work with the Matrons or the Senior Mission Auxiliary.[11]

PROGRAM OF THE SIXTY-SECOND ANNUAL SESSION OF THE WOMEN'S MISSIONARY AND EDUCATIONAL CONVENTION OF FLORIDA

Auxiliary of the
PROGRESSIVE MISSIONARY and EDUCATIONAL
CONVENTION OF FLORIDA

Dr. J. C. Sams, President
To Convene with
MT. PLEASANT BAPTIST CHURCH
314 South Parramore Ave., Orlando, Florida

THEME:
"Christ's Responsible Church In An Irresponsible World"
Matthew 5:13–16, 25:35–36; Micah 6:8

Convention Officers

Mrs. Hannah B. Miller 1117 Durkee Drive, Jacksonville	President Emeritus
Mrs. Amelia E. Houston P.O. Box 884, Belle Glade	President
Mrs. Annie L. Brigham 645 Oklahoma St., Bonifay	First Vice President

Mrs. Maude M. Fowler — Second Vice President
1314 Lemon Street, Tampa
Mrs. Mary L. Black — Third Vice President
Box 47, Gretna
Mrs. Janie L. Nails — Fourth Vice President
3506 Lindell Avenue, Tampa
Mrs. Rosa Lee Carwise — Recording Secretary
855 Sears Avenue, Winter Haven
Mrs. Callie D. Granberry — Assistant Recording Secretary
Box 330 Greenwood
Mrs. Shirley Laffitte, Sarasota — Assistant Corresponding Secretary
Mrs. Anna Gayle, Palmetto — Corresponding Secretary
Mrs. Ruby L. Herndon — Financial Secretary
2527 Lantana Avenue, Jacksonville
Mrs. Alexina Johnson — Treasurer
1424 West 15th Street, Jacksonville
Mrs. Maretta Stokes — Assistant Treasurer
Mrs. Estella Dickson — Historian
1015 South Delaney Avenue, Avon Park
Mrs. Marzella Brown — Assistant Historian
Mrs. Juanita Reynolds — Musician
1814 West 11th Street, Jacksonville
Mrs. C. M. Graham, Orlando, Fla — Assistant Musician
Mrs. Angeline Russ — Director of Music
2503 27th Avenue, Tampa
Mrs. Marion Myrick — Assistant Director of Music
Mrs. Wilma W. Thompson — Dean of Workshop
37890 St. Augustine Road, Jacksonville
Mrs. Betty Harris — Assistant Dean of Workshop
Mrs. Cora Walker — Assistant Dean of Workshop
Mrs. Alberta J. Williams — Public Relations Editor
629 West Church Street, Jacksonville
Mrs. Gladys C. Vaught — Coordinator
2220 Spires Avenue, Jacksonville

District Presidents

1. First South Florida — Mrs. W. A. Smart
   206 W. 7th St., Lakeland

2. East Florida and Bethany Baptist
   1137 W. 21st. St., Jacksonville — Mrs. M. L. Johnson
3. Middle Florida and Clay County, Hibernia
   Route, Box 166,
   Green Cove Springs — Mrs. Janie Phillips
4. Greater South Florida — Mrs. Amelia Houston
   P.O. Box 884 Belle Glade
5. South Florida Progressive — Mrs. Esther Green
   121 Jordan Park, St. Petersburg
6. Mt. Pilgrim — Mrs. M. M. Fowler
   1314 Lemon St., Tampa
7. Union Foreign — Mrs. Creola Shepherd
   1022 E. Yukon St., Tampa
8. New Central — Mrs. M. L. Avery
   444 Keech St., Daytona Beach
9. Kissimmee Valley — Mrs. Susan Beckton
   Rt. 2 Box 54, Clewiston
10. Gulf Coast — Mrs. Janie Williams
    3506 Lindell Ave., Tampa
11. Greater Union — Mrs. Ruth C. Gaines
    1457 NE 154th Terr., Miami
12. Second West Florida — Mrs. Callie D. Granberry
    Box 330 Greenwood

Field Secretaries

1. Superintendent,
   Mrs. Pauline Stokes — Kissimmee Valley
2. Assistant Superintendent,
   Mrs. Lester Spivy — Union Florida
3. Mrs. Ruby Mitchell — First South Florida
4. Mrs. Cora Samuels — Greater South Florida
5. Mrs. Catherine Farragut — So. Fla. Progressive
6. Mrs. Minnie Dukes — Mt. Pilgrim
7. Mrs. Minnie Marshall — Middle Florida and Clay County
8. Mrs. B. L. Clay — Gulf Coast
9. Mrs. Lelia Hayes — New Central
10. Mrs. R. L. Colvin — Great Union
11. Mrs. Collis Quarterman — East Florida and Bethany

Mrs. Josephine Williams, Mrs. Lillie Kimble,
Mrs. Fannie Daniels
Each Field Secretary is asked to report $50.00 (Fifty Dollars)

Chairmen and Co-Chairmen

Finance — Chairman, Mrs. Estella Dickson

District Presidents Council — Chairman, Mrs. Susie Beckton
Co-Chairman, Mrs. Ruth Gaines

District Vice Presidents Council — Chairman, Mrs. Annie L. Green
Co-Chairman, Mrs. Nellie Williams

Business and Professional Women — Chairman, Mrs. W. H. Brunson
Co-Chairman, Mrs. F. R. Davis
Secretary, Mrs. Louvenia Wooten

Secretaries Council — Chairman, Mrs. Rosa Lee Carwise
Co-Chairman, Mrs. Anna E. Gayle

Music — Chairman, Mrs. Angeline Russ
Co-Chairman, Mrs. G. Laffitte

Treasurer Council — Chairman, Mrs. Daisy Foster
Co-Chairman, Mrs. Minnie Thomas

Dramatic Arts — Chairman, Mrs. Arlie P. Holmes
Co-Chairman, Mrs. Lillie Brooks

Executive Board — Chairman, Mrs. E. R. Simpson
Co-Chairman, Mrs. Annie Green and Mrs. Carrie Long

Usher Board — Chairman, Mrs. Beatrice Williams
Co-Chairman, Mrs. Annie Campbell

Workshop — Chairman, Mrs. Wilmer D. Thompson
Co-Chairman, Mrs. Betty Harris and Mrs. Cora Walker

Education — Chairman, Mrs. Algertha Jenkins
Co-Chairman, Mrs. Princess Harris
Secretary, Mrs. Grace Robinson

Badges — Chairman, Mrs. Susie Sandlin
Co-Chairman, Mrs. Mable Stephens

Local Presidents — Chairman, Mrs. Mary Newby
Co-Chairman, Mrs. Margaret Thompson
Secretary, Mrs. Ethel Pitts

Local Secretaries	Chairman, Mrs. Estelle Conners Co-Chairman, Mrs. Marie Barrows Secretary, Mrs. Naomi Jones
Personal Service	Chairman, Mrs. Lillie Sands Co-Chairman, Mrs. Josephine Smith
New Societies	Chairman, Mrs. Minnie Bolden Co-Chairman, Mrs. Fannie Henry
Track Distributors	Chairman, Mrs. Mary White Co-Chairman, Mrs. Georgia Williams
Gleaners	Chairman, Mrs. Stella Robinson
Open Door	Chairman, Mrs. Elouise Kelly Co-Chairman, Mrs. Daisy Edwards Secretary, Mrs. Marie Lambert
Tape Measure	Chairman, Mrs. Lauretha King Co-Chairman, Mrs. Mary F. Dunkley Secretary, Mrs. M. Newson and Mrs. Annie L. Richardson
Christian Birthdays	Chairman, Mrs. Lucile Scott Co-Chairman, Mrs. Susie Hammonds Secretary, Mrs. Dorothy Hicks and Mrs. W. C. Graham
Widows Council	Chairman, Mrs. Georgia Myers Co-Chairman, Mrs. Annie M. Doles Secretary, Mrs. Rachel Brown and Mrs. Bessie Birdsong
Nurses	Chairman, Mrs. Arlene S. Neugin Co-Chairman, Mrs. Nettie Pelham Secretary, Mrs. Marie Brewton
Temperance	Chairman, Mrs. Ethel Daughtry Co-Chairman, Mrs. Essie Collins Secretary, Mrs. Ella P. Burroughs and Mrs. Josephine Wilson
Summer Camp	Chairman, Mrs. Annie Huff, Mrs. H. L. Alexander Mrs. L. H. King, Mrs. W. B. Cooper, Mrs. Theresa Helms, Mrs. Arlene Tolver, Mrs. Gladys C. Vaught, Mrs. V. A. Toomer, Mrs. Agnes Speights, Mrs. Lucille Scott and others
Needle and Art	Chairman, Mrs. Carrie Stephens Co-Chairman, Mrs. H. L. Bradley Secretary, Mrs. Easter Marion

Committee on President's Hour Chairman, Mrs. Ruby Herndon
Co-Chairman, Mrs. B. H. Hartley, Mrs. Minnie Marshall Mrs. Minnie Dukes, and Mrs. Alice Frierson
Ways and Means Committee Chairman, Mrs. Gladys C. Vaught
Co-Chairman, Mrs. Creola Shepherd
Secretary, Mrs. Annie Green
Circle Committee Chairman, Mrs. Rosa Redding
Co-Chairman, Mrs. Thelma Brown and Mrs. Josephine Deatwiley
Calendar Committee Chairman, Mrs. Angeline Wooten
Co-Chairman, Mrs. Beatrice Hankerson
Secretary, Mrs. Esther Green
Welcome to Visitors Committee Chairman, Mrs. Sallie Smith
Co-Chairman, Mrs. Josie Jones and Mrs. Mammie Mannings
Courtesy Committee Chairman, Mrs. Vera Whitfield
Co-Chairman, Mrs. Nettie Pelham, Mrs. Mildred Dawson, Mrs. Norman Austin
Woman's Hour Committee Chairman, Mrs. Annie Patterson
Co-Chairman, Mrs. Fanny Dawson, Mrs. Charlotte Sims, Mrs. Hattie Kelly

PROGRAM OF THE SENIOR WOMEN'S AUXILIARY OF THE PROGRESSIVE MISSIONARY & EDUCATIONAL BAPTIST STATE CONVENTION OF FLORIDA, INC.

SIS. RUBY F. HERNDON, PRESIDENT

Sister Barbara R. Wright, Corresponding Secretary
The Reverend Madison Murray, Minister-Advisor
Dr. Henry T. Rhim, Convention President

Theme:
"A New Look At An Old Mission"
Matthew 28:19–20

Convening with
The Greater Peace Missionary Baptist Church
102 4th Street
Fort Walton Beach, Florida
The Reverend Clanston Seymore, Pastor

SENIOR WOMEN'S SESSIONS
WILL BE HELD AT
The Ramada Beach Resort
1500 Miracle Strip Parkway
Ft. Walton Beach, Fl

PRESIDENT
SISTER RUBY F. HERNDON

First Vice President	Sister Ida M. Spires
Second Vice President	Sister Mary H. Miller
Third Vice President	Sister Aquilla Morgan
Recording Secretary	Sister A. Pearl Boatman
Assistant Rec. Secretary	Sister Idella Hayward
Corresponding Secretary	Sister Barbara Wright
Secretary to the President	Sister Ruth Devoe
Financial Secretary	Sister Mary S. Kendall
Treasurer	Sister Frankie Whitfield
Chairman of Finance	Sister Elowisa S. Cox
Director of Music	Sister Elizabeth Whitehead
Assistant Director of Music	Sister Daisy Jenkins
Pianist	Sister Lillian Parker
Assistant Pianist	Sister Shirley McCauley
Workshop Director Emeritus	Altermese Smith Bentley
Workshop Director	Sister Joy Bradley-Leonard

Asst. Workshop Director — Sister Ann Hagin
Asst. Workshop Director — Sister Ernestine Butler

Chairman of Ushers — Sister Aslen O. Gilley
Devotional Chairman — Sister Jacqueline Staton
Devotional Co-Chairman — Sister Pearl Jennings

Minister Advisor — The Reverend Madison Murray

1996 CALENDAR

FEBRUARY 1996 — MID-WINTER BOARD
National Baptist Convention of America
Jacksonville, Florida

JANUARY 1996 — PLANNING CONFERENCE
Jacksonville, Florida

Y.W.A. & JUNIOR WOMEN'S MINISTRY

Sister Willean T. Hadley, President

Sister Blanche Raymond, Advisor
Reverend S. L. Maxwell, Ministerial Advisor
Reverend H. T. Rhim, General President

Officers

Sister Linda Lewis—First Vice President
Sister Sonya Davenport—Second Vice President
Sister Virginia Striggles—Third Vice President
Sister Regina Harris—Recording Secretary
Sister Lisa Rozier—Assistant Recording Secretary
Sister Corliss Jones—Corresponding Secretary
Sister Connie Cross—Assistant Corresponding Secretary
Sister Bonnie Blake—Financial Secretary
Sister Terri Emerson—Assistant Financial Secretary
Sister Brenda Bradley-Walter—Treasurer

Sister Carolean Sanders—Dean of Workshop
Sister Debra Davis—Bible Teacher
Sister De'Lois Barge—Director of Music
Sister Sonya Cambridge—Assistant Director of Music

YOUNG WOMEN'S AUXILIARY AND JUNIOR WOMEN

In March 1945, the Young Women's Auxiliary and Junior Women were organized at an annual session of the Progressive Baptist State convention. This was during the administrations of Reverend C. J. Smith and Mrs. Theresa H. Moore, President of the Senior Women. The first president was Mrs. Agnes Dean of Sebring who served for nineteen years, and was followed by Mrs. Rosa S. Lee. Mrs. Lee filled the office from 1964–1970.

These young women served the following years as presidents:

Mrs. Barbara W. Wright, Belle Glade	1970–1979
Mrs. Nora Woodard, Orlando	1979–1982
Ms. Eleanor Ball, Sarasota	1982–1987
Ms. Linda Lewis, Ft. Mead	1987–1989
Ms. Paquetta McCray Freeman, Panama City	1989–1991
Ms. Patricia Lott, Panama City	1991–

PRESIDENT'S RECOMMENDATION

Reverend H. T. Rhim, President, recommended:

> That the age limit for the Young Women's Auxiliary and Junior Women's Auxiliary will be enforced; that age is 18–35. Persons age 36 and older may work with the matrons or the Senior Mission Auxiliary.[12]

PROGRAM OF THE THIRTY-THIRD ANNUAL SESSION OF THE JUNIOR WOMEN'S AUXILIARY OF THE PROGRESSIVE MISSIONARY AND EDUCATIONAL BAPTIST STATE CONVENTION OF FLORIDA

to convene with
THE MT. GILBOA BAPTIST CHURCH
Bartow, Florida
March 18–23, 1975
Reverend Eddie Burroughs, Pastor

Mrs. Barbara W. Kight	President
Dr. J. C. Sams	General President
Mrs. Carolyn Burney	Counselor
Rev. J. W. Daughtry	Minister-Advisor

PROGRAM OF THE JUNIOR WOMEN'S AUXILIARY TO THE PROGRESSIVE MISSIONARY AND EDUCATIONAL BAPTIST STATE CONVENTION OF FLORIDA

to convene with
THE MOUNT PLEASANT BAPTIST CHURCH
Orlando, Florida
March 24–28, 1976

The Reverend J. F. Hargrett, Host Pastor
(The Junior Women's Auxiliary will meet at the St. John Baptist Church 2035 W. Central Blvd. 843-2649)

Sister Barbara W. Kight, President

OFFICIAL STAFF

President	Barbara W. Kight
First Vice President	Mary Miller
Second Vice President	Barbara Barbes
Recording Secretary	Annie O. Godbee
Assistant Recording Secretary	Pequetta McCray

Corresponding Secretary	Mary S. Kendall
Financial Secretary	Barbara Austin
Treasurer	Elowisa S. Holliday
Historian	Geraldine Stovall
Study Course Dean	Jacqueline Staton
Chairman of Finance	Deloris Johnson
Musician	Cynthia Glenn
Organist	Gwendolyn McCree
Bible Teacher	Lutrell Simmons
Assistant Bible Teacher	Coretha Brown
Missionary	Mary H. Smith
Reporter	Henrietta S. Alexander
Advisor	Carolyn Burney
Minister-Advisor	Rev. J. W. Daughtry

THE MATRON'S AUXILIARY

The first session of the Matron's Auxiliary was held at the Zion Hope MB Church, Jacksonville, Reverend S. P. Donald, Pastor. According to the minutes of that session, the following officers were present.[13]

President:	Miriam Ruth Newsom, Progressive West Florida Association
First Vice President:	Anita Goodman, New Gulf Coast Association
Second Vice President:	Dessie Morris, East Florida & Bethany Association
Third Vice President:	Barbara Austin, Mt. Pilgrim Association
Recording Secretary:	Gwendolyn Wright, Second West Association
Asst. Recording Secretary:	Deloris Gallon, Kissimmee Valley Association
Corresponding Secretary:	Linda West, First South Florida Association
Asst. Corresponding Secretary:	Dannie Speights, New Gulf Coast Association
Financial Secretary:	Patricia Hutchinson, East Florida & Bethany Association

Asst. Financial Secretary: Dora Davis, New Gulf Association
Treasurer: Ruth Johnson, South Florida Progressive Association
Asst. Treasurer: Janice Bennerman, Kissimmee Valley Association
Secretary to the President: Margaret Kirkman, Progressive of West Florida Association
Organist: Parthenia Davis, Mt. Pilgrim Association
Workshop Director: Mamie Rogers, South Florida Progressive Association
Asst. Workshop Director: Janie Walker, Union Foreign Association
Advisor: Dorothy Borroughs, East Florida & Bethany Association
Convention President: Rev. H. T. Rhim, East Florida & Bethany Association

The second Women's Intermediate Auxiliary Mission Encounter Weekend was held Friday and Saturday, December 3–4, 1993, hosted by the St. John Missionary Baptist Church, Panama City, Florida, Reverend Roy L. Bedford, Pastor. The musical worship service was rendered by the St. John Gospel Choir host church and the New Gulf Coast Association Youth Choir. The sermon was brought by Reverend Henderson Powell, Pastor, Greater Union Missionary Baptist Church, Century, Florida. The Prayer Breakfast was held Saturday morning at 7:00 a.m., with Sister Susan L. Turner, past Women's Intermediate Auxiliary National President, Main Street Missionary Baptist Church, Biloxi, Mississippi, as the Speaker. Theme: **"Christian Women Dealing With The Storms of Life,"** II Corinthians 4:8–10. Three things we need to deal with the storms: Prayer, Faith, and Endurance. We can endure if we hold on to God. Galatians 6:16. The question was asked, "Why do we experience pain and trouble?" They exist to remind us that we are still in the wilderness. The benefit of trouble opens up the gate of compassion. We must handle the storms in our lives. Sometime we weather the light breeze, but when the hurricane comes we want to give in, God is able to deliver. We as a people must realize that God can handle all things. First Vice President, Reverend E. B. Williams closed the breakfast with a prayer. The breakfast was followed by four 30 minute concurrent workshop clusters and the noon sermon.

The noon sermon was brought by Rev. Rufus Wood. Topic: "**Woman Among Women,**" St. Luke 1:26, 38–42. God has always used women in a special way. God can use anybody. "Do you want to be a woman among women?" Immediately following the noon sermon the state WIA's went out witnessing in the city of Panama City with numerous contracts made and with several accepting Christ. God has continued to bless our efforts with souls saved.

Respectfully submitted,
Patricia Lamar, Historian
St. Joseph Missionary Baptist Church
Jacksonville, Fl
President H. T. Rhim, Pastor

HISTORY OF THE WOMEN'S INTERMEDIATE AUXILIARY

Progressive Missionary and Educational Baptist State Convention of Florida, Inc.

The Third Annual Session of the Women's Intermediate Auxiliary was held during the Seventy-Ninth (79th) Annual Session of the Progressive Missionary and Educational Baptist State Convention of Florida, Inc. Our third session was hosted by the First Providence Baptist Church, Bartow, Florida, First Vice President Reverend E. B. Williams, Pastor. The Welcome Program was hosted by the WIA of First Providence Missionary Baptist Church, Bartow, Florida.

PASTOR H. T. RHIM
President

Progressive Missionary and Educational Baptist
State Convention of Florida

MERGER SERVICE FOR SENIOR MISSION
AND MISSION NUMBER TWO AUXILIARIES
AND ORGANIZATIONAL SERVICE FOR
THE MATRONS' AUXILIARY

SATURDAY, MARCH 24, 1990 - 9:00 A.M.

New Friendship Missionary Baptist Church
3107 East Lake Avenue - Tampa, Florida
The Reverend H. L. Daniels, Pastor

THE REVEREND H. T. RHIM,
PRESIDENT, PRESIDING

CHORAL CALL TO WORSHIP	COME, WE THAT LOVE THE LORD
INVOCATION	
PREPARATORY HYMN	HAVE THINE OWN WAY
HEARING OF THE WORD	Ephesians 6:10–23 The Reverend Rollie Murray, Sr.
THE OCCASION	Sister Barbara Wright Gary
HYMN OF ONENESS	BLESS BE THE TIE
MERGING CEREMONY	LITANY OF UNITY PLEDGE OF COMMITMENT PRAYER FOR UNITY
PRESENTATION OF OFFICERS OF THE SENIOR WOMEN'S AUXILIARY	PRESIDENT RHIM
PRESENTATION OF OFFICERS OF THE MATRON'S AUXILIARY	PRESIDENT RHIM
HYMN OF ASSURANCE	BLESSED ASSURANCE
REMARKS AND BENEDICTION	

Installation ceremony of the new State Matron's Auxiliary and the merged Missions #1 and #2. July 1990, Lakeland, Florida Convention Headquarters.

The installation of officers for the Matron's Auxiliary was held at the James Carl Sams Conference Congress, Rev. Alex Harper, Sr., President.

PROGRAMME OF THE WOMEN INTERMEDIATE AUXILIARY OF THE PROGRESSIVE MISSIONARY & EDUCATIONAL BAPTIST STATE CONVENTION OF FLORIDA

to convene with
Greater Peace Missionary Baptist Church
102 Fourth Street
Fort Walton Beach, Fl

March 21–25, 1995
Theme: A New Look At An Old Mission
Matthew 20:19–20

The Women Intermediate Auxiliary Will Meet At the
Beulah First Baptist Church
109 McGriff Street
Ft. Walton Beach, Fl

Sister Meriam Newsome, Auxiliary President

THE REVEREND H. T. RHIM,
CONVENTION PRESIDENT

PROGRESSIVE MISSIONARY & EDUCATIONAL BAPTIST STATE CONVENTION OF FLORIDA, INC.

OFFICERS

President	Meriam Ruth Newsome—Progressive of West Florida Association
First Vice President	Anita Goodman—New Gulf Coast Association
Second Vice President	Dessie Morris—East Florida & Bethany Baptist Association
Third Vice President	Barbara Austin—Mt. Pilgrim Baptist Association
Recording Secretary	Dorothy P. Davis—Second West Baptist Association
Asst. Recording Secretary	Deloris Gallon—Kissimmee Valley Baptist Association
Asst. Recording Secretary	Geraldine Stovall—Union Foreign Baptist Association
Corresponding Secretary	Dannie Speights—Progressive of West Florida Association
Asst. Corresponding Secretary	Tina Brown—New Central Baptist Association
Financial Secretary	Patricia Hutchinson—East Florida & Bethany Association
Asst. Financial Secretary	Dora Davis—New Gulf Coast Association
Treasurer	Ruth Johnson—South Florida Progressive Baptist Association
Asst. to Treasurer	Janice Bannerman—Kissimmee Valley Baptist Association

Secretary to President	Gerry Stovall—Union Foreign Baptist Association
Historian	Patricia Lamar—East Florida & Bethany Association
Director of Music	Vanessa Bank—Mt. Pilgrim Baptist Association
Asst. Director of Music	Judy Cook—Equal Right Baptist Association
Musician	Carrie Williams—Mt. Pilgrim Progressive Baptist Association
Director of Workshops	Mamie Rogers—South Florida Progressive Baptist Association
Asst. Director of Workshops	Janie Walker—Union Foreign Baptist Association
Advisor	Dorothy Borroughs—East Florida & Bethany Association
Ministerial Advisor	Rev. Earl Tyler—Progressive of West Florida Association
Convention President	Dr. H. T. Rhim—East Florida & Bethany Association

STATE DEACONESS' COUNCIL

(Formerly the Ministers' Wives and Deaconesses State Council or Ministers' and Deacons' Wives Council.)

This Auxiliary observed twenty-five years of ministry on March 23–27, 1966, when the Progressive Baptist State Convention met with the Mt. Ararat Metropolitan Baptist Church, Dr. D. J. Graham, Pastor in Jacksonville. It was organized in March of 1941.

"Twenty-five years ago our Ministers' and Deacons' Wives Council had its origin under the late Dr. C. J. Smith. It has become one of the beacon lights of the Progressive Baptist State Convention. The Ministers' and Deacons' Wives have supported it wholeheartedly. We are interwoven into this great Auxiliary," stated Mrs. W. A. Smart, President in her Annual Letter.[14]

PROGRAM OF THE SIXTY-SECOND ANNUAL SESSION OF THE MINISTER WIVES AND DEACONESS STATE COUNCIL

Auxiliary to the SENIOR WOMEN'S MISSIONARY and EDUCATIONAL CONVENTION OF FLORIDA

To Convene with the
MT. PLEASANT MISSIONARY BAPTIST CHURCH
ORLANDO, FLORIDA
The Reverend J. F. Hargrett, Pastor

MARCH 23–28, 1976

Convention Officers

Mrs. W. A. Smart 206 W. 7th Street, Lakeland	State Chairman
Mrs. Lillie Mae Bogan 401 Naloniz Street, Pensacola	First Vice Chairman
Mrs. Carrie Long 1022 20th Street, St. Petersburg	Second Vice Chairman
Mrs. Mary White 391 Rardin Avenue, Pahokee	Third Vice President
Mrs. Pauline Stokes 284 West 5th Avenue, Pahokee	Recording Secretary
Mrs. Fannie Mae Henry 721 Avenue R.N.E., Winter Haven	Assistant Recording Secretary
Mrs. Estella M. Conyers 817 S.W. Avenue D., Belle Glade	Corresponding Secretary
Mrs. Dorothea D. Miller 806 15th Avenue S., St. Petersburg	Assistant Corresponding Secretary
Mrs. Rachel Brown N.T.P.O. Box 9044, Sarasota	Financial Secretary
Mrs. Annie Mae Doles P.O. Box 3813, Winter Haven	Treasurer
Mrs. Nettie E. Pelham 933 Bethune Drive, Orlando	Musician
Mrs. Lillie Mae Harris 2995 St. Charles Street, Ft. Myers	Dean of Workshop

Mrs. Cora Walker — Assistant Dean of Workshop
1100 E. Baars Street, Pensacola
Mrs. Alberta J. Williams — Public Relations Editor
629 W. Church Street, Jacksonville

PROGRAM
Saturday Morning

7:30 A.M.	Study Course—Mrs. Lillie Mae Harris, Dean of Workshop and Mrs. Cora Walker, Assistant Dean of Workshop Instructors—Mrs. Lillie Brooks, Mrs. Ruby R. Mitchell and Mrs. Darthuea Dean
9:00 A.M.	Call of Worship: Mrs. L. W. Williams and Mrs. Mary Holland Selection: Convention Chorus Theme: Mrs. Evelyn Welch Theme Song: "Stand Up, Stand Up for Jesus"
10:00 A.M.	Presentation of Chairman by Mrs. Lillie Mae Bogan, First Vice Chairman Greetings for the Chairman, Mrs. W. A. Smart Roll Call of Officers Organization of Districts Report of Finance Committee
11:00 A.M.	Sermon: The Reverend C. P. Epps, Mt. Olive Baptist Church, Tampa, Florida, Choir and Ushers Serving Alternate: The Reverend J. E. Harmon, Pastor, Oak Hill Baptist Church, Tampa, Florida, Choirs and Ushers Serving Chairman Smarts Annual Address presentation by Mrs. Lillie Mae Bogan, First Vice President Solo: Mrs. T. W. Streeter Appreciation Hour: Mrs. Annie Mae Doles, Chairman and Mrs. F. R. Davis, Co-Chairman Election of Officers

Introduction of New Workers and Visitors:
Mrs. Ruby R. Mitchell
Meditation Period: Mrs. Frances Williams

Saturday Afternoon

2:00 P.M.	Vice-Chairman, Mrs. Lillie Mae Bogan, Presiding	
	Song and Prayer period: Mrs. Lillie Brooks	
	Highlights from the Mission and Fellow ship Conference: Lake Yale	
	Mrs. Dorothea D. Miller	
	Report to Parent Body	
3:00 P.M.	*Report of Committees*	
Education		Mrs. Lillie Mae Harris, Chairman
Christian Birthdays		Mrs. Bessie Birdsong, Chairman Mrs. Viola Johnson, Co-Chairman
Business Women		Mrs. Viola Scrivens, Chairman Mrs. Elizabeth Jackson, Co-Chairman
Personal Service		Mrs. Osie Mae Sailes, Chairman Mrs. Lottie Brown, Co-Chairman
Widows Council		Mrs. Lillie M. Brooks, Chairman Mrs. Mamie Manning and Mrs. Mattie L. Watson, Co-Chairman
Ushers Committee		Mrs. Mary Boatman, Chairman Mrs. Rosa Newsome and Mrs. Lottie Leonard, Co-Chairman
Mission		Mrs. Frances Williams, Chairman Mrs. Dorothea D. Miller and Mrs. L. Owens, Co-Chairman
Bible Committee		Mrs. Mildred R. Dawson, Chairman Mrs. Inon Anderson and Mrs. Grace McDonald, Co-Chairman
New Councils		Mrs. Willie B. Cooper, Chairman Mrs. M. B. Broxton, Mrs. Doretha Grander, and Mrs. Pauline Stokes, Co-Chairman
Open Door		Mrs. Jessie M. Anderson, Chairman Mrs. J. W. Streeter and Mrs. Ada M. Davis, Co-Chairman

Needle and Art	Mrs. Hattie Kelly, Chairman
	Mrs. Mary Holland and
	Mrs. Ella P. Burroughs, Co-Chairman
Temperance	Mrs. Fannie B. Henry, Chairman
	Mrs. Nettie E. Pelham and
	Mrs. H. B. Hopkins, Co-Chairman
Tape Measure	Mrs. Dorthua Dean, Chairman
	Mrs. Mattie Smith and
	Mrs. Laura Pugh, Co-Chairman
Obituary	Mrs. Bridgett Simmons, Chairman
	Mrs. Mildred Warren and
	Mrs. Susie Jackson, Co-Chairman
Courtesy	Mrs. L. W. Williams, Chairman
Music	Mrs. Osie Lee Sailes, Chairman
	Mrs. Nettie E. Pelham and
	Mrs. Mildred R. Dawson, Co-Chairman
Women's Hour	Mrs. J. E. Harmon, Chairman
	Mrs. Marjana Lopez, Mrs. Ruth Gains,
	Mrs. Lester M. Spivey
	Mrs. Essie Mae James and Mrs. Ruth Gains
Finance	Mrs. Arlene S. Neugin, Chairman
	Mrs. Rachel Brown, Mrs. Cora Samuels and
	Mrs. Annie Mae Doles

SPECIAL NOTE: *State Chairman Smart is asking all Chairmen of Deaconess Councils to please do more for Education this year, and have your money for Thursday. The financial goal is $2,000.00*

Enrollment

Class A—;$20.00 Class B—$15.00
Class C—$12.00 Class D—$10.00
Council Enrollment $3.00, Officers $5.00,
Messengers $1.00
Personal Enrollment: Mrs. Cora Samuels

PROGRAM FOR THE STATE DEACONESS COUNCIL OF THE PROGRESSIVE MISSIONARY AND EDUCATIONAL BAPTIST STATE CONVENTION OF FLORIDA, INC.

Sister Hazel N. Jones, President
Reverend E. E. Cross, Minister Advisor
Reverend Dr. H. T. Rhim, State Convention President

Fort Walton Beach Florida
1995

Elected Officers for 1995

President Emeritus	Sister Lillie Mae Bogan
President	Sister Hazel N. Jones
First Vice President	Sister Louise James
Second Vice President	Sister Elouise Bythwood
Third Vice President	Sister Edna Smith
Recording Secretary	Sister Dorothea Miller
Asst. Recording Secretary	Sister Mercedes Anderson
Corresponding Secretary	Sister Annie L. Henderson (Deceased)
Asst. Corresponding Secretary	Sister Juanita Maybin
Finance Secretary	Sister Lottie B. Johnson
Assistant Finance Secretary	Sister Beulah Savage
Treasurer	Sister Mildred Dawson
Workshop Director	Sister Cora Walker
Assistant Workshop Director	Sister Edna M. Smith
Chairman of Finance	Sister Patricia Westbrook
Minister Advisor	Reverend E. E. Cross

COMMITTEES

Education
Sisters:
Lottie B. Johnson, Chairman
Elouise Bythwood
Hazel N. Jones

Nomination
Pastor E. E. Cross, Chairman
Mildred Dawson
Dorothea Miller

Lillie Mae Bogan

Mission
Sisters:
Annie L. Robinson, Chairman
Viola Johnson
Betty Jenkins

Open Door
Sisters:
Osie M. Sailes, Chairman
Mildred Dawson

Local Presidents
Sisters:
Louise James, Chairman
Elouise Bythwood
Edna M. Smith
Mattie L. Green

Women's Hour
Sisters:
Edna M. Smith
Mildred Dawson, Chairman
Edna M. Smith
Viola Scrivens

District Presidents
Sisters:
Sarah Jones, Chairman
Charlie Mae Wilder
Dorothea Miller
Mittie J. Mullins
Ora V. Ogden

Badges
Sisters:
Lillie Mae Bogan, Chairman
Chairman
Estelle Conyers

Charlie Mae Wilder
Edna Smith
Mittie J. Mullins
Carrie Hinton

Business & Professional Women
Sisters:
Dorothea Miller, Chairman
Louise James
Beulah Savage
LuNell Lilly

New Councils
Sisters:
Cherry Crum, Chairman
Carrie Hinton
Carolyn Wilson

Workshop
Sisters:
Cora Walker, Chairman

Courtesy
Sisters:
Deothia Baker, Chairman
Mercedes Anderson

Benevolent
Sisters:
Mittie J. Mullins, Chairman
Queenie Powell
Ann Teal
Hazel N. Jones
Lillie Mae Bogan

President's Appreciation
Sisters:
Juanita Maybin, Chairman
Beulah Savage
Dorothea Miller
Mildred Dawson
Louise James
Sarah Jones
Elouise Bythwood

Christians Birthday
Sisters:
Iola Upshaw,
Lillie P. Brown

MINUTES OF THE 50TH GOLDEN JUBILEE SESSION OF THE MINISTERS' WIVES AND DEACONESS CONVENTION

CONVENED WITH THE
MT. PLEASANT BAPTIST CHURCH
ORLANDO, FLORIDA
REV. L. J. JENKINS, MINISTER

SISTER W. A. SMART
PRESIDENT

OFFICERS OF M.D.W.C.

Mrs. W. A. Smart	President
Mrs. Bertha Binyard	First Vice President
Mrs. Mary White	Second Vice President
Mrs. Georgia D. Smith	Recording Secretary
Mrs. Rachel Brown	Financial Secretary
Mrs. Elizabeth Miller	Corresponding Secretary
Mrs. Janie Williams	Treasurer

COMMITTEE CHAIRMEN

Finance	Mrs. Ollie Banks
Enrollment of Councils	Mrs. Ruth Ferrell
Personal	Mrs. Elizabeth Miller
Letters	Mrs. Rachel Brown
Temperance	Mrs. Lillie Scott
New Councils	Mrs. Viola Scrivens

Society	Mrs. Ollie Bryant
Courtesy	Mrs. Flossie Hills
Obituary	Mrs. Maggie Taylor
Art Work	Mrs. Logenia Smart
Mission	Mrs. Harmon

HISTORY OF MINISTER WIVES & WIDOWS AUXILIARY

PROGRESSIVE MISSIONARY and EDUCATIONAL BAPTIST STATE CONVENTION

"A WOMAN THAT FEARETH THE LORD, SHE SHALL BE PRAISED."
Proverbs 31:30b

The wife of the Minister faces numerous challenges that are unique *only* to those women who are married to a clergyman. Sometimes the inner needs become so vast, she must try to restrain herself. Wives felt that they needed opportunities to discuss topics pertinent to them.

Thus, in March, 1988, during the Progressive Missionary and Educational Baptist State Convention; hosted by Saint Paul Missionary Baptist Church, Lakeland, FL. Reverend N. Sanders, Pastor; the Ministers Wives and Widows were organized as an Auxiliary; under the leadership of General President, Reverend H. T. Rhim. Previously, they had been combined with the Deaconess Council.

The Ministers Wives and Widows Auxiliary meets at each session of the convention. There is an outlined program which includes spiritual enrichment, prayer sessions, study courses, sermons, and a fellowship luncheon. The sessions are geared toward "Total Growth: as a Minister's/Pastor's Wife/Widow.

The Auxiliary Purposes are:

1. Provide opportunities for Spiritual Growth.

2. Provide study and discussions on topics important to their needs; and those of their husbands.
3. Gain information and suggestions on being a better support to husbands.
4. Allow time for interaction and reactions.
5. Become more familiar with scriptures that will strengthen the areas of need.
6. Develop a close bonding in a "Sisterhood of Love."
7. Increase one's sensitivity toward the other Sister.
8. Maintain confidentiality of concerns discussed.
9. Develop and maintain a prayerful, humble attitude at all times.
10. Encourage each other in attaining a "Totally Fulfilled Life."

The first officers were:

President	Sister Victoria Kirkland
Vice President	Dorothy Davis
First Vice President	Mildred Jackson
Second Vice President	Susie Hammond
Activities Coordinator	Barbara Gary
Recording Secretary	Gloria Murray
Assistant Recording Secretary	Brenda Turner
Financial Secretary	Pearlie Robinson
Assistant Financial Secretary	Willie Mae McCray
Treasurer	Betty Pegram
Assistant Treasurer	Ruby Hendrix
Historian	J. B. Adams
Assistant Historian	Sadie Burt
Dean of Workshop	Mary E. Streeter
Assistant Dean of Workshop	Ruby Byrd
Music Committee	Mildred Dawson, Chairperson
	Betty Sanders
	Edna Hargrett
	Ruby Hendrix
	Vanessa Banks
	Sylvia Leonard
	Linda Crews

Devotional Leaders	Mattie Murray Polly Rentz Allie Biggs
Ministerial Advisor	Reverend S. P. Donald
General President	Reverend H. T. Rhim

Sister Victoria Kirkland resigned as President, March 1990. Sister Dorothy Davis was elected President, and is presently serving.

While our auxiliary was still a "Baby", Progressive M&E Baptist State Convention hosted the National Baptist Convention of America, Inc. at Mount Pleasant M.B. Church, Orlando, Florida. The late Reverend Joseph Hargrett was Pastor.

This was a tremendous task, yet a joyous experience. This aided us in establishing a united bond of support, strength, confidence and love.

The Ministers/Wives/Widows Auxiliary has increased in attendance and participation. The study and sharing sessions are appropriate for the needs of the attendees. One of our present study courses is "WINNING WAYS FOR MINISTERS WIVES" by Shirley E. Montgomery.

Our prayer is - "As we grow chronologically, we will grow in love and fellowship; and, will be an example of "SISTERLY LOVE" for other MINISTERS WIVES/WIDOWS.

PROGRAM OF THE MINISTERS WIVES/WIDOWS AUXILIARY

Sister Gloria Murray
Auxiliary President

DR. H. T. RHIM, CONVENTION PRESIDENT

1995 Official Staff

President	Sis. Gloria Murray

First Vice President	Sister Mary Williams
Second Vice President	Sister Allie Biggs
Third Vice President	Sister Mattie Murray
Recording Secretary	Sister Willie Mae McCray
Corresponding Secretary	Thelma Farmer
Treasurer	Sister Jovanare Giles
Chairman of Finance	Sister Cynthia Savage
Pastoral Advisor	Reverend S. B. Donald

PROGRAM

THEME: "MINISTERS' WIVES/WIDOWS
Pressing Onward and Upward."
Philippians 3:14

Theme Song: "Higher Ground" (#309 The New Baptist Hymnal)

Tuesday, March 21, 1995
8:00 a.m.–8:30 a.m. REGISTRATION

SESSION I

8:30 a.m.–9:00 a.m.

Theme Hymn	"Higher Ground"
Devotion	Sisters Polly Rentz & Allie Biggs
Theme	Sister Massalena B. Echols
Official Opening	President Gloria Murray
Welcome	Sister Delois Thigpen
Officers Introduction	President Gloria }Murray

9:00 a.m.–10:15 a.m.
Panel: **"You—The Minister's Wife!" (Five minutes each)**

Panelist 1	**"The Minister's Mate"**	
		Sis. Victoria Kirkland, Tampa
Panelist 2	**"Ministerial Support Person"**	
		Sister Martha Harper, Bradenton
Panelist 3	**"Personal Identify"**	
		Sis. Cynthia Savage, Arcadia

Interaction Period

10:15 a.m.–10:30 a.m.	Break
10:30 a.m.–11:30 a.m.	President's Hour
11:30 a.m.–1:00 p.m.	Luncheon

Appendix III

THE ASSOCIATIONS BRIEF HISTORICAL EXCERPTS

EAST FLORIDA AND BETHANY BAPTIST ASSOCIATION, 1893–

In 1972, the Reverend B. H. Hartley, moderator, appointed Mrs. Ruby F. Herndon, Ms. A. N. Sessions, and Mr. George Walker to research and compile the History of East Florida and Bethany Baptist Association.

The committee stated:

> As we began the task of compiling and gathering this information, we were faced with the problems of gathering data from reliable and available sources. We found persons who remembered names but no dates, and too often we found past officers with no written records.
>
> The object of the Association as found in the first Constitution states: "The object of this Association shall be to create and perpetuate a union among the ministers and churches to collect monies to carry on the missionary and educational work; the spreading of gospel throughout the world and the advancement of the cause of Christ in every possible way."[15]

The History of the Association as submitted included this information: 1932, the Association met with the St. Mary's Baptist, St. Augustine, Florida, Reverend W. M. Banks Pastor.

ROSTER OF OFFICERS

Moderator	Reverend J. M. Royster, Jacksonville
Vice Moderator:	Reverend J. M. Bind, Jacksonville
Recording Secretary:	Reverend A. B. Eady, Green Cove Springs
Corresponding Secretary:	Reverend W. R. Mack, Jacksonville
Treasurer:	Reverend M. B. Britton, St. Augustine

MEMBERS

Dr. John E. Ford, Jacksonville
Prof. N. W. Collier, St. Augustine
Rev. J. W. Callaway, Jacksonville
Rev. M. B. Britton, Jr., Picalatto
Rev. W. A. Weaver, Jacksonville
Rev. A. C. L. Arbourne, Jacksonville
Rev. A. L. Wilson, Jacksonville
Rev. W. M. Hill, Jacksonville
Rev. R. T. Wimberley, Jacksonville

EXECUTIVE BOARD MEMBERS 1893–1972

Rev. W. M. Banks, St. Augustine
Rev. W. B. Mathis, Jacksonville
Rev. H. H. Robinson, Jacksonville,
Rev. K. D. Britt, Jacksonville
Rev. J. B. Green, Jacksonville
Rev. I. S. Hudson, Jacksonville
Rev. A. G. Hardy, Palatka
Rev. A. B. Eady, Green Cove Springs

Rev. M. B. Britton,
St. Augustine
Rev. G. W. Jenkins
Jacksonville,
Rev. E. D. White,
Jacksonville
Rev. E. D. Martin,
Palatka
Rev. G. H. Hawkins,
Jacksonville

EDUCATION AND MISSION BOARD

Rev. R. J. Hagins,
Jacksonville
Rev. E. D. Martin,
Palatka
Rev. A. F. Harrison,
Palatka
Rev. J. F. Mann, Jr.,
Jacksonville

MODERATOR'S ANNUAL LETTER TO THE OFFICERS AND MEMBERS EAST FLORIDA BETHANY BAPTIST ASSOCIATION

September 14, 1945

GREETINGS:

In a few more days we will assemble with the St. Thomas Baptist Church, Reverend W. Neal, pastor, Jacksonville, in the Fifty-second Annual Session of the East Florida and Bethany Baptist Association. We are praying for your cooperation that this will be the banner year, especially so spiritually and financially. The demands of the kingdom are great; we must do bigger things this year than ever before, both for missions and Christian education. Our finance report depends largely upon the interest the pastors manifest; you can, if you will bring up from your church, the amount asked for simply by asking and working with your committee. May we depend upon you? Please don't fail us this time. "Quit ye like men, be strong."

Reverend K. David Britt, Moderator
Office: 954 Kings Road, Phone 3-1561-J
Residence: 1345 W. 6th Street, Phone 5-8575-W
Jacksonville, Florida

MODERATORS

To the date of this report (1972), the following people have served as moderators:[16]

Rev. J. M. Bing, Day Spring Baptist Church
Rev. J. M. Royster, Pastor, First Baptist Eastside
Rev. A. C. Porter, Pastor, First Baptist Eastside
Rev. C. T. Darrah, Pastor, Shiloh Baptist Church
Rev. Reuben Thomas, St. Thomas
Rev. R. T. Wimberly, Mt. Calvary
Rev. C. M. Vaught, St. John
Rev. C. Williams
Rev. John E. Ford, Bethel Baptist Institutional Church
Rev. K. D. Britt, Second Baptist Church
Rev. W. M. Hill, Mt. Calvary Baptist Church, elected 1958
Rev. B. H. Hartley, Friendly Baptist Church, elected 1968

As of the writing of this report, the following people were officers:

Moderator:	Rev. B. H. Hartley
First Vice Moderator:	Rev. Charles B. Dailey
Second Vice Moderator:	Rev. G. T. McCall
Third Vice Moderator:	Rev. J. J. Jones
Recording Secretary	Deacon W. G. Patterson
Financial Secretary:	Rev. Theodore R. Lee
Corresponding Secretary	Rev. G. W. Mitchell
Statistical Secretary:	Rev. N. B. Williams
Treasurer:	Rev. H. T. Overstreet
District Missionary:	Rev. J. T. Daniels
Chm. Mission Board:	Rev. A. J. Hughes
Chm. Education Board:	Rev. B. J. Lane
Auditor:	Rev. W. C. Neal

AUXILIARIES SENIOR WOMEN'S CONVENTION

Organized in 1907, this auxiliary is observing its 65th Annual Session. Some of the early presidents were:

Mrs. Idella Cason	Mrs. E. M. Lewis
Mrs. Essie Hightower	Mrs. M. J. Walker Thomas
Mrs. E. Lena Williams	
Mrs. M. L. Johnson	1952–1971

President officers [as of 1972] are:

President:	Mrs. M. L. Johnson
First Vice President:	Mrs. Lena George
Second Vice President:	Mrs. Susie Sandlin
Third Vice President:	Mrs. Renalda Jenkins
Recording Secretary:	Mrs. Bessie Hill
Corresponding Secretary:	Mrs. Mary Washington
Treasurer:	Mrs. Rosa Mozell
Organist:	Mrs. Hortense Neal
Pianist:	Mrs. E. M. Singleton

JUNIOR WOMEN'S CONVENTION

Organized in 1946, under the leadership of Rev. K. D. Britt as Moderator is observing its 26th Annual Session. First officers were:

President:	Mrs. M. K. Gibson
Vice President:	Mrs. Roberta A. Hall
First Vice President:	Mrs. Willie M. Thomas
Recording Secretary:	Mrs. Annie L. Flowers
Financial Secretary:	Mrs. Ruby F. Herndon
Asst. Recording Secretary:	Mrs. Lillian P. King
Corresponding Secretary:	Mrs. Ada Reeves
Treasurer:	Mrs. Cola McCoy
Editorial Secretary;	Mrs. A. J. Williams
Organist and Chorister:	Mrs. Hortense Neal
Assistant Chorister:	Mrs. Edith Jones
Chairman of Finance:	Mrs. Annie L. Patterson

USHERS

Organized in 1947, with Reverend K. D. Britt as moderator, the Ushers are now observing their 25th Annual Session. Some of the early Presidents were:

Mr. Eddie Vereen Mr. Parker Mr. Dunbar

BROTHERHOOD

Organized in 1962 under Reverend W. M. Hill as Moderator. The first officers were:

President:	Deacon George Walker
CUL:Vice President	Deacon John Francis
Secretary	Deacon I. M. Jones
Corresponding Secretary:	Deacon Oris L. Merriett
Financial Secretary:	Deacon John Lowery
Treasurer:	Deacon Isaiah Fields

NURSES' GUILD

Organized in 1968, Reverend B. H. Hartley, Moderator, is presently observing its 4th Annual Session. The first president was Mrs. Susie D. Thompson.

SENIOR MISSION

Organized in 1969, with Reverend B. H. Harley as Moderator, the Senior Mission is now observing its 3rd Annual session. Its first officers were:

President:	Mrs. Miranda Tennant
Vice President:	Mrs. M. D. Hudson
Recording Secretary:	Mrs. Helen Wright
Financial Secretary:	Mrs. Ernestine Cross
Corresponding Secretary:	Mrs. Claudette Bryant
Treasurer:	Mrs. Frankie S. Whitfield

SOUTH FLORIDA PROGRESSIVE

The South Florida Progressive Association was organized on January 27, 1916.

That same year the first session was held in Arcadia with H. L. Stephens as moderator.[17]

The Rev. W. R. Wright, served as the clerk.

The following served as moderators from 1916–1961:

H. L. Stephens	1916–1918
J. H. Brown	1919–1921
J. C. Daniels	1919–1921
S. Randolph	1930–1931
S. C. Caldwell	1932–1968
W. J. Glover	1969–1987
Joseph Gordon	1988–

NEW CENTRAL BAPTIST ASSOCIATION HISTORY

In November 1945 a group of pastors and ministers met at the New Salem M. B. Church in Maitland, Florida. The purpose was to discuss the organizing of a new Association. The ministers wanted an Association with the same goals and affiliations as their parent body, First South Florida. Thus the new Central Baptist Association was organized and the following officers were elected:

Moderator:	Rev. C. L. Jones, New Hope M. B. Church, Winter Park and Zion Hill M. B. Church, Orlando
Vice Moderator & Bible Expositor:	Rev. H. L. Bradley, St. Luke M. B. Church, Sanford
Secretary:	Rev. Thomas, Open Door M. B. Church, Eatonville
Treasurer:	Rev. J. M. Brown, Friendship M. B. Church, Orlando
Missionary:	Rev. J. B. Webb

Other ministers and pastors present were: Rev. B. T. Williams, St. Luke M. B. Church, Altamonte Springs; Rev. A. D. Avery, President, Sunday School and BTU Congress, Mt. Mission M. B. Church, Daytona Beach; Rev. A. D. Raines, Bethlehem M. B. Church, DeLeon Springs.

Rev. Epps
Minister P. M. Mount
Minister Hal B. King
Rev. B. T. Smith, John M. B. Church, Sanford

HISTORY OF THE NEW GULF COAST MISSIONARY BAPTIST ASSOCIATION

Port St. Joe, Florida
April 18, 1941

After the devotional exercises, Rev. W. J. Johnson stated the object of the meeting and read the roll of the Commission appointed to take part in the deliberations. The following named persons constituted the Commission for the New Orange Association: Reverends W. J. Johnson, B. A. Allen, W. R. Walker, W. S. Drayton, L. D. Brown, and A. D. Bower; Deacons W. C. Brown, J. R. Bower, H. Washington, and Rich Berry. The Commission from the New Coast Association: Reverends F. Byrd, D. F. Battle, J. W. Whitly, W. Martin, G. B. Baker, T. J. Jones, P. D. Hopkins, R. B. Booth, and Deacon J. B. Byrd.

Note that the Old Orange Hill and the New Hope Associations merged to form the New Orange Association in 1931. The first moderator of this new association was Rev. John E. Lytes followed by Rev. William Gipson. Rev. W. J. Johnson was the last moderator of that association which held its last session in October 1941 at the Macedonia Baptist Church, Panama City, FL, of which the Rev. W. J. Johnson was pastor.

These two commissions met together in session and discussed at length the great good to be derived, as well as the feasibility of combining the two associations into one body. Nearly every phase of the work was brought under discussion, after which it was the unanimous opinion of both of the commissions that these two Associations should proceed to merge into one body thirty days after the October sessions.

A motion passed the house that these two commissions recommend the merging of the two bodies into one body thirty days after the October sessions, that both of these associations meet at the St. John Baptist Church, Panama City, Florida, to perfect the new body; and that Reverend F. Byrd be the chairman and Reverend W. R. Walker be the recording secretary until the meeting be accomplished.

Panama City, Florida
November 6, 1941

Deacons Stallworth and Willis opened the Praise Services. Rev. W. J. Johnson announced the purpose of the meeting and the chairman, Rev. Byrd, took charge of the meeting. Rev. Johnson obtained the floor and declared all officers suspended. A motion then prevailed, without a single dissenting vote, that the name of the Gulf Coast Association and the New Orange Association be done away with, to be buried in history. It was motioned and carried that Rev. J. P. Glover act as chairman of the meeting to hold the election and that Rev. N. B. Blackshear act as recording secretary; after which, the house asked for the election of all officers and a new name, which resulted as follows:

NAME

A motion prevailed that this Association shall be known as the New Gulf Coast Missionary Baptist Association.

OFFICERS

Then a motion prevailed that Rev. D. F. Battle be moderator; Rev. W. S. Drayton, vice moderator; Rev. W. R.

Walker, recording secretary; Rev. R. H. Bass, corresponding secretary; Deacon H. T. Sorey, treasurer; and Rev. J. W. Whitly, missionary. Executive Board: Reverends F. Byrd, W. J. Johnson, P. D. Hopkins, B. A. Allen, T. J. Jones, and G. B. Baker.

OFFICERS FOR THE UNION MEETING

Rev. P. D. Hopkins, Chairman; Rev. T. J. Jones, Vice Chairman; Rev. P. O. Glover, secretary; Rev. A. D. Bower, treasurer.

OFFICERS FOR THE WOMEN'S HOME & FOREIGN MISSION SOCIETY

President	Mrs. Rosa Lucas
Vice President:	Mrs. Stella Battle
Recording Secretary:	Mrs. Annie L. Walker
Corresponding Secretary:	Robbie Williams
Treasurer:	Mosetta Edwards
Organizers:	Mrs. Minnie Dawson and Mrs. Lula McClinton

Executive Board: Mss. Lena Prow, Lucille Mons, Keturah Hodge, Bobbie Bass, V. S. Cooper, and Hannah Goods

OFFICERS FOR THE SUNDAY SCHOOL CONVENTION

President:	Rev. C. P. Price
Vice President:	Rev. P. L. Glover
Recording Secretary:	Mrs. Verna M. Rouse and Mrs. Lena Prow
Treasurer:	Dollie Miller
Executive Board:	Bertha Johnson, Hatte Russ, Viola Cain, W. J. Jones, H. T. Sorey, J. B. Byrd

OFFICERS FOR THE BYPU CONVENTION

President:	Rev. G. B. Baker
Vice President:	Clifford Wood

Recording Secretary:	Velma Miney
Corresponding Secretary:	Rev. George Prow
Executive Board:	Catherine Patterson, Lula McClinton, Lossie Gautier, Rev. W. S. Drayton, Minnie Hogan, Viola Cain

MODERATORS—THEN AND NOW

Of those who have served the New Gulf Coast Missionary Baptist Association as moderator, God has called from labor to reward all but the current moderator. They have been:

Rev. D. F. Battle	serving for 17 years
Rev. W. R. Walker	October 1958–October 1959
Rev. W. M. Sutton	October 1959–October 1963
Rev. C. P. Price	October 1963–October 1967
Rev. Chris Brown	October 1967–October 1970
Rev. H. L. Long	October 1970 until his death in August 1975
Rev. Butler Jones	October 1975–1981
Rev. H. C. McCray, Jr.	October 1981–present

During Rev. McCray's tenure, the association was blessed with 10 acres of land in Fountain, Florida. A church in Wewahitchka, Florida, and land in Carrabelle, Florida. A dream came true—at one time New Gulf Coast Association had a church in Fountain, Florida. Today, Rev. McCray, with God's help, led us back to the land where we started.

NEW GULF COAST ASSOCIATION RETREAT

In 1972, Rev. Harold Long, Jr., dreamed that one day the New Gulf Coast Association would be the proud owners of their very own land. Moderator Butler Jones, sent a committee to look into the possibility of the New Gulf Coast Association purchasing and occupying the land. Moderator McCray, driven by a force not seen by any man and understood by few, pursued that dream.

Here, in Fountain, Florida, on May 25, 1985, the Lord our God fulfilled a promise. God made the dream of three successive New Gulf Coast Association moderators come true. On this day, the land was blessed and dedicated to the Lord. Fellowship dinner followed and some chose to spend the night and camp out.

REFLECTIONS OF HISTORICAL REFERENCES OF THE GREATER SOUTH FLORIDA DISTRICT BAPTIST ASSOCIATION 1939–1989

God of our weary years,
God of our silent tears,
Thou who hast brought us thus far
on the way,
Thou who hast by Thy might,
led us into the light,
keep us forever in the path, we pray.

The Greater South Florida Baptist Association was organized by a group of dedicated Baptist ministers on a very cold night in February, 1939 at the First Baptist Church of Belle Glade, now named the St. John Missionary Baptist Church.

The Reverend William Smith was elected Moderator, Reverend S. Randolph, Vice Moderator, Reverend G. J. Martin, Corresponding Secretary, Reverend T. C. Callahan, Recording Secretary, and Reverend J. H. Carswell, Treasurer. Other members included Reverend J. S. Scott, Reverend Engran, Reverend Cooper, Reverend J. P. Austin, Sr., Deacon Brooks Bacon, Reverend E. Coffee, Deacon Willie Riggs, Reverend F. D. Williams, Deacon Joe Foster, Deacon Bolden, Deacon James Poe, Deacon A. Z. Morgan, Deacon Lovett Cooper and others.

The object of the Association shall be to collect money for missions and Christian education, to do missionary work by supporting competent and efficient men in the field and to do educational work by donating to some and giving scholarships to unfortunate, underprivileged and worthy children of Baptist families and Baptist parentage who have finished their high school course, who attend a school supported by this Association, also young men who were desirous of entering the ministry.

The association is comprised of auxiliaries: The Senior Women's Mission, The Mission No. 2, The Junior Women, Youth, The Brotherhood, Minister's Wives and Deaconess Council, The Children's Department and the Missionary and Educational Congress.

God has blessed us spiritually and financially during these 50 years and we are thankful and give him the praise.

We are greatly blessed to have had only two Moderators, Dr. William Smith, D. D., who served as Moderator until the year of 1951 and Dr. J. B. Adams, our present Moderator who became acting Moderator and in the year of 1952 was duly elected as the official Moderator.

Under the leadership of Dr. Adams, this Association is known as "The Greater South Florida District Baptist Association" and progress has continued to move higher and higher.

This Association is celebrating its 50th Golden Anniversary and has nine (9) churches, and they are:

First Institutional Baptist Church
Lake Wales, Florida
Rev. Alphonso Battle, Pastor

Gethsemane Baptist Church
St. Petersburg, Florida
Rev. F. Ford, Pastor

St. John Missionary Baptist Church
Belle Glade, Florida
Rev. J. B. Adams, Pastor

Northside Baptist Church
Lakeland, Florida
Rev. M. Q. Williams, Pastor

St. John Baptist Church
Palmetto, Florida
Rev. J. D. Johnson, Pastor

Mt. Calvary Baptist Church
South Bay, Florida
Rev. R. Cooper, Pastor

Mt. Calvary Baptist Church
Raderville, Florida
Rev. L. Camel, Pastor

Bethel Baptist Church
Okeechobee, Florida
Rev. L. Camel, Pastor

New Mt. Temple Church
Tampa, Florida
Rev. N. L. Hagan, Pastor

This Association has within it State and National Officers, and they are:

1. Dr. J. B. Adams, Moderator
   (a) State and National Chairman of the Educational Board
   (b) Member of the Executive and National Board
2. Deacon P. J. Bryant
   (a) Past Vice President of the State Brotherhood
3. Sister Jeresa C. Austin
   (a) Financial Secretary—State Children Department
   (b) Past Recording Secretary of NBC Children Department
4. Reverend A. Battle
   (a) member of the State Educational and Home Mission Boards
5. Sister Amelia Houston
   (a) Past National Historian
   (b) President Emeritus of the Progressive State Women's Convention
6. Sister Rosa L. Carwise
   (a) Past Recording Secretary, Women's State Convention
7. Reverend L. C. Carwise
   (a) Past Minister advisor for the Women's State Convention
8. Reverend J. D. Johnson
   (a) Recording Secretary, P. M. & E. State

OFFICERS—1989

Dr. J. B. Adams	Moderator
Rev. Leon Camel	Vice Moderator
Rev. Roosevelt Cooper	Treasurer
Rev. J. D. Johnson	Recording Secretary
Rev. Alphonso Battle	Financial Secretary
Bro. P. J. Bryant, Jr.	Financial Secretary
Rev. O. Robinson	Historian and Statistical Secretary
Rev. M. Q. Williams	Chairman of Education
Sis. Mamie Mitchell & Sis. Mary Audrey	Musicians
Sis. Carrie Barfield	Chorister

The Senior Women's Auxiliary was organized during the year of 1940 with Sister Fannie Mack Batista serving as the first President, following her were Sister Carrie Harris. Sister Amelia Houston served as President for several decades until her retirement. Sister Sallie Lee Smith has served as President for several years and has continued to raise financial support for Florida Memorial College in Miami. Sister Rosa Lee Carwise also served as Recording Secretary for many years, Sister Mamie Mitchell served as pianist for many years and Sister Josette Duval served as Chorister for several years.

Officers for the Senior Mission No. 2: Sister Julia Tyler, President; Sister Carrie Barfield, Vice President; Sister Christine Benjamin, Secretary; Sister Ernestine Massey, Financial Secretary;

Junior Women's officers: Sister Elnora Bailey, President; Sister Diane Wells, Vice President; Sister Veronica Miller, Recording Secretary.

Appendix IV

Moderator's Address

Delivered 1920

Brother Vice Moderator, Messengers, Brethren, Ladies and Gentlemen:

I assure you that it is a source of inexpressible pleasure to me to have the pleasure of presenting to you my sixth annual address. We have come over a twelve month's journey. We met last a Friendship Baptist Church, Apalachicola, Florida, where we had a great meeting, and today finds us assembled at St. Mary's Baptist Church to do more and better work for the Master this year than we did last year. I am sure you are cognizant of the fact that more is required of us. The church is passing through one of the most trying ages that ever history recorded. You realize that it takes more work now to keep the church moving than it did a few years ago. It takes more praying, singing, preaching, lecturing than ever before. The propositions that you go up against now are harder. It requires of us more faith, and in short, more actual consecrated service. There is a great feeling of unrest existing throughout the world. . . .

Instead of the war being over, it seems like it has just begun. Of course, there is a cessation of hostilities in parts of the country, still we are in a worse condition today than we were when the cannons were firing on the battlefields. I cannot recall in my mind if there ever was a time when our government was in such a restless condition politically than it is now. There is a bitter war between capital and labor. Strikes and rioting seem to prevail the country over. The high cost of living seems to be a menace to the country and as the poet would have it: "The hosts of sin are pressing hard, to draw thee from the skies."

THE RACE

In proving education in the common schools and otherwise for the Negro, it is but natural that he has attained some qualifications that carry with them changes in surroundings and conditions. His habits, his tastes, his dress, his general deportment are entirely new and different from many years ago, and his white neighbor must take these matters under consideration, especially when it comes to dealing with him. Therefore, education is the way of preserving and guiding progress. The greatest life that we can lead is one of service. The greatness of God is that of service. True greatness lies in character. The man who lives to render service is despised, because there is a strange ambition ruling in the hearts of multitudes of people to be ministered to instead of ministering. People wish to receive rather than to give.

OUR DUTY

Duty's call is heard throughout the country, and especially in our district. There is uprising here and there throughout the country. Anti-Christ and the time is here that our Lord said would come when they would tell you that He (Jesus) is here at this place. And if it were possible, would deceive the very elect. He said, believe him not, nor go after him. And my brethren, do you see the need of preaching and teaching the gospel as never before? Our people have set under the sounding appeal of the untarnished gospel of the Son of God for years perfectly deaf and idle in a manner, and numbers of them have confessed under the sound of the same gospel, the gospel that saved you and my mother. I call to remembrance some of her last dying remarks in which she said, "I will soon be done with the troubles of this world, and will fly away," and many testimonies from countless numbers of our loving dead. They are apostatizing, saying, "We never heard the gospel before now." I have just received the Blessing of the Holy Spirit.

Our district is in fairly good condition and is doing some constructive work, but there is room for improvement, and I believe we have the material in our boundaries to do the work. Yet there are some of our leading ministers and deacons who can find time to be idle.

Our mission work is somewhat delinquent. Neither of the missionaries, for some cause, have been very active. If there ever was a time in the history of our existence that we need good strong missionaries, it is now. To neglect mission work means almost instant death to the district.

EDUCATIONAL WORK

We need a better system of education. Our Educational Board of the district has not reported to the association since it has been appointed. Might I say that the great possibility of the educational work rests upon our shoulders. A religious education is the only education that will stand the crucial test of this age. To educate means to prepare. Preparedness means readiness, and to be ready is the Master's watchword to us. The Lord has said, "Be ye also ready for ye know not what hour your Lord doth come." We must lay the foundation for the preparation of our people.

The district needs a good strong missionary—one who will go into all of the needful places and preach and teach our people, and organize our people, hold convocations and revivals, etc. In fact, we need a prepared man.

Our women's work also needs stimulating from the pulpit as well as from the pews, and it also needs a good strong woman organizer who is endowed with the mission spirit who will go and teach our women to be sober and chaste housekeepers. My brethren, to neglect our women's work means almost instant death to the cause. I am speaking to the conservative brethren of the church.

I am speaking to the exceptional few who stand hard by the women, who stand hard by the church. The majority of the men seem to have gone on a strike against the church. Very few men you can find now that are very active in the church or anywhere else. It seems to be another time when God would have it that women should lead. It must be another time when we must have a Deborah to lead the army of the Lord.

Before I close these remarks, let me thank you for having repeatedly given me the honor of presiding over the business of the district as your moderator, an honor that I feel hardly worthy to accept.

RECOMMENDATIONS

I recommend that this association put on a drive for five hundred dollars to foster the cause of education.

I recommend further, that a ministerial institute be held yearly somewhere, at some central point in the district for the better preparation of our ministers and leaders.

I further recommend that a campaign team be appointed by the association to manage the affairs of the drive.

I further recommend that the campaign team hold convocations or whatever they deem best, to raise these funds and that these teams report quarterly to the Executive Board of this association.

Yours for the Master's Cause,
F. Byrd

MIDDLE FLORIDA AND CLAY COUNTY ASSOCIATION

The Association was organized September 1931, at the St. Luke Baptist Church, Hibernia, Florida, Reverence Mack Spencer was founder and moderator.

Reverend Emory Bradly is presently serving as moderator.

NOTICE
to the
Union Missionary Baptist Association

You are called to meet with the Bethel M. B. Church at River Junction, Fla., October 14, 1937

Rev. B. B. Stuart, Pastor

The pastor and his good people are not leaving a stone, unturned in making it ready to receive you.

I have belonged to this District 43 years and am the oldest Minister in the Association. I am going to offer my resignation as Moderator. If am physically able I will do my best to give an educational sermon on Friday night.

Rev. J. E. Highsmith

THURSDAY MORNING

10:00 A.M. The Association opens with Introductory Sermon by Bro. D. Nealy. Prayer, Collections, appointment of Finance Committees and Adjournment.

THURSDAY EVENING

2:00 P.M. The Association opens in the usual form with the moderator in chair.

	Calling for letters from different churches. Enrollment of Dele gates.
3:00 P.M.	All dues paid for 1937. No one will have a voice till claims are paid.
5:00 P.M.	W. H. M. in session until six o'clock
7:00 P.M.	Prayer service by appointment. Preaching at 7:30.

FRIDAY MORNING

9:00 A.M.	The Association opens in usual form with moderator in chair. Reading and Prayer. Appointment of Committees. W. H. M. in session.

FRIDAY EVENING

2:00 P.M.	Hearing of reports of Committees. Devotional Service Friday night by appointment.

SATURDAY MORNING

9:00 A.M.	Session opens in usual form with moderator in charge. The hearing of all reports. Moderator's Address. Election of officers and adjournment.

SATURDAY EVENING

2:00 P.M.	Closing of the business of the session.
7:30 P.M.	Literary Program rendered by Sister L. J. West

SUNDAY

9:00 A.M.	Front Line Sunday School.
11:00 A.M.	Preaching Services
	Executive Board is asked to come to my house Wednesday P.M.

HISTORY OF THE KISSIMMEE VALLEY MISSIONARY BAPTIST ASSOCIATION

The Kissimmee Valley Missionary Baptist Association was organized in October 1924 at the First Missionary Baptist Church, Okeechobee, Florida. Reverend M. J. Lambert of Bainbridge, Georgia, was elected Moderator of the Association.

October 1925 the First Annual session of the Association was held at the First Missionary Baptist Church of Okeechobee, Florida. During this session Rev. Connie (C) Dean was elected Moderator of the Association. Rev. C. Dean served from 1925 til 1933. The Rev. A. J. Shaw was elected to served as Moderator of the Association. Rev. A. J. Shaw served from 1933 to 1935. After this period Rev. C. Dean was re-elected Moderator of the Kissimmee Valley Missionary Baptist Association. Rev. C. Dean served as Moderator from 1935 until God called him from labor to reward March 20th 1960.

Dr. O. D. Williams, vice Moderator was elected Moderator of the Association during the year of 1960. Dr. O. D. Williams served from 1960 until May 10 1972 when God called him off the battle field.

Vice Moderator Rev. L. W. Williams was elected Moderator of the Association in 1972. Moderator L. W. Williams served faithfully from 1972 til 1977. Moderator Williams' health prevented him from continuing as Moderator of the Kissimmee Valley Missionary Baptist Association.

The year 1977 Dr. Aaron Drayton II was elected Moderator from 1977 until 1982. The year of our Lord 1982 Rev. W. M. Davis was elected Moderator of the Kissimmee

Valley Missionary Baptist Association. Dr. Davis is still at the Helm, leaning and depending on the Lord.

Courtesy of Sister Emma L. Jackson
Okeechobee, Florida

HISTORY OF THE EQUAL RIGHTS PROGRESSIVE MISSIONARY BAPTIST ASSOCIATION

Six ministers met on February 5, 1947 at the Emmanuel Baptist Church, Pensacola, Florida, to plan for the organization of an Association. The ministers were:

Reverend John Rhoden,	Emmanuel	Pensacola
Reverend E. V. Wilson	New Hope (Goulding)	Pensacola
Reverend G. W. Trawick	Friendship	Pensacola
Reverend W. G. Green	Tabernacle	Pensacola
Reverend W. M. Johnson	Little Rock	Pensacola
Reverend D. W. Webb		Pensacola

Later, on February 26, 1947 the following ministers joined the movement to bring about a productive organization:

Reverend S. L. Leggett	Morning Star	Pensacola
Reverend A. D. Darden	New Hope	
Reverend J. W. McCants	St. Luke	Cantonment
Reverend N. Mills		Pensacola
Reverend Blackwell		Pensacola
Reverend J. S. Porm	Englewood	Pensacola
Reverend E. L. Causey		Pensacola
Reverend O. R. Robinson		Pensacola

March 7, 1947 a meeting was called for a preplanning session at the Little Rock Baptist Church to draft an agenda for a proposed election of officers.

March 12, 1947 with Reverend John Rhoden, Pastor of Emmanuel Baptist, after a brief opening presented the Chairman Reverend G. W. Trawick. The Chairman, announced the purpose of the meeting and opened the house for the formal election of officers. The officers elected:

Reverend S. L. Leggett	Moderator
Reverend G. W. Trawick	First Vice Moderator
Reverend W. M. Johnson	Second Vice Moderator
Deacon Will Sampson	Secretary
Reverend O. R. Robinson	Treasurer

March 28, 1947 Installation Services for officers was held at the Little Rock Baptist Church, Reverend D. W. Webb was the speaker. Text, John 21:9.

At a called meeting, April 10, 1947, at the Emmanuel Baptist Church several names were suggested for the newly formed association. The Reverend S. L. Leggett submitted the name Equal Rights Progressive Baptist District Association, which was accepted and approved.

AUXILIARIES: June 1947

June 1947 (Fourth Sunday) The Hopewell Sunday School and Baptist Training Union Convention was organized.

Reverend J. H. Rhoden was elected President of the Sunday School Department.
Reverend E. V. Wilson, President of the Baptist Training Union Department.
Mrs. Phyliss Wilmer, President, Women's Mission.
Reverend W. G. Green, President Ministers and Deacons Union.
Mrs. E. V. Wilson, President Ministers and Deacons Wives.
Reverend G. W. Trawick, Historian.
Reverend J. T. Thomas, Missionary.
Mrs. C. Fitchew, Musician.

1950—Deacon L. Sheppard, President Choir and Ushers.
1960—Mrs. Della Savage, Directress Youth Department.
1963—Mrs. N. Moore, President District Chorus, reorganized.

Properties Purchased

On May 17, 1948 The Equal Rights Association acquired 4 acres of land from Mr. Henry and Annie Maud Duncan. Description—210 feet by 420 feet in the Northwest Corner of the SW 1/2 of section 10. Township 1 North, Range 31 West. Cantonment, Florida.

On January 15, 1950, the Association began the construction of a building on the site. The building description: 50 × 30 with six (6) rooms; two (2) baths; two (2) halls; one 14 × 30 and the other 4 × 16. Completed with electric pump and equipped kitchen.

On January 15, 1951 the Association purchased five (5) additional acres of land from Mr. J. R. and Jessie Stokes. Description: 617 feet × 217 feet in SW 1/4 of SW 1/4, 217 feet east of Northwest corner, 101 m 31 W, Cantonment, Florida.

The rentals from the Association's home was used for years to aid needed families within the Association.

Progress and growth has continued over the years with full focus on mission and education.

Officers 1993–1994

Moderator	Reverend Ceasar Smith
First Vice Moderator	Reverend J. J. Miller
Second Vice Moderator	Reverend Nathaniel Wilson
Third Vice Moderator	Dr. W. E. Bruner
Secretary	Sister Aserdean Soles
Treasurer	Reverend Joe Bryant

Senior Women

President	Sister Bessie Rice
First Vice President	Sister Lillie M. Bogan
Second Vice President	Sister Zetherine Lee
Advisor	Dr. W. E. Bruner

Intermediate Mission

President	Sister Judy Cook
Advisor	Reverend Alvin Smith

Appendix V

Position Paper

The Reverend J. F. Hargrett

CENTENNIAL CELEBRATION
First South Florida
Missionary Baptist Association
1888–1988

Mt. Carmel Missionary Baptist Church
Dr. Mac J. Williams, Host Pastor
Clearwater, Florida
November 16–19, 1988

THE BLACK CHURCH: CHALLENGE OF THE PAST, HOPE OF THE FUTURE

Prepared by the Reverend Joseph F. Hargrett, Pastor
Mt. Pleasant Missionary Baptist Church
Orlando, Florida
First Vice Moderator, First South Florida Baptist Association

Moderator Jackson, Vice Moderator Johnson, Officers and members of the First South Florida Missionary Baptist Association, visitors, friends, and sinner friends if there are any present. God is good. Thank you for the opportunity to discuss with you the theme of the association. It is a privilege and an honor to have been chosen to appear as a speaker on this 100th birthday of this grand old Association. All praises go to God.

Black Americans have such a rich heritage. Fact! Their history has not been made fully reported in the usual way in which the significant aspects of its development. Black Americans need to know who they were and who they are if they are seriously interested in whom they can become. The "Black Church" has been a vital part of the Black American history from slavery to a freedom that is yet to be perfected. The Black Church accepted a daring challenge of the past and now stands today as hope for the future.

Black America is what it is today and what it can become because of the "Black Church." Not just Black America but white America must respect the facts of history which records that the "Black Church" has been the protective plate in the development of a nation. The Black experiences in America was made less [*odious*] because of the Black Churches.

Believe it, accept it, agree with the statement or not, there is in the American society, the "Black Church." Otis Moses, Jr. in his essay, "Black Church Distinctives" states:

> "For better or for worse in the North American section of the Western hemisphere, we do have what can be relatively designated as the Black church and the white church. The Black church is the product of one of the agonies in Christian history. There are four compelling agonies in Christendom. These are: war, anti-Semitism, capitalism, and racism."

This church which is known as the Black Church is a fellowship of Christian believers which had its beginnings in the fields of the white slave owners. Its government, administration, functional life, and structure are in the hands of Black people.

The "Black Church" for discussion sake is the church which surrounds itself with Black concerns. A notable study of the Black Church attributes its origins to five challenging characteristic forces:

1. growing racial consciousness,
2. individual initiative,
3. splits and withdrawals,
4. the migration of Blacks from rural areas in the south to the north, and
5. the missions started by other churches.

Mays and Nicholson in their accounts of the Black Church, say that the Black Church began as a means of separating an unwanted racial group from common worship and that the Black Church accepted the challenge of survival and survived because of the economic, sociological, and psychological forces in the church and its environment. Black churches originating from discrimination and racial consciousness had their appearance well ahead of Black churches originating from groups desirous of having the "Black Church" to conduct and direct his own religious activities. Churches resulting from schisms also developed rapidly. In later years the most influential factor in development of the New Black Church was the migrating movements of "Blacks."

The challenge of the "Black Church" in the past was to develop the whole Black man, and this was done in one way by providing places of assembly for her people. The "Black Church" served as a community center. The "Black Church" was the organizing principal around which their life was built. Their church was their political arena, their social club, their art gallery, and even their conservatory of music. All this and more, especially in the south where there were few, if any, places or buildings, for recreational purposes. The exception to this trend was the larger cities. To the black Church came the lecturers asking for hearings. To the Black Church came the foreigners asking for collection to help them on their way. To the church came race leaders demanding the rostrum from which the alarms were sounded for an advance of the bold enemy who, if not checked, would fix upon the race disabilities and burdens until all hope of liberty was lost. The Black Church was the unique sustaining force that gave Black Americans the strength to endure when endurance gave no promise, and the courage to be creative in the face of their own dehumanization.

The "Black Church" further served as a mutual aid center from which all types of aid was given to all types of people.

During the ages past, the Black church was faced with the challenges of bringing freedom from slavery of the black race and increasing the Black faith and building the Black solidarity. But, too, in the face of despair and discontentment, Black *found* gratification through the expressive patterns provided by the church. Such expressions as singing together, praying together, engaging in the formal expression of religious fellowship, and celebrating special occasions. Another challenge of the Black church has been its provision of release from frustration which accompanied economic and political restrictions. In the social and moral isolation of the Black masses, the church has been "a nation within a nation."

The distinct challenge of the Black church has been that of setting at liberty those that are bound. The black church has been known as the church of the oppressed. She is known for her theology of survival, generally, and as a carrier of the Black folk culture.

The challenges of the Black church in the past have been that of being used as a way of creative hope, have made provisions for integrity. Integrity means wholeness. When the world and society were constantly tearing the Blacks apart, the church continued to help get the Blacks together. When Blacks were torn apart all the week, for a few fleeting moments in that worship service the Blacks had an experience of togetherness.

The Black church provided social unity. It provided limited educational support. It provided a meaningful spiritual legacy.

The thrust for freedom by Black Americans found a home in the black church. The black church accepted the challenge of yesterday and converted oppression into poetry, exploitation into creative force, humiliation into a hunger for justice, haunting fears into hymns of faith.

The Black church in her challenge of the past now stands as hope of the future. If the Black church is to remain relevant, she must convert a praying people into a positive power-conscious people. As in the past, the Black church kept the race from committing suicide. When Blacks were living under the conditions of genocide, the Black church kept them alive on the inside. Yet, today, too many Blacks are living in a hopelessness with no hope in sight. Blacks need somebody or something to transport hope in this hopeless world. The Black church should be that means of transport; it should be the vehicle of hope to a hopeless people.

The pluralistic context of American culture and its encounter with Blacks affords another potent challenge to traditional Black church life. More and more, society is facing new forms of Christian witness as well as the rise of other world religions in this American culture. Everywhere there are new cults, denominations, and new faith movements encountering the life of Blacks. Many of these movements tend to prey particularly on the Black church. Black churches seem especially vulnerable to these religionists because of their historic failure to be equipped educationally for meaningful dialogue with such groups.

The Black church is a distinct part of the development of Christianity. A rich history and heritage are filled with stories of advance and decline, joys and sorrows, and growth toward maturity.

What will the future bring? The future will escape the one who seeks to predict what will happen. Nevertheless, the Black Church will continue to be involved in and make major contributions to the continuing growth and development of Blacks in the world. The Black church is the hope of the future because she had been anointed to preach the gospel to the poor, sent to heal the broken-hearted, to preach deliverance to the captives, and recover sight to the blind, and preach the acceptable year of the Lord.

Appendix VI

Open Letter

July 15, 1988

My Dear Member of NBCA, Inc.:

I feel it necessary to inform you of a most recent convention happening and why it happened. An action of critical importance was taken by the National Baptist Convention of America, Inc. in its recent summer session in San Antonio, Texas, on Thursday, June 23, 1988. Under the 1979 mandate of the convention, meeting in its annual session on September 6, 1979, in San Antonio, Texas, the constitution was amended for the convention to have a congress and the convention voted on June 23, 1988, to carry out this mandate. Please believe me this is not harsh action, but a meditative and prayerful execution to implement the Kingdom's Agenda as a convention. The National Baptist Congress of the National Baptist Convention of America, Inc. will hold its first session in June of 1989 in Shreveport, Louisiana.

I want you to know why this action was taken. The National Baptist Sunday Church School and Baptist Training Union Congress, of which Dr. T. B. Boyd, III, is Executive Secretary/Director, is not an auxiliary of the National Baptist Convention of America, Inc. As I stated previously in the 1987 Board Meeting in Mobile, Alabama, that the said congress is incorporated without any members (Article 7, Charter of the National Baptist Sunday Church School and Baptist Training Union Congress, June 20, 1979). It is owned, operated, and under the control of the Publishing Board and is in no way subject or answerable to the National Baptist Convention of America, Inc., not even to the sanctioning or election of its Publishing Board members who, by the way, are members of our convention.

The members of the Convention voiced their beliefs that it is wrong for a Sunday School to operate independently of the local church of which it is a part. The Convention feels it is equally wrong for a National Sunday School Congress whose constituency is made up of the National Baptist Convention of America, Inc. to operate independently of the National Baptist Convention with which it is supposed to be affiliated! BECAUSE OF NO INPUT: NO SAY SO ABOUT WHO OR WHAT IS PROGRAMMED, NO SAY SO ABOUT TAXATION, EXPENDITURES OR DISBURSEMENTS, IT IS NECESSARY FOR THE NATIONAL BAPTIST CONVENTION OF AMERICA, INC. TO ORGANIZE ITS OWN CONGRESS. WE EXPECT THE FULL AND COMPLETE SUPPORT OF EACH MEMBER OF THIS CONVENTION.

The Congress that meets in June in Shreveport, Louisiana, will be an auxiliary of the National Baptist Convention of America, Inc. The National Baptist Convention of America, Inc. will elect congress officers as we do all other officers of the convention, and it will be subject to the parent body. I ask your prayers, concern, and cooperation for this significant and historical step in the life of our convention. Information concerning the dates of the Congress will be forwarded soon.

May God richly bless your field of labor as we, as a convention, strive to do for Him what we cannot do for the Kingdom alone.

Sure of Eternal Life.

E. Edward Jones, President
NBCA, Inc.[18]

805 Florida Avenue
Sarasota, Florida 34236

August 30, 1993

Mrs. Altermese S. Bentley
612 East Ninth Street
Sanford, FL 32771

Dear Mrs. Bentley:

Dr. N. S. Sanders received a letter from you requesting a brief history of the Mount Pilgrim Missionary Baptist Association. After a diligent search, we found that this Association was organized in 1908. The idea was born in the minds of the late Reverends N. W. King, W. M. Dillard, S. J. Johnson and a Reverend Jordan (whose first name or initial is not documented). The organizational meeting was held in Tampa, FL at Saint John Baptist Church, where the Reverend W. M. Dillard was Pastor.

The Mount Pilgrim Missionary Baptist Association has continued to make great strides in kingdom building for our great God, Creator and Maker of all things, under the leadership of the following Moderators:

Rev. N. W. King	1908–1931
Rev. Scott Davies	1932–1938
Rev. Fluker	1939–1942
Rev. G. W. Jones	1943–1949
Rev. R. D. Dawson	1950–1952
Rev. E. D. Burnett	1953–1960
Rev. I. Anderson	1961–1969
Rev. C. H. Bolden	1970–1980
Rev. J. E. McCrary	1981–1982
Rev. F. G. Hilton	1982–1985
Dr. N. S. Sanders	1986–Present

My prayer is that God bless you in this great work. I hope this information is adequate, if not please feel free to contact me.

Your in Christ Jesus,

Sister Susie Hammond
Historian

Rev. Dr. N. S. Sanders,
Moderator
Mount Pilgrim Missionary
Baptist Association

UNION FOREIGN
1908
Moderators

Reverend John Kayen,
Oakhill Baptist Church, Fort McCoy
Reverend N. Burnett
1912–1913
Reverend A. W. Crawford
1913–1914
Reverend N. Burnett
1914–1915
Reverend G. W. Blackston
1915–1923
Reverend H. M. Dillard
1923–1938
Reverend J. D. Dupree
Reverend Frank Cubby
Reverend L. S. McCree
Reverend J. E. Harmon
Reverend S. N. Lumpkin

It has also been determined that the First Annual Session of the Union Foreign Mission Baptist Association was held in the year of Our Lord. Nineteen-Hundred and Eleven. The Reverend John Kayen served as the first Moderator. This Association has consistently met on a annual basis since that time. From 1911 until 1990 there has been nine previous Moderators. It has been my good fortune and blessings to have been seeked out and encouraged by four of those great leaders: Reverend J. D. Dupree, Revernend Frank Cubby, Reverend L. S. McCree and Moderator emeritus J. E. Harmon under whose guidance I reverently pursue. These men have done great works for this Association, having placed it at one-time among the leading District of the Progressice Missionary & Educational Baptist State Convention, Inc. of Florida. It was Union Foreign Association who led as host of the National Baptist Convention of America at St. Petersburg, Florida in September

1969. The Mt. Zion Progressive Baptist Church and Reverend L. S. McCree served as host.

Since the year 1924, this Association has hosted the State convention six times and just this past June 1992, assisted the South Florida Progressive Baptist Association as they hosted the National Baptist Congress of Christian Workers with its 8,000 or so workers and delegates in St. Petersburg, Florida.

The Moderators before me left behind a true and genuine legacy and a steadfast-solid foundation for which I am to build upon. I thank God for these great men of determination, faith, dedication and vision for the future. Most assuredly, they were men amongst men; giants amongst giants and real champions of their era. In retrospect these man have done for me just what General Colin L. Powell, the Military's Joint Chiefs of Staff said in a recent speech of the ***Tuskegee Airmen*** (the first all Black Fighter-Escort Pilots). "I didn't get where I am by my self—I got here on the wings of men like you."

This is no indication that we should forget our cherished past, but rather hold it always at the very center of our hearts; to be inspired by it as we move forward. There is much work for us to do as we are faced daily with many new challenges. Our churches, our congresses and association have all been tapped by both the state and the national conventions to support various associations, but many community service organizations for support as well.

Brethren, I urge you to do the best that you can and urge you to also help this association to live up its expectations in supporting these causes. It is my goal to make Union Foreign Missionary Baptist Association one of the greatest and influential religious groups in all of Florida. We must build a better world for ourselves, our children, our successors. We must win more souls for Christ and prepare for His coming back.

I pray God's blessings and solicit each of your prayers and continued support as we go forth.

S. N. Lumpkin, Moderator
October 20, 1992

Union Foreign Association
Roster of Officers
1992–1993

Reverend S. N. Lumpkin	Moderator
Reverend J. E. Harmon	Moderator Emeritus
Reverend Madison Murray	First Vice Moderator
Reverend Willie McDaniel	Second Vice Moderator
Reverend J. W. Cooper, Sr.	Exec. Recording Secretary
Reverend W. R. Roberts	Corresponding Secretary
Reverend J. A. Stephens	Treasurer
Mrs. Gerry Stovall	Public Relations and Financial Secretary

UNION FOREIGN ASSOCIATION
13484 121ST STREET
LARGO, FL 34648

July 15, 1993

Mrs. Altermese Smith Bentley
Historian, Progressive M&E Baptist State Convention
612 East 9th Street
Sanford, FL 32771

Dear Mrs. Bentley:

Moderator S. N. Lumpkin asked that I respond to your request of April 14, 1993 for information regarding Union Foreign Association. My apologies for the delay in complying. Listed below are the current officers for 1992–1993:

Reverend J. E. Harmon, Moderator Emeritus
Pastor, Oakhill M. B. Church
4202 East Palifox
Tampa, FL 33610

Reverend Madison Murray, First Vice Moderator
Pastor, Greater Friendship M. B. Church
4413–35th Street238
Tampa, FL 33610

Reverend Willie McDaniel, Second Vice Moderator
Pastor, Mt. Olive M. B. Church
13207 Pine Street North
Largo, FL 34638

Reverend J. W. Cooper, Sr., Exec. Recording Secretary
Pastor, First Missionary Baptist Church
11504 Bessie Dix Road
Seffner, FL 335484

Reverend W. R. Roberts, Corresponding Secretary
Pastor, Piney Grove M. B. Church
P.O. Box 990
San Antonio, FL 33576

Reverend J. A. Stephens, Treasurer
Pastor, Mt. Olive M. B. Church
P.O. Box 191
Bradley, FL 33835

Mrs. Gerry Stovall, Public Relations Secretary
Financial Secretary, Galilee M. B. Church
505–35th Street South
St. Petersburg, FL 33711

Enclosed is a copy of Moderator Lumpkin's 1992 Annual Address which gives a brief history of the Association. I hope this meets with your request. If the 3 × 5 photograph is not concise, please contact me.

Sincerely,

Gerry Stovall, Public Relations
Secretary
1355–40th Street South
St. Petersburg, FL 33711
813-321-3821

Encl.

In an editorial, Dr. T. B. Boyd, III had this to say:

"I feel compelled at this time to make a statement concerning an article from the *Lantern*, the official newsletter of the National Baptist Convention of America, Inc. The fifth statement under the heading reads as follows:

The CHRISTIAN EDUCATION COMMITTEE and the President are making the following recommendations concerning literature to be used by member churches of the convention:

5. The presidents recommendation is if you feel helpless and don't know quite what to do, order your materials from your former source for this year. (Do this only in a case where you are truly "helpless.")

"While it is very unfortunate for our Christian Brothers to have ever been led to a state of helplessness, this statement seems to give credence to the perception held across the nation, that negotiations between the National Baptist Convention of America, Inc. and the white-owned Cook Publishing Company failed, or at least has not materialized to any great extent.

This "Former Source" would by all logic, be the majority of those few customer accounts that withdrew their quarterly subscription from the National Baptist Publishing Board.

"For nearly one hundred years, the Publishing Board has provided our churches with the best available Christian Education literature that is on today's market for use. We take pride in the fact that our churches are receiving the best source of information available that addresses the needs of our people. That is the reason the Publishing Board was started in the first place, to meet the needs of our constituents.

"We are a Publishing Board that understands the needs of our constituents. Through the years, we have been able to design and perfect a product that meets the needs of Black Baptists across America and abroad. Our literature is for Black Baptist, written by Black Baptist, and designed for use in the Black church. We welcome the return of those churches who wish to renew their affiliation with us, because we are about advancing the Kingdom of God in knowledge through the literature which we offer.

"I believe that there are many people who missed seeing this article who may still be members of the NBCA, Inc. Therefore, I wanted to take this opportunity to inform these persons of the statement.

"I have known as unyielding fact—as have so many persons whose minds have remained open to the truth—that we were faced with a situation built on a whole mass of misinformation—a situation that should have never occurred. Contributing substantially to the "convention shift," for example, was the unsubstantiated statement that the National Baptist Publishing Board did not share benefits with the convention in anyway. Also, it was further implied, and stated, that the National Congress was not "their" organization.

"Finally, after many years of trying to convince doubters of the truth told and retold that "the Congress belongs to everybody, and everybody is the Congress," it is a sad note that only now are many of these same individuals able to "see the light." Only now have we seen the benefit of the Publishing Board providing literature for Church training programs, Sunday Church School and Baptist Training Union, Auxiliaries Guides, and Vacation Bible School. Only now do many of these brethren realize the significant financial contributions, along with spiritual and physical assistance whenever called upon. The Publishing Board has consistently gone well "beyond the call."

It is a matter of record that the Publishing Board has been over the years, a tremendous asset to the National Baptist Convention of America, Inc. A review of the Audit Report of 1986 in the Official Journal shows as a qualified fact that the Publishing Board, over a span of five short years, contributed a total of $800,000 to the convention and its causes to promote and further the work of Christian Education through scholarships, donations, donations of literature, direct Church contributions, Foreign Mission, Home Mission, and other Boards and Auxiliaries of the Convention.

"The Publishing Board holds no malice. God in his infinite wisdom has brought the Publishing Board and our dynamic National Missionary Baptist Convention of America into a harmonious relationship as one which will benefit this nation and the world. We take no joy in the discomfort or struggles of others. We are solely concerned with the building up of God's kingdom—not tearing it down. The Publishing Board stands ready to assist and help its brethren in Christ. It doesn't matter what unbelief or misinformation is held by others, the Publishing Board welcomes opportunities to show the way to what is truthful about its work, while helping to lighten the load of others in any it can."[19]

Endnotes

APPENDICES

1. McKinney and McKinney, *History of the Black Baptists of Florida, 1850–1985,* pp. 261–263.

2. Minutes of the State Sunday School and BYPU (Baptist Young People Union) convention, held at Zion Hill Missionary Baptist Church, Sebring, Florida, July 19–23, 1951, Rev. C. Dean, Pastor.

3. Program of the 43th Annual Session of the Progressive Baptist State Sunday School and BYPU Convention. To be held at the Harmony Baptist Church, Lakeland, Florida. Rev. J. J. McGriff, Pastor, July 23–27, 1958.

4. Minutes of the 49th Annual Session of the Progressive Baptist State BTU. Held with the Mt. Zion Progressive Baptist Church, St. Petersburg, Florida. Rev. L. S. McCree, Pastor, July 16–21, 1964, pp. 119–120.

5. Souvenir Program Golden Jubilee 50th Annual Session of the Progressive Baptist State Sunday School and BTU Convention.

6. Program of the 51st Annual Session of the Progressive Baptist State Sunday School and BTU Convention.

7. Program of the 58th Annual Session of the Progressive Baptist State Sunday School and BTU Convention, St. John Missionary Baptist Church, Orlando, Florida. Rev. F. L. Maxwell, Pastor, July 17–22, 1973.

8. Historical Facts of the Women's Missionary and Educational State Convention of Florida, p. 8.

9. *Ibid*, p. 9.

10. *Ibid*, p. 9.

11. Official Journal of the Seventy-Sixth Annual Session of the Progressive Missionary and Educational Baptist State Convention of Florida, Inc. and Its Auxiliaries, 1990, The Reverend Henry T. Rhim, President, pp. 71–72.

12. Official Journal of the Seventy-Sixth Annual Session of the Progressive Missionary and Educational Baptist State Convention of Florida, Inc. and Its Auxiliaries, 1990, The Reverend Henry T. Rhim, President, pp. 71–72.

13. Minutes of the First Session, Matron's Auxiliary, pp. 55–56.

14. Mrs. W. A. Smart, Annual Letter to the Ministers' and Deacons' Wives, March 23–27, 1980, Jacksonville, Florida. Sixty-Sixth Annual Session of the Progressive Missionary and Educational Baptist State Convention.

15. Historical Information: East Florida and Bethany Baptist Association, by Herndon, Sessions and Wilson, October, 1972, pp. 1–10.

16. *Ibid.*

17. Combined minutes of the 46th Session of the South Florida Missionary Baptist Association and Auxiliaries, November 22–26, 1961.

18. Open letter from the National Baptist Convention of America, Inc., dated July 15, 1988, signed by E. Edward Jones, President.

19. *The National Baptist Union Review*, 94 (June 1990), p. 4.

Appendix VII

FIRST ANNUAL PASTOR'S CONFERENCE OF THE PROGRESSIVE MISSIONARY AND EDUCATIONAL BAPTIST STATE CONVENTION OF FLORIDA

The Reverend H. D. Rucker, Acting Chairman
Monday, March 21, 1988
2:00 p.m.–6:00 p.m.

Theme
"The Pastor-Preacher Executing the Great Commission in This Present Age"
Matthew 20:19 Mark 16:15
at the Ramada Inn

Greater St. Paul Baptist Church
Host Church
Lakeland, Florida

The Reverend N. S. Sanders, Pastor
The Reverend H. T. Rhim, President

The Chairman's Message:

It is most pleasant to have been asked to be the Chairman of the First Pastors' Conference of the Progressive Missionary and Educational Baptist State Convention of Florida. Therefore, I greet you as chairman of this great responsibility. For many years, it has been in the minds of the pastors that the Pastors' Conference be born in this our great Convention. Keeping in mind the bringing of outstanding Black Theologians and ministers, not only from Florida, but from across the Nation for the business of perfecting the Preacher-Pastor of today.

God has blessed many of us in various ways through the challenges in our churches, communities, and our preaching experiences. This Conference will afford chances to share the ministry with each other. For it is here that principles, ideas, and experiences which have been proven to be essential in the growth and development of a blessed pastorate, spiritual and financially will be shared.

It is truly gratifying to know that all the participants on this Conference program were glad to accept this task of illuminating the minds of the Preacher-Pastor with their knowledge and wisdom as laborers together with him for the perfecting of the saints.

God Bless and Keep Each of You.

Harry D. Rucker
AA, BA, MDIV.

The Conference Schedule

1:30 p.m.–2:00 p.m.	Registration Session
2:00 p.m.	Devotion
	The Reverend A. L. Phillips
	The Reverend C. Smith
The Reverend H. D. Rucker,	Chairman
Presiding	
2:15 p.m.	Devotional Message.
	The Reverend Carl Brooks
2:30 p.m.	Statement of Purpose
	Chairman Rucker
	Greetings
	Host Pastor Sanders
2:45 p.m.	Theme Implications.
	The Reverend R. Robinson
3:00 p.m.	The Commission To Go

	"Go Ye Therefore . . . " Matthew 28:19 The Reverend Rollie Murray, Jr.
3:20 p.m.	The Commission To Preach " . . . And Preach the Gospel" Mark 16:15a The Reverend Bobby Jones
3:40 p.m.	Offerings, Remarks, and Break
	The Reverend H. H. Wynn, Vice Chairman Presiding
4:00 p.m.	Congregation Singing "The Commission to Baptize" "Baptizing Them . . . " Matthew 28:19c The Reverend G. I. Bradley
4:20 p.m.	"The Commission to Teach" "Teaching Them . . . " Matthew 28:20 The Reverend N.F. Sumpter
4:40 p.m.	Congregation Hymn
4:45 p.m.	Introduction of Speaker The Reverend Rudolph McKissick
Keynote	The Reverend Hayward Wiggins, Pastor Gethsemane Baptist Church Houston, Texas
5:30 p.m.	Remarks: The Reverend H. T. Rhim, President The Reverend H. D. Rucker, Chairman
Benediction	The Reverend Hayward Wiggins

Tentative Officers

The Reverend H. D. Rucker	Chairman
The Reverend H. H. Wynn	Vice Chairman
The Reverend James Bush, Sr.	Secretary
The Reverend Price Wilson	Treasurer
The Reverend Hugh Brockington	Musician
The Reverend Rudolph McKissick	Dean
The Reverend H. T. Rhim	President

THE COMMISSION TO GO
"Go Ye Therefore. . . . " Matthew 28:19
Presented by : Reverend Rollie Murray, Jr.

Introduction

Jesus is about to ascend to his Father, following his resurrection, at the end of the forty (40) day period which he remained on earth. Before he ascends he gives to his disciples, the eleven Apostles that were standing there with him, and to the Preachers and the church that were to come after them, the Great Commission. He began that Commission with the Commission to Go. "Go ye therefore." This commission is set in the frame work of the Power and Authority of Jesus. "All power is given unto me in heaven and in earth," he declared and then, immediately, gave this commission to go. Because all power is mine, go. This command from Christ to involves more than just an action and encompasses the entire universe.

I. The Commission to Go is a Command of Christ

A. The definition of Commission.
The term commission is defined as the act of granting authority to someone to carry out a certain job or duty. The commission to go is the job or duty assigned by Jesus to the pastor-Preacher in this present age.

B. The Command is "To Go."
*Before we can begin discussing any other part of the commission we must discuss the "Go." This is the first thing our Lord said. Before he said preach, baptize or teach, he said "Go." In

order for any other part of the Great Commission to be carried out, the command to go must be heeded. Before any amount of evangelism can be initiated, we must "Go." This command is plain and simple, "Go ye therefore." In the command to "Go" are words of strong authority from the Captain to the Soldier; from Master to Servant; from redeemer to Redeemed; from King to Subject. No doubt as to possibility, not discussing of dangers, no calculating of results—"Go!" Great oceans, high mountains, wide deserts are in the way; shipwreck, fever, starvation, death—"Go!" The people are brutish and hard of hearing; they have slain the Lord; they will not hear the disciple—"Go!" I am but a child, a man of unclean lips; I forsook the Lord and fled; I denied Him—"Go!"

Jesus was saying that because all power is mine, go. I can defend you. The world is placed under my control. Calvary didn't take away any of my authority. The crucifixion didn't rob me of any power. The resurrection assured my victory over all foes, go. The world is redeemed. It is given me in promise by my Father, as the purchase of my death. Though you are weak yet I am strong. Though you will encounter many troubles and dangers, yet I can defend you. Though you die, yet I live, and the work shall be accomplished. In this command is word of encouragement. Go and fear not for I have sent you. Go and make a business of this work. You must not take state and issue out summons to the nations to attend upon you; but you must go and bring the gospel to their doors. "Go ye therefore."

II What is Involved in the Commission to Go?

A. This is a Purposeful "Go."

There is definitely a purpose in this "Go." You are not being sent out simply because there is nothing else that you can do. You are being sent out because I need you to venture on a mission from me. "Go Ye Therefore."

B. Faith is in this "Go."
The Faith of Christ is exemplified in this Commission. He knew what was to be faced. He knew the weakness of those to whom He gave this commission both of that time and the future, but he still said, "Go Ye Therefore." From the basis of his omniscience he gave this commission to "Go." He knew that the victory was assured.

C. Agency is in this "Go."
As his agents we act in his name and for his sake.

D. Assurance is in this "Go."
He is with everyone sent. "Go Ye Therefore," and be assured that
"I am with you."

III. This Commission To Go Encompasses The World.

A. "Go Ye Therefore," Where? The command is to go "into all the world." When Jesus said this to the disciples He was indicating to them that they were to go to the Gentiles as well as the Jews: This was contrary to the opinions of the Jews, that the Gentiles be admitted to the privileges of Messiah's Kingdom or that the partition wall between them should be broken down. (Acts 22:21,22). It was long before the disciples could be trained to the belief that the gospel was to be preached to all men; and that it was only by special revelation, even after this command, that Peter preached to the Gentile Centurion, Acts 10. Jesus has graciously ordered that the preaching of the gospel shall be stopped by no barriers. Wherever there is man, there it is to be/proclaimed, to every sinner he offers life; and all the world is included in the message of mercy, and every descendant of Adam offered eternal salvation.

B. Why Does It Encompass the World? "All the World"—because all the world is involved in transgression. (Romans 3:19, 23) "All the world"—because man's wants are the same everywhere. All need pardon; all need enlightenment; all need peace.

"All the World"—because God has designed to collect a people for himself from all the tribes and families of the men.

CONCLUSION

The Commission to Go demands an immediate and definite response from us. We must Go. There is no choice. Hear Him still saying "Go ye therefore." If we don't go. . . .

THIRD ANNUAL PASTOR'S CONFERENCE OF THE PROGRESSIVE M&E STATE BAPTIST CONVENTION OF FLORIDA

March 20, 1990 Tampa, Fl
"The Business Of The Spoken Word"
II Timothy 2:15c
Lewis C. Lampley

I. Introductory Comments

A. Commendation & Appreciation

We owe Chairman Rucker a great deal of commendation and appreciation for this fine program of challenge and concern. He is correct when he states, "The nineties present us with a most challenging and difficult age." The question comes, then, are we equipped for the task? The answer could be yes and no . . . at any rate, this kind of conference should (will) greatly thrust us forward in the business of communicating the Truth in these challenging times.

B. Communication & Application

Truth, that is, God's Word is to be communicated and applied. In other words, the Pastor/Teacher or any Preacher should make sure of three (3) things when he stands or sits to speak. God's Truth needs to be expounded accurately, illustrated clearly, and applied practically.

II. Characteristics of Faithful Minister

The passage chosen for these discussions is profound for Truth proclaimers. Mater of fact, the twenty-six (26) verses of II Timothy 2 can be designated as the characteristics of a faithful minister: Flow via these two chapters with me. . . .

1. The Discipling Teacher 2:1,2
2. The Single-minded Soldier 2:3–5
3. The Enduring Farmer 2:6–13
4. The Diligent Workman 2:14–19
5. The Sanctified Vessel 2:20–23
6. The Gentle Servant 2:24–25

A. <u>The Diligent Workman</u>

I want to single the Preacher out as the diligent Workman. As such, Paul gives him a series of imperatives in Chapters 1 & 2.

1. **1:8** "Therefore do not be ashamed of the testimony of our Lord, or of me His prisoner; but join with me in suffering for the gospel according to the power of God."
2. **1:14** "Guard, through the Holy Spirit who dwells in us, the treasure which has been entrusted to you."
3. **2:1** "You therefore, my son, be strong in the grace that is in Jesus Christ."
4. **2:2** "And the things which you have heard from me in the presence of many witnesses, these entrust to faithful men, who will be able to teach others also."
5. **2:3** "Suffer hardship with me, as a good soldier of Christ Jesus."
6. **2:7** "Consider what I say, for the Lord will give you understanding in everything."

7. **2:8** "Remember Jesus Christ, risen from the dead descendant of David, according to my gospel."
8. **2:14** "Remind them of these things, and solemnly charge them in the presence of God not to wrangle about words, which is useless, and leads to the ruin of the hearers."
9. **2:19** "Nevertheless, the firm foundation of God stands, having this seal, 'The Lord knows those who are his,' and, 'Let everyone who names the name of the Lord abstain from wickedness'."
10. **2:22** "Now flee from youthful lusts, and pursue righteousness, faith, love and peace, with those who call on the Lord from a pure heart."
11. "But refuse foolish and ignorant speculations, knowing that they produce quarrels."

All of those commands are present imperatives! It is my task to expound the last clause of verse 15. On the surface, this verse also appears to be an imperative, but it is not. The basic grammar here is in the aorist tense . . . "study to show" . . . aorist infinitive. In other words, the infinitive is a verbal noun . . . and in Greek it has many more uses than it does in English . . . the most common is . . . "to see, to study." List to at least four (4) translations of verse 15.

> "Study to show thyself approved unto God, a workman that needeth not to be ashamed, *Rightly Dividing the Word of Truth."* (KJV) Do your best to present yourself to God as one approved, a workman who does not need to be ashamed who *Correctly Handles the Word of Truth."* (NIV)
>
> "Be diligent to present yourself approved to God as a workman who does need to be ashamed, *Handing accurately the Word of Truth."* (NASB)

Be eager thyself approved to present to God, a workman unashamed, *cutting straight the Word of Truth."* (N.T. Greek)

III. Cutting It Straight

The word for "rightly dividing" or "handling accurately" is one Greek word . . . orthotomeo, and means to cut long a straight line; to cut a straight road. The metaphor could be that of *plowing a straight furrow* or of a road maker *driving his road straight* or of a mason squaring and *cutting a stone to fit* in its proper place of the *cutting of a sacrifice or food* for household use. It is the Pastor-Teacher's responsibility, then to cut it straight. What? God's infallible, inerrant Word. The question comes, "How?" Let me suggest at least two specific ways: Approaching the Word of God exegetically and avoiding errors.

A. Approaching God's Word Exegetically

Definitions

1. **Exegesis** is the process of extracting the accurate interpretation of every text preached or taught. It is to draw out.
2. **Eisegesis** is the faulty interpretation and reading into scripture ideas and meanings that are not there.
3. **Apogesis** is looking at the text or passage and missing altogether what is there.
4. Theology is a word or discussion about God . . .

Cutting it straight involves exegeting/expounding the text accurately, illustrating the text of the passage clearly and applying the text practically. . . . this approach is assured as we:

a. observe the text closely.
b. investigate the text by consulting other sources.
c. interpreting the text *linguistically, culturally, historically,* and *geographically*. Thus, closing four gaps.

That is the three-fold approach, exegetically speaking. It is at this point of interpretation where we go astray. Thus, as Pastor-Teachers and Preachers, we need to make sure that we do not follow the wrong school of interpretation. Interpretation is about Original Meaning!

Three Schools of Thought
Classical Liberalism, Neo-Orthodoxy, and Orthodoxy

a. Classical Liberalism employs Historical-Critical Methods of Interpretation. This school of thought also employs textual criticism to identify the original reading . . . this school rejects inerrancy, infallibility and verbal, plenary inspiration. Sees the Bible as a book of *Jewish Mythology* and ethical *insight.*
b. Neo-Orthodoxy employs Historical-Critical Methods of Interpretation . . . employs textual criticism to identify original reading . . . rejects inerrancy completely. Also rejects verbal, plenary inspiration. Some advocates (in most denominations) accept "infallibility, or purpose" by which they mean that the Bible is infallible in its spiritual teaching. The "thoughts" are inspired but not necessarily the words. This school of thought sees the Bible as a record of Revelation which at times may not be entirely accurate. It records the author's religious experiences.[1]
c. Orthodoxy (to cut straight) This school of thought employs Grammatical-Historical Method of Interpretation. Employs textual criticism to identify original reading. Accepts full inerrancy and infallibility of the Bible, believing in verbal, plenary inspiration.

B. Avoiding Common Errors Made by Many Preachers and Teachers

What are some of these errors?

1. Prooftexting
2. Isolationism
3. Spiritualizing
4. Nationalizing
5. Defining or Redefining
6. Anglicizing

7. Mysticizing
8. Letterism
9. Legalizing
10. Domatizing
11. Embellishing
12. Methodologizing
13. Culturalizing
14. Accommodation
15. Dispensationalizing

PROOFTEXTING—Takes place when we string together an inappropriate or inadequate series of Bible verses to prove our Theology. Put another way . . . it's enticing, but wrong to form one's theology from a complete inductive study of scripture. For example, Isaiah 53:5 and I Peter 2:24 have been misinterpreted regarding physical healing in the atonement. We need to avoid Prooftexting.

ISOLATIONISM—Occurs when we fail to interpret a single scripture text in light of its context. We isolate the scripture from its immediate literary surroundings. ". . . . When two of three have gathered . . . " (Matthew 18:15–18) What's the context? It's not a prayer meeting . . . it's church discipline! There are three major rules for correct interpretation: 1. Context, 2. Context, 3. Context.

SPIRITUALIZING—This happens when we read spiritual or historical truth into a text rather than extracting truth from it. Song of Solomon 2:1 has been ascribed to Christ. . . . "Rose of Sharon and Lily of the Valley." Those are the words of the Bride . . . "I am the Rose of Sharon, The Lily of the Valley."

NATIONALIZING—Although it's akin to spiritualizing, Nationalizing is different. . . . This type of Misinterpretation happens when we see our own country as the recipient of national promises made by God in the Bible to Israel. II Chronicle 7:14 "If my people . . ." This is not the Church . . . Context begins with Verse 12–22 . . . America is not Israel. . . .

EMBELLISHING—Occurs when we read current thinking into the Bible. We all strain at times to make the

Bible seem more contemporary by garnishing scripture's truth with the latest in modern thought. Take the subject of creation for instance. Even since the days of Darwin there has been great pressure brought by the scientific community to explain origins according to the latest scientific theory. . . . Even some Christians advocate theistic evolution. They are not sure that God really created everything that's seen . . . Creation resulted from the . . . the Big Bang, steady state or evoluted over billions of years. Yet, Genesis 1–2 contains the salient biblical facts. Another example of Reading current thinking into the Bible is the present stress on self-love. . . . Remember the two commands in Matthew 22:37–40. "Thy shalt love?" . . . Not Jesus, other, you! No, Love God and your neighbor as yourself.

METHODOLOGIZING—Occurs when the scriptures are interpreted by means of an unproved theory about the Bible's literary origin. Scholars have hypothesized about how or why a part of the Bible came into existence and then used their theory to interpret the text. For example, The Graf Wellhausen Documentary Hypothesis . . . holds that the Pentateuch (Gen-Deut) has multiple authors. The "J" Document, "E" Document, "D" Document, and the "P" Document. We believe that Moses is the human author—both the external and internal evidence point to him. What's my Point? *Let's Cut it Straight! Let me share just two more errors to Avoid.*

ACCOMMODATION—it is viewing scripture through the lens of human reason. This doesn't have to take the form of denying the supernatural. It is also manifested in the subtle practice of diluting the full impact of the scripture to accommodate or excuse sinful practices or behaviors. (I Thessalonians 4:3 & I Corinthians 7:2), Both of the passages are clear—we are to abstain from sexual immorality. In other words, physical love outside of marriage is sin. Let's not be guilty of accommodation. Sin needs to be confessed and forsaken (Proverbs 28:13).

CULTURALIZING—Societal demands produce great pressure to "RESTUDY" and "RETHINK" time-honored doctrines because they do not march to the beat of contemporary drummers, thus Culturalizing limits a text to a specific time in history or culture, when in reality the text demands a wider application in time.

1. Husband leadership in Ephesians 5:22–24 One head not two
2. Male Church leaders I Timothy 2:11–12, I Timothy 3:1–13

Conclusion: II Timothy 2:15 says, "Be diligent to present yourself approved to God as a workman who does not need to be ashamed, handling accurately the word of truth.

The Demand is to Cut it Straight—How?

1. Approaching God's Word Exegetically.
   A. Observation
   B. Investigation
   C. Interpretation
2. Avoiding Common Errors.
   A. Don't add or edit God's word, Cut It Straight. "*That The Business of the Spoken Word*!" WHY? Because every text still means what its original author meant and no next can ever mean what it never meant!

SOCIAL ACTION

July 1988

The Reverend Jesse Jackson
The Convention Center
Jackson Headquarters
Atlanta, Georgia

Congratulations on your achievement at the Democratic National Convention.

The Progressive M.E. Baptist State Convention is in session on the beautiful campus of Florida Memorial College, Miami, Florida of which Dr. Willie C. Robinson is the president.

The presidents of both august bodies wish to offer you their deepest commendation for the way you met the tremendous challenge of the hour while the world's eyes were focused on Atlanta, Georgia. At the same time, we wish to express our deep commitment and support to your organization and future plans.

Yours in the Strong Name of Jesus,
General President H. T. Rhim

President A. H. Parker

Chairman of Social Justice,
Comm. J. E. Atkins

PROGRESSIVE MISSIONARY AND EDUCATIONAL BAPTIST STATE CONVENTION OF FLORIDA, INC.

Dr. Henry T. Rhim
Convention President

FIRST ANNUAL SESSION
YOUTH/CHILDREN'S CONVENTION

Dr. T. G. Bess, Executive Director
Lakeland, Florida
July 21–24, 1992

Kathleen Senior High School
2600 Crutchfield Road
Lakeland, Florida
(MORNING SESSIONS)

New Bethel African Methodist Episcopal Church
2122 Martin Luther King Jr. Avenue
Lakeland, Florida
(EVENING WORSHIP SERVICES)

Greetings From Dr. T G. Bess

Welcome to each of you who have followed the roads that leads to Lakeland, Florida to share in this historical event of this Great Convention. We thankfully embark upon the untamed and unfamiliar seas of a new beginning.

This first Young People's Convention, promises to be the launching pad to the 21st Century. This is an unexpressible time of rejoicing, because of what God is doing in our human frailty. We can never understand God! But we must be grateful that God does allow us to see and experience portions of his divine movement.

I am grateful that God, in his infinite wisdom, has allowed us to gather together to ask his blessings and share in all planned Christian experiences. It is our desire to implement a Godly, scriptural, and baptistical upward mobility among young people of Florida. Thusly, ushering in the "Newness of Life" that's needed and demanded through the conventional encounter. I give admiration to all Pastors, churches, directors/ directresses, and parents for your loyal and pleasant support. I am thankful for the leadership of this Convention and Congress in your support roles.

We must always encounter some turbulent weather as we sail upon the seas of life. Therefore, let us keep ready to weather the storms through continued prayer and communication. I request special supplication unto God for the clients we serve, as well as the entire staff and workers of this Convention. My prayers for our Children/Youth Convention and our Congress, is that we use the accomplishments and failures of our past as stepping stones toward spiritual development, while we objectively analyze our present situation relative to being good servants.

Remember: "You don't fail unless you stop trying."

Yours in His Service,

T. G. Bess, Executive Director, '92

FIRST CHILDREN/YOUTH CONVENTION BLASTS OFF

by Dr. T. G. Bess
State Executive Director
Children/Youth Convention

This great convention of Florida gave genesis to an upward move in that the first Annual Session of the Children/Youth Convention convened July 21–24, 1992, in Lakeland.

This uniqueness of time and session gave credence to the fact that change can be positive!! The Convention opened with a spirit-filled musical at 7 p.m. at the New Bethel A.M.E. Church. As the melodic sounds caressed the ears of the listeners, the Holy Spirit lifted the house to an enchanting ecstasy! After being energized through planning, prayer and more planning, this opening supplied the motivation needed for a successful Convention. The Convention shared in Christian education, through class work for youngster and adults alike, sing alongs, powerful devotions, workshop services, (Christian) interactions and encounters, local Church pride by wearing Church T-shirts and much more! A special thanks to Dr. Clinton Wright, principal of Kathleen Senior High School, where our daily operations were held; Bethel A.M.E. Church for hosting the nightly services! Please note: Thanks to Sisters Elizabeth Rozier, Hattie Alexander and D. Bolden, convention directresses; Pastor James White, Dean; Paster J. L. Downing, registrar, and Sis. Jackie Staton, assistant registrar; Sis. Lynda West, administrative secretary; Sis. P. Glover, Finance; Pastor E. E. Cross, counselor; Sis. Bennet and Sis. Banks and Bro. Darby for music and staff members for loyal support as we sailed uncharted waters. Praise God we lost none!

OUTLINE PROGRAM OF THE THIRTEENTH ANNUAL SESSION OF THE YOUTH CONVENTION

Auxiliary to the
PROGRESSIVE MISSION AND EDUCATION CONVENTION OF FLORIDA
Dr. J. C. Sams, President

To convene with
MT. GILBOA BAPTIST CHURCH
Bartow, Florida
Rev. Eddie Burroughs, Host Pastor
March 18–23, 1975

Officers

President	Brother Eugene Parker
First Vice President	Brother Frederick Brinson
Second Vice President	Sister Linda Mathis
Third Vice President	Brother Frank Butler (M & E)
Fourth Vice President	Sister Norma J. Hall (M & E)
Recording Secretary	Sister Margaret Cason
First Asst. Recording Secretary	Mrs. Valeria Perry
Second Asst. Recording Secretary	Sister Shirley Banks
Financial Secretary	Brother Willie C. Barnes
First Financial Secretary	Sister Marilyn Whitehead
Second Vice Financial Secretary	Brother Andrew Jenkins
Corresponding Secretary	Sister Cecilia Epps
Asst. Corresponding Secretary	Sister Janice Johnson
Treasurer	Sister Linda Samuel

Committee on Finance	Brother Leroy Bell, Chairman
Counselor on Finance	Sister Q. E. Williamson
Pianist	Brother Kenney Marshall
Asst. Pianist	Brother Rufus Woods (M & E)
Director of Music	Sister Constance Harry (M & E)
Historian	Brother Henry Cason
Secretary to Counselors	Sister Tommisinia Williams
Ushers	Sister Ida Young, Chairman
	Sister Yvette Crawford
	Brother Carey Brooks (M & E)
Counselor	Sister Hattie L. Alexander
Asst. Counselor	Sister C. D. Bolden
Chieftain	Rev. N. F. Sumpter (M & E)
General President	Dr. J. C. Sams

Committees

Education	Sister C. D. Bolden
Counselor	Sister Doretha Wilcox
Chairman	Sister Patricia Mathis
Co-Chairman	Sister Shirley Gibbon
Badges	Sister Thelma Thompson, Counselor
Chairman	Sister Ida M. Young
Co-Chairman	Valencia Smith
Counselors Enrollment	Sister Rosa Cobb, Counselor
	Sister Tommisenia Williams
Chairman	Brother Clarence Chester
Co-Chairmen	Brother Wilbert Johnson
	Brother John Powell

Evangelical Board	Brother Alvin McWhorter, Orlando Brother James Cobb, Tampa
Counselor	Rev. N. F. Sumpter
Mission	Sister Alice Hanible
Counselors	Sister Vivian Chester, Sister A. K. White
Chairman	Martha Tony
Co-Chairman	Gwen Hud
Co-Chairman	Polly Davis
Regional Conference	Sister Ernestine Sermon Sister Cornelia Prime, Sheryl Jennings, Harriet Byrd

OUTLINE PROGRAM OF THE FOURTEENTH ANNUAL SESSION OF THE YOUTH CONVENTION MARCH 25–27, 1976

THEME
"Christ's Responsible Church In An Irresponsible World"
St. Matt. 5:13; Matt. 25:35–36; Micah 6:8

MOTTO
Jesus Answer for the World Today

THEME SONG
The Light Of The World

YOUTH WILL MEET

Thursday Morning, March 25, 1976

9:30 A.M. Joint Session with Parent Body For Social Hour Session

Thursday Afternoon

12:30–2:00 P.M. Dinner
2:00 P.M. Devotion and Testimonial
Sermon
Rehearsal for Program
4:00–6:00 P.M. Workshop for Counselors and Youth

Thursday Evening

6:30 P.M. Welcome Program, Host Church and Community Churches (Jointly with the children).
7:30 PM. Response
Offering, Remarks, Benediction
Go to Parent Body for Education Night

Friday Morning, March 26, 1976

9:00 A.M. Brother Porter, Presiding
Call to Worship(Ephesians 6:1–4)
Selection, Young People's Chorus
Discussion of Theme: Bro. George C. Bowers, Liberty Hill, Bason, Florida
Theme song: "Jesus Is All the World to Me"
9:45 A.M. Presentation of Youth Officers

Chieftain, Counselors, Sis. Debra Cooper, St. Paul, Lakeland
Reading and Adoption of Program, Secretary, Margaret Cason, Bethel, Orlando
Selection: Youth Chorus

11:00 A.M. Workshop Topic: The Role of the Christian Youth
Dedication and Commitment Romans 12:1–21
Panelists: (3 minutes each) Martha White, St. John, Orlando; Andrew Jenkins, Bethlehem, Winter Garden; Angelcian Green, St.Joseph; Leroy Cooper, Buckhorn, Marianna
Moderator: Kenny Marshall, Beth lehem, Orlando
Church Music: Constance Harris

Friday Afternoon

12:00 P.M. Offering, Report of Committees, Election of Officers
Progress Report, Remarks, Benediction

12:45 P.M. Rehearsal and Dinner

2:00 P.M. Go to Parent Body for President's Address
(Attire in Light Green & White)

5:00 P.M. Music, New Mt. Zion, Lakeland, St. John Progressive, Tampa, Fl

Friday Evening

6:00 P.M. President's Hour, President's Address
Counselors for President's Hour: Sis. D. M. Bolden, New Mt. Zion,

Lakeland; Sis. Thelma Thompson, Little Rock, Jacksonville; Sis. E. D. Graham, First Providence, Bartow; Curtis Doltie, Bethel, Orlando

Theme song: "Jesus Is All the World to Me"

Presentations:

Selection: Youth Chorus

7:00 P.M. Discussion: Jesus Christ, The Panacea for the World's Ills

St. John 15:1–2

8:00 P.M. Brother Frederick Brinson, Presiding

Panelists: Glenda Nelson, Belle Glade; Willie C. Barnes, Bethlehem, Orlando; Curtis Doltie, Bethel, Orlando; Valerie Perry, Shiloh, Orlando; Monica Wynn, First Providence, Bartow; Rosalyn Lawson, Bethel, Orlando

Moderator: Harrington Covington, Jr.

Selection-Music: New Mt. Zion, Lakeland, St. John Progressive, Tampa

Sermon: Rev. Thomas Leonard, St. Paul, St. Petersburg

Alternate: Rev. Ralph Rivers, St. Luke, Plant City (Choir and Ushers serving)

Invitation to Joiners, Offering, Remarks

Benediction

Saturday Morning, March 27, 1976

9:00 A.M. Counselors and Messengers meet for Prayer

President Presiding

Devotion: All Districts
Selection: Youth Chorus
Theme: "Christ's Responsible Church In An Irresponsible World" (St. Matt. 5:13–16; Micah 6:8; St. Matt. 25:35–36)
Theme Song:Jesus Is All The World To Me

10:00 A.M. Christian Birthday, Led by Sister Angeline Russ, St. John Progressive, Tampa, Fla.
Committees Report
Topic Discussion: Pre-Marital Intropersonal Relations
Panelists: Glenda Nelson, Belle Blade; Margaret Cason, Bethel, Orlando; Ernestine Crum, Bethlehem, Orlando
Moderator: Willie C. Barnes
Church Music: Brother Kenneth Marshall
Discipleship—Offering, Bulletin
Remarks, Benediction

Saturday Afternoon

12:00 P.M. Dinner
2:00 P.M. Go to Parent Body (Attire, Green & White)
4:00–6:00 P.M. Fellowship Hour
7:30 P.M. Variety program, Searching for Talents
Devotion: Fourth Vice President
Selection: Youth Chorus
Selections from invited Chorus
March of Queens, Crowning of Queen
Offering, Remarks
Resolution of Thanks, Sister Harriett Wynn

STATE YOUTH OFFICERS OF THE PROGRESSIVE MISSIONARY AND EDUCATIONAL BAPTIST STATE CONVENTION OF FLORIDA 1975–76

President	Brother Eugene Porter
First Vice President	Brother Frederick Brinson
Second Vice President	Sister Linda Adams
Third Vice President (M&E)	Brother Harrison Covington, Jr.
Fourth Vice President (M&E)	Brother Leroy Cooper
Recording Secretary	Sister Margaret Cason
First Assistant Recording Secretary	Sister Valeria Perry
Second Assistant Recording Secretary (M&E)	Sister Shirley Banks
Financial Secretary	Brother Willie C. Barnes
First Assistant Financial Secretary	Sister Marilyn Whitehead
Second Assistant Financial Secretary	Brother Andrew Jenkins
Corresponding Secretary	Sister Martha White
Assistant Corresponding Secretary (M&E)	Sister Janice Johnson
Treasurer	Sister Winifred Dallas
Chairman Committee on Finance	Brother Leroy Bell
Counselor on Finance	Sister Q E. Williamson
Pianist	Brother Kenny Marshall
Assistant Pianist (M&E)	Brother Rufus Woods
Director of Music (M&E)	Sister Constance Harrison
Historian	Brother Henry Carson
Secretary to Counselors	Sister Tomasina Williams
Ushers (M&E)	Sister Jennifer Baker & Brother Knight

Counselor	Sister Hattie L. Alexander
Assistant Counselor	Sister D. M. Bolden
Chieftain	Reverend N. F. Sumpter
General President	Dr. J. C. Sams

PROGRAM OF THE FORTY-NINTH ANNUAL SESSION OF THE GIRLS AUXILIARY TWENTY-SECOND ANNUAL SESSION OF THE SHEPHERD BOYS' LEAGUE

Auxiliary to the
PROGRESSIVE MISSIONARY AND EDUCATIONAL STATE CONVENTION OF FLORIDA MARCH 23–28, 1976

CHILDREN'S DEPARTMENT PROGRAM

Officers

Sister E. L. Jenkins, Directress
P.O. Box 304, Plant City Florida
Sister Loretta King, Assistant Directress
P.O. Box 115, Clewiston, Florida
Sister Maggie Marzell Brown, Assistant Directress
600 W. Lloyd Street, Pensacola
Rev. L. H. King, Chief Shepherd
P.O. Box 115, Clewiston, Florida
Sister Karen Hall, President Girls Auxiliary
1904 Warren Street, Plant City, Florida
Sister Sonja Davenport, First Vice President
401 W. 5th Street, Lakeland, Florida
Brother Harold Byrd, President Shepherd Boys' League
1309 14th Street, East Bradenton, Florida
Brother Cedric Brown, Second Vice President
Sister Valorie Mitchell, Recording Secretary
519 W. 7th Street, Lakeland, Florida

Fredie Packard, Corresponding Secretary
812 E. 7th Court, Panama City, Florida
Mrs. Elizabeth Rosier, Supervisor of Secretaries
519 W. 7th Street, Lakeland Florida
Mrs. Jeresa Austin, Finance Secretary
602 North Avenue, Lake Wales, Florida
Mrs. Pauline Glover, Treasurer
925 23rd Avenue S., St. Petersburg, Florida
Mrs. Argretha Jenkins, Tiny Tots Directress
1060 Spearing Street, Jacksonville, Florida
Sister G. B. C. Clay, Assistant Directress
2801 19th Street, Jacksonville, Florida
Miss Willean Tarver, Pianist
Jacksonville, Florida
Mrs. Betty Sanders, Music Director
1108 W. 13th Street, Lakeland, Florida
Dr. J C. Sams, President of Parent Body
Sister Amelia Houston, President of Senior Women

PROGRAM

Theme: "Christ's Responsible Church
In An Irresponsible World"
Matthew 5:13–16, 25:35–36; Micah 6:8

Motto

He hath shewed thee, o man, what is good, and what doth the Lord require of thee, but to do justly, and to love mercy, and to walk humbly with thy God?

Micah 6:8

Songs

"He's Got The Whole World In His Hands"
"Onward Christian Soldiers"
(action)
"Lift Him Up"

Special Committees

Education:	Mrs. Elizabeth Rosier and Mrs. Emma Lou Adams
Badges:	Mrs. L. H. King and Mrs. Estella Snelling
Mission:	Mrs. Rutha Frazier and Mrs. T. R. Helms
Music:	Mrs. Eula P. Jenkins and Mrs. Annie Holmes
Arts and Crafts:	Mrs. Mattie Bell and Mrs. Vera Whitfield
Fellowship:	Mrs. Lois Johnson and Mrs. Lila Weston
Entertainment:	Mrs. Mary Daniels and Mrs. Rossie Lee Killings
Finance:	Mrs. Earnestine Brooks and Mrs. G. C. B. Clay
Social Hour:	Mrs. Marzella Brown
Fieldworkers:	Mrs. Lillie M. Wilkerson, Mrs. Annie Holmes, Mrs. Rutha Lee Frazier
Dean of Workshop:	Sister Elizabeth Barkley

PROGRAM OF THE FORTY-EIGHT ANNUAL SESSION OF THE GIRLS AUXILIARY TWENTY-FIRST ANNUAL SESSION OF THE SHEPHERD BOY'S LEAGUE

Auxiliary to the
PROGRESSIVE MISSIONARY and EDUCATIONAL BAPTIST STATE CONVENTION OF FLORIDA

March 1975

Children's Department
PROGRAM

Officers

Sister E. L. Jenkins, Directress
1002 Renfro Street, Plant City Florida
Sister Loretta King, Assistant Directress
P.O. Box 115, Clewiston, Florida
Sister Maggie Marzell Brown, Assistant Directress
600 W. Lloyd Street, Pensacola
Rev. L. H. King, Chief Shepherd
P.O. Box 115, Clewiston, Florida
Sister Karen Hall, President Girl's Auxiliary
1904 Warren Street, Plant City, Florida
Sister Sonja Davenport, First Vice President
401 W. Fifth Street, Lakeland, Florida
Brother Harold Byrd, President Shepherd Boy's League
1309 14th Street, East Bradenton, Florida
Brother Anthony Glover, First Vice President
925 25th Avenue S., St. Petersburg, Florida
Bardan Lewis, Second Vice President
Sister Valorie Mitchell, Recording Secretary
519 W. 7th Street, Lakeland, Florida
Fredie Packard, Corresponding Secretary
812 E. 7th Court, Panama City, Florida
Mrs. Elizabeth Rosier, Supervisor of Secretaries
519 W. 7th Street, Lakeland, Florida
Mrs. Jeresa Austin, Finance Secretary
602 North Avenue, Lake Wales, Florida
Mrs. Pauline Glover, Treasurer
925 23rd Avenue S., St. Petersburg, Florida
Mr. Argretha Jenkins, Tiny Tots Directress
1060 Spearing Street, Jacksonville, Florida
Sister G. B. C. Clay, Assistant Directress
2801 19th Street, Tampa, Florida
Sister Venita Smith, Pianist
Dr. J. C. Sams, President of Parent Body
Sister Amelia Houston, President of Senior Women

Program

Theme: "The Gospel of Liberation for the Sin-Bound"
John 8:32–36

Motto
"Ye Shall know the Truth and the Truth Shall Make You Free
John 8:32

Songs
Jesus Paid it All
Onward Christian Soldiers
Lift Him Up

A BRIEF HISTORY OF THE NURSES' CORP

On March 22, 1969 at 11:00 a.m.the Progressive Baptist State Convention of Florida Nurses' Corp was organized at the Zion Hill Missionary Baptist Church of Winter Haven, Florida, Reverend J. E. Adkins Pastor. Eleven members were Present. They were:

Sister Ida Cooper
Sister Ida Tucker
Sister Mary Alice Goodman
Sister Pauline Eaton
Sister Iris Jenkins
Sister Annie Bell Cheatum
Sister Carol Myles
Sister Maggie Hunter
Sister Bertha Thomas
Sister Sarah Allen
Sister S. W. Grimsley

Reverend J. Hargrett, First South Florida Association, presided over the election of officers. The parent body elected Sister W. W. Grimsley, First South Florida Association, to serve as president for the year 1969–70. The following persons were recommended to the parent body as officers:

The late Reverend P. E. Devanport	Counselor
Sister Annie Bell Cheatum	Vice President
Sister Ida Cooper	Recording Secretary
Sister Charlie M. Flowers	Corresponding Secretary
Sister Susie Thompson	Treasurer
Sister Annie O'Neal	Financial Secretary
Sister Iris Jenkins	Financial Committee Chairman
Sister Mamie Starling	Coordinator

These officers were approved by the parent body and became the official staff.

March 1970, the first session of the Nurses' Corp was held in Fort Myers, Florida, at St. John First Baptist Church, Reverend J. L. Stephens, Pastor.

The second session convened March, 1971 with New Bethel Baptist Church, Belle Glade, Florida, the late Reverend O. D. Williams Pastor.

The third annual session was held at the Shiloh Baptist Church, Orlando, Florida, Reverend J. W. Toomer, Pastor.

March 1972 with many hours of hard work and sincere leadership of Sister W. Grimsley, this auxiliary had grown with the Nurses' Guild in many of our churches throughout the state of Florida. To the regret of the State Nurses' Corp, we accepted the resignation of Sister Grimsley as president. The following officers were recommended and accepted by the Parent Body:

Sister Veronica Fung	President, First South Florida Association
Sister Susie Thompson	Vice President, East Florida and Bethany Association
Reverend B. H. Hartley	Moderator

Sister Magnolia Rhodes	Recording Secretary, South Florida Progressive Association
Reverend W. J. Glover	Moderator
Sister Doris Talbert	Corresponding Secretary, Mt. Pilgrim Association
Reverend C. H. Bolden	Moderator
Sister Grace Middlebrook	Financial Secretary, First South Florida Association
Reverend P. H. Jackson	Moderator
Sister Dorthy Mott	Treasurer, Union Foreign
Dr. L. S. McCree	Moderator

In July 1972, the State Board meeting was held in Jacksonville, Florida. Sister Dorthy Chambers was appointed Parliamentarian and Sister Hellen Lundy was appointed Historian.

The Fourth annual session was held in March 1973 with the Galilee Missionary Baptist Church in St. Petersburg, Florida, the late Reverend Frank Cubby, Pastor and Past Moderator of the Union Foreign Association. At this session our convention merged with the Missionary and Educational Baptist State Convention of Florida. The office of the second Vice-President was opened to accept a recommendation from the West Florida Section. Sister Minnie Paramore was recommended and accepted. Sister Florence Gilmore was accepted as Assistant Secretary. Both were from the West Florida Section.

The Fifth Annual Session was held in March 1974 with the New Bethel Baptist Church, Panama City, Florida, where Reverend P. L. Glover is pastor.

In March 1975 the Sixth Annual Session was held with the Mount Gilboa Baptist Church, Bartow, Florida, Reverend Eddie Burrough, Pastor. Sister Letrice Franklin was elected Financial Secretary.

The Seventh Annual Session was held with the Mount Pleasant Baptist Church, Reverend J. F. Hargrett, Pastor. Sister Lizzie Shaw was elected Historian, Union Foreign Association, Sister Margie Williams, Parliamentarian, Union Foreign Association and Dr. L. S. McCree Moderator.

The New Hope Baptist Church in Pensacola, Florida, hosted the Eight Annual Session in March 1977, Reverend E. L. Causey, Pastor. Sister Daisy Washington was elected Second Vice President, Union Foreign Association and Dr. L. S. McCree, Moderator.

The March 1978 Ninth Session was held with the New Mount Zion Baptist Church, Lakeland, Florida, Reverend Bolden Pastor. Sister Edith Hankerson Moran of the Union Foreign Association became Assistant Recording Secretary and Sister Bernice Scott, Musician.

In July 1978 the Annual Board meeting was held at the St. John Baptist Church with Reverend Alex Harper, Pastor in Arcadia, Florida. Sister Margie Williams was elected Parliamentarian and Secretary of the President, Union Foreign Association.

The March 1979 Annual Session met at the St. John Baptist Church. The Reverend F. L. Maxwell Pastor. Sister Florence Hayes was elected Recording Secretary and Sister Grace Middlebrook, Assistant Financial Secretary, First South Florida. Reverend P. H. Jackson, Moderator.

December 1, 1979 the First State Nurses Corp fellowshiped together. A one day session was held with the St. John Baptist Church, Reverend Eddie Newkirk, Pastor. The State Nurses Corp advisor, Reverend Earl B. Williams attended. He was accompanied by Reverend Powell.

Humbly Submitted,
Sister Lizzie Shaw, Historian.

THE HISTORY OF CHURCH NURSING

"A good Nurse is God's love on display." "Nursing" is a participle coming from the transitive verb, to nurse. It means to care for the sick, the informed, and to protect persons who need protecting. It is Curative Care which means to nourish, to keep in good health, and to supply whatever promotes growth, development and progress. Nursing is older than medicine. That is, Nursing as a practice, is older than professional and instructional medicine. Nursing has been regarded as a Christian Calling. Jamieson and Sewall traced the origin of the nursing profession to early Christian orders of Deacons and Deaconesses.

In 1910, under the leadership of Major Charles Lynch, the Red Cross First Aid effort was begun. First Aid Training Programs were initiated in a wide variety of industries.

In the 1920's and the 1930's, the Red Cross broadened its program of activity, developing new techniques. The public health nursing program was active in more than half the countries of the nation.

In the early forties it was recognized that the church should become directly interested and involved in the immediate and temporary care to the sick and injured. Church nurses had an opportunity to better prepare themselves to render such services throughout the nation through the Red Cross activity. Out of the movement has grown our volunteer church nurses. What a job they have done! Mouth-to-mouth resuscitation a method of artificial respiration, was drawn from the Bible by the Red Cross from 2 Kings 4:34, the story of Elisha restoring the Shunammite's son, which reads: "And he went up, and lay upon the child, and put his mouth upon his mouth, and his eyes upon his eyes, and his hands upon his hands: and he stretched himself upon the child; and the flesh of the child waxed warm."

The Church nurse must be a dedicated Christian person. She has a grand opportunity to render service for God through serving humanity, and by the same token, the nurse has a great responsibility to prove herself as a follower of Christ.

OFFICERS

President	Veronica Fung
First Vice President	Daisy Washington
Second Vice President	Martha Whitney
Recording Secretary	Edith Morgan
Assistant Recording Secretary	Clementine Davis
Corresponding Secretary	Doris Talbert
Financial Secretary	Letrice Franklin
Assistant Financial Secretary	Helen Lundy
Treasurer	Mattie Boyd
Historian	Florence Hayes
Advisor	The Reverend Henderson Powell

PROGRAM OF THE SEVENTH ANNUAL SESSION OF THE NURSES CORPS AUXILIARY TO THE PROGRESSIVE MISSIONARY AND EDUCATIONAL BAPTIST STATE CONVENTION OF FLORIDA

Dr. J. C. Sams, President

To Convene with the
NEW MT. ZION BAPTIST CHURCH
Tampa, Florida
Rev. B. J. Jones, Pastor

March 1976

THEME
"Christ's Responsible Church In An Irresponsible World"
Matthew 5:13–13; Malachi 6:8; Matthew 25:35–36

Officers

Mrs. Veronica Fung	President
Mrs. Susie D. Thompson	First Vice President
Mrs. Minie L. Paramore	Second Vice President
Mrs. Florence Gilmore	Recording Secretary
Mrs. Magnolia Rhodes	Assistant Recording Secretary
Mrs. Doris Tolbert	Corresponding Secretary
Mrs. Daisy Washington	Assistant Corresponding Secretary
Mrs. Letrice Franklin	Financial Secretary
Mrs. Inez Cobb	Assistant Financial Secretary
Mrs. Dorothy Mott	Treasurer
Mrs. Dorothy Chambers	Parliamentarian
Mrs. Helen Lundy	Historian
Rev. J. C. Sams	Advisor

PROGRAMME OF THE NURSES CORPS OF THE PROGRESSIVE MISSIONARY & EDUCATIONAL BAPTIST STATE CONVENTION OF FLORIDA, INC.

to convene with
THE GREATER PEACE
MISSIONARY BAPTIST CHURCH
102 Fourth Street
Fort Walton Beach, Florida

May 21–25, 1995

Theme: "A New Look At An Old Mission"
Matthew 20:19–20

Headquarters Hotel: RAMADA BEACH RESORT
1500 Miracle Strip Parkway Highway 98 East
Fort Walton Beach, Florida

The Nurses Corps Auxiliary
will meet at the Headquarters Hotel
(Ramada Beach Resort)

Sister Daisy Washington
President

THE REVEREND HENDERSON POWELL-ADVISOR
DR. HENRY T. RHIM-CONVENTION PRESIDENT

NURSES CORPS' OFFICERS

Sister Daisy Washington, President
3217 E. Hanna Avenue
Tampa, Florida

Member of ST. JOHN MISSIONARY
BAPTIST CHURCH
The Reverend Eddie Newkirk, Pastor
and Member of
UNION FOREIGN BAPTIST DISTRICT
ASSOCIATION

Sister Veronica Fung
President Emeritus

Sister Martha Whitney
First Vice President

Sister Louise Daniels
Second Vice President
Sister Edith Moran
Recording Secretary

Sister Helen Lundy
Assistant Financial
Secretary
Sister Mattie Boyd
Treasurer
Sister Florence Hayes
Historian

Sister Clementine Davis Assistant Recording Secretary	Sister Lottie Johnson Workshop Instructor
Sister Doris Tolbert Corresponding Secretary	Rev. Henderson Powell Minister-Advisor
Sister Leatrice Franklin Financial Secretary	Dr. H. T. Rhim Convention President

HOME MISSION REPORT

The Chairman's Report
Dr. T. G. Bess
Chairman, Home Mission Board
Progressive Missionary and Education
Baptist State Convention of Florida

James 1:2–20

Key Verse: 2–4 "Consider it all joy, my brethen, when you encounter various trials, knowing that the testing of your faith produces endurance. And let endurance have its perfect result, that you may be perfect and complete, lacking nothing." N.A.S.

Greeting in the name of Jesus Christ:

Again this year, it has been my pleasant experience to do the work of the Church through this board. It is because of willing workers across this great state that produces an acceptable level of success. It must become paramount in our minds that if we're going to experience Spiritual growth in our Churches, strength in our personal conviction and stimulate the spread of God's work through Jesus Christ, we must become joyfully sold out to the cause of the King's Agenda. The work demands a Biblical mind set, Spiritual Conditioning and broad shoulders. There is a need to face the adversary's counter attacks with the powerful sword of the Gospel. "Count it all joy, my brethen, when you encounter various trails," James 4:2. There must be a realization that in this struggle, adversity will arise. When he does, people of God must arise and enter the Garden of prayer.

The Lord has showered us with unique individual abilities to do our share in the cause of Kingdom building. The cause is just, the cause is right, righteous and the cause is divinely mandated by Christ! We experience a high level of love objectives in our songs of praise, sermons and work. The Lord Himself has advised and commanded us when He said, "Little children love one another!" Love will make things happen Spiritually in Christ. We must become lovers of souls rather than faces and personalities. When one reaches the Holy perfection, of loving souls, then and only then, the laborer will enter the field of labour set forth through God's Holy Word. We are just trail blazers for the Lord trying to address our work to the needs of the human race. Will you help? Can the Lord depend on you? Will you tell Him, Lord, I am just willing. . . . ?

The Lord almighty has blessed us to share across the State in all area regions. It has been my good pleasure to give service to this ministry. I would like to take this opportunity to extend a heartfelt thanks to all of you for your loyal and continual support.

I remain

Yours in His Service,
Dr. T. G. Bess, Chairman

ANNUAL REPORT

MARCH 1993–MARCH 1994

Income:

Churches		$ 411.39
Associations		$ 1,000.00
South Florida Progressive	$ 750.00	
Kissimmee Valley	$ 250.00	
State Convention '93		$ 2,831.50
Enrollment	$1,931.00	
Offering	$ 950.00	
North West Florida Regional Conference '93		$ 1,976.00
Church Enrollment		$
Personal Enrollment		$
Offerings		$
North East Mass Meeting '93		$ 620.85
Progressive M & E	$ 110.00	
East Florida & Bethany	$ 390.00	

South Central Regional Conference '94
. . . .$ 2,129.72
Church Enrollment . . . .$ 985.00
Personal Enrollment . . . .$ -0-
Offering . . . .$ 120.80
Total Income 1992–1994 . . . .$ 8,969.46
Total Brought Forward . . . .$ 2,256.60
Total Operating Funds $11,226.06

DISBURSEMENTS

Administration:
Clerical, Office Supplies, Printing & Postage
. . . .$ 980.00
Travel Expense State Convention . . . .$ 600.00
Staff Travel Expense State Convention . . .$ 600.00
Donation—Office . . . .$ 600.00
Associational Representation Travel/Expenses
. . . .$ 225.00
Benevolent Aide to Church/Ministers
The Reverend C. C. Reeves . . . .$ 100.00
Annual Report Expense . . . .$ 150.00
Staff Donations and Expense State
Convention '93 Bartow . . . .$ 123.20
Board Secretary Travel Expense . . . .$ 175.00
Commissions . . . .$ 300.00
North/West Conference '93
Donations to Staff members . . . .$ 1,152.00
Donations to Host Church & Pastor . . . .$ 100.00
Printed Materials & Clerical Donations .$ 25.00
Total . . . .$ 1,777.00
Mass Meeting
Love Offering . . . .$ 123.00
South/Central Conference '93
Donations to Staff Members . . . .$ 1,590.50
Donations to Church & Pastor . . . .$ 325.00
Printed Materials & Donations . . . .$ 142.50
Total . . . .$ 2,058.00
Total Disbursements $10,040.20

SUMMARY REPORT

Total Brought Forward	$ 2,256.60
Total Receipts	$ 8,969.46
Total Disbursements	$10,040.06
Balance on Hand	$ 1,186.06

PROGRESSIVE MISSIONARY AND EDUCATIONAL BAPTIST STATE CONVENTION OF FLORIDA, INC.

Pastor H. T. Rhim
President

August 8, 1994

TO: ALL PASTORS, MODERATORS, BOARD CHAIRMEN AND AUXILIARY PRESIDENTS

RE: RELIEF ASSISTANCE FOR FLOOD VICTIMS IN THE WEST FLORIDA AREA

"Now there are diversities of gifts, but the same Spirit. And there are differences of administrations, but the same Lord. And there are diversities of operations, but it is the same God which worketh all in all. And God hath set some in the church, first apostles, . . . then gifts of . . . *helps* . . . " (1 Cor. 12:4–6,28)"

My brothers and sisters, this letter comes to formally introduce to you the *Chairman of Home Mission Board, Rev. J. J. Downing*. In our last session of the convention, July 1994, he accepted the appointment to this monumental post. His first commission is to spearhead the assistance to the victims of the *flood* in the panhandle area. We would like to assist those in need. You will be receiving a letter from him within the next few days outlining specific items that we would like to see donated and drop-off locations around the state. Please work with him, as this is his first act as chairman, we need to make as many curves straight for him so that the insurmountable job can be done as methodically as possible with as little problems as possible.

In addition to (or in lieu of) your donated items, any financial assistance you can afford to this effort is appreciated. **Please make your check payable to the convention and mail them to my office: P.O. Box 2949, Jacksonville, Fl 32203.** Distribution to the Home Mission Board's activities and needs will be made from this office so that we will have complete records of the assistance provided.

There will be assistance pleas from all over the state, however, only requests/pleas from Rev. Downing will reflect the voice of the Progressive M & E. Please do all you can to assist our Home Mission Board as they do the necessary to alleviate the pain caused by the flood.

Dr. T. G. Bess is still working as a part of the Home Mission Board; currently, he is serving as consultant to Rev. Downing. Inasmuch as they have worked together before, Dr. Bess has graciously advised me of his willingness to continue the work on the board and provide as much leadership knowledge to Rev. Downing.

Thank you for your fellowship. A complete report will be provided you at our next meeting time and during the convention setting when all board will make their reports.

May God continuously bless you and your congregation/ministry as you continue your efforts of kingdom building.

Yours In His Service,
H. T. Rhim, President

FIRST SOUTH FLORIDA MISSIONARY BAPTIST DISTRICT ASSOCIATION

Office of the Moderator
Dr. M. C. Johnson, D. D.
1302 Arch St.
Tampa, Florida 33617

Urgent! Urgent! Urgent!
Emergency Flood Relief—Mission Project!

Dear Pastor & Congregation:

Jesus said, "I was hungry, and ye gave me meat; I was thirsty, and ye gave me drink; I was a stranger; and ye took me in; Naked and ye clothed me; I was sick and ye visited me; I was in prison and ye came unto me," Matthew 25:35–36

The First South Florida Missionary Baptist District Association in cooperation with the Progressive Missionary and Educational Baptist State Convention of Florida Home/State Missions Board is organizing an Emergency Flood Relief Mission Project to the Florida Panhandle and South Georgia.

There is an immediate need for many items. We are asking that your Church receive a Special Offering to assist the flood victims. Please make your checks payable to: First South Florida Baptist Association. Please mark your check: Flood Relief.

We will be going on a Mission Tour to the affected areas on Wednesday, August 10–11, 1994. We have designated County-Area Coordinators to Assist us in the collection of donations and goods. We will certainly appreciate your support of this Missions Project.

We do not know when our day will come, when we too may become victims of some natural disaster. If you are interested in sharing in a personal way or accompanying us on this Missions Tour or, if there is a need for additional information please contact Dr. L. Howard at 813-447-7092 or Pastor Turner at 813-533-4539.

Yours for the Cause of Christ,
Dr. L. Howard, Missions Chairman Dr. M. C. Johnson, Moderator
First South Florida Baptist Association First South Florida Association

BIOGRAPHICAL SKETCH

The Late Rev. Henry L. Bradley, Sr humble birth on August, 3rd, 1916 in Lake Helen, FL. was the beginning of a journey of servanthood for the Master. His conversion took place at the age of twelve and two years later he was called to the gospel ministry.

Rev. Bradley embarked on his continuous study of God's word and his spiritual growth by attending and graduating from Florida Seminary, Inc. Birmingham, Alabama where he obtained the Doctor of Divinity. He did further studies at Stetson University, Deland, FL.

Rev. Bradley was forever seeking for more depth, width, and length of the Christian faith so he could be a better servant in his ministry.

His pastorage included 5 years at New Providence Baptist Church, Lake Monroe; 15 years at St Luke M. B. Church, Sanford, FL. 5 years at St. John M.B. Church, Altamonte Springs; 2 years at St. John Baptist, Ocala, FL. 15 years at St. Paul Baptist Oakland and 23 years at Zion Hill M.B. Church, Orlando. Under his leadership each congregation experienced spiritual growth in soul-winning, spiritual motivation, and scriptural study for better Christian living and service. Four of the churches built new sanctuaries and one church was completed.

The late Rev. Bradley and his wife, Johnnie Mae Robinson have a loving family of four sons and seven daughters. Their strong belief in God and their training led their children to strive for the highest goals they could achieve in life with God as their source.

Though he never sought a place of prominence, his faithfulness and his sacrificial and servant-like spirit led to his offices in his district including Moderator of the New Central Baptist Association. He served in the Progressive M & E Baptist Convention and the National Baptist Convention of America under the leadership of the Late Dr. Sams.

Reverend King David Britt

Reverend Britt was born at Marianna, Florida, Jackson County, April 14, 1882. He was converted at the age of twelve. He was baptized by the late Rev. G. H. Hill, pastor of the St. John Baptist Church where he served seven years as chorister. It was at this church where he was divinely called. He preached his trial sermon August 1901 and was granted license the same day. The same year was called to Oak Grove Mission Church, Sneads, Florida. He found there a people who needed the gospel. They accepted his leadership and he was quite successful in that field of labor. He was ordained in 1902 by the late Rev. J. C.

Blackshear. He attended State Normal (the present Florida A & M University) two years under the auspices of the State Board of Education, the honorable G. N. Sheats was State Superintendent at that time. He attended the Phelps Bible School at Tuskegee Institute under the late Dr. Penney. He holds diplomas from Princeton University, also he finished the ministerial course at Florida Normal College during the presidency of the late Dr. N. W. Collier and the late Dr. J. E. Ford was Dean. He taught in Public Schools for ten years and for fifteen years he taught in some of the best private schools in West Florida.[1]

Dr. G. J. Martin

The late Dr. G. J. Martin served as First Vice Moderator of the Greater South Florida Baptist Association, Treasurer of the Progressive Baptist State Convention, Treasurer and Business Manager of the Florida Seminary of Lakeland and Pastor of the Greater St. Paul Missionary Baptist Church, 1931–1966.

Reverend Earl B. Williams

The Reverend Earl B. Williams was born in Pelham (Mitchell County) Georgia, November 24, 1933. He is the son of Mrs. Willie A. Williams of Jacksonville, Florida. He received his early education in the Duval County School system. Upon graduation from high school he entered the United States Air Force in March 1952 and served 24 years. He retired honorably with decorations, and the ranking of Master Sergeant (E-7).

Rev. Williams was converted as a youth and was Baptized from the Mt. Sinai Missionary Baptist Church by the late Rev. H. H. Robinson. He served in the Sunday School, Baptist Young People Union (BYPU), participated in the Youth Choir, and the Boy Scouts of America.

Reverend Williams served as corresponding secretary, Vice Moderator, and Moderator to the Progressive Missionary Baptist District Association of West Florida for thirteen years.

Reverend Williams served as Advisor to the Nurses Corps, Assistant Financial Secretary, 3rd Vice President, and presently serving as First Vice President of the Progressive M&E Baptist State Convention, Inc., Dr. H. T. Rhim, President.

Reverend Williams served as Advisor to the Nurses Corps, Assistant Financial Secretary, 3rd Vice President, and presently serving as First Vice President of the Progressive M&E Baptist State Convention, Inc., Dr. H. T. Rhim, President.

Reverend Williams earned his A. A. Degree from Okaloosa Community College, Nicevice, Florida. Advance Bible, Pineland Baptist College, Pineland, Florida. Further studied Philosophy and Religion at the University of West Florida, Pensacola, Florida.

Reverend Williams pastored the St. Mark Missionary Baptist Church, Flowersview, Florida; Temple Missionary Baptist Church, Defuniak Springs, Florida; First Mt. Zion Missionary Baptist Church, Century, Florida; currently pastoring the First Providence Missionary Baptist Church, Bartow, Florida.

Reverend Williams is the father of six children; two sons, four daughters. He is married to the former Mary Lee Mincey, R.N., of Chipley, Florida.

Reverend N. S. Sanders
Pastor
Greater St. Paul Missionary Baptist
Institutional Church
1130 N. Webster Ave
Lakeland, Florida

Marital Status: Married
Children: 1 Son
Health: Excellent

Employment:

1974–Present	Pastor, Greater St. Paul M.B.I. Church, Lakeland, Florida

1959–1974	Pastor, Jacobs Chapel, Tallahassee, Florida
1965–1975	Pastor, St. James, Moultrie, Georgia
1965–1975	Counselor, Division of Youth Services, Tallahassee, Florida

Education: ITC—Atlanta, Georgia (Theology)
Florida A&M University (Theology)
Night courses for four years

Special Accomplishments:

Presently Moderator of the Mt. Pilgrim District Association
Presently 2nd Vice President of the Progressive M&E Baptist State Convention of Florida
Presently Secretary-Treasurer Benevolent Board, National Baptist Convention of America
Presently President of the Inter-Denominational Ministerial Alliance
Board Member of the United Way FEMA Program

Special Recognitions:

Who's Who in American Christian Leadership Council, 1989 Edition
Honorary Doctor of Divinity Degree from Florida Baptist Seminary, 1988
Proclamation from the City of Lakeland November 1, 1988

as "Rev. N. S. Sanders Day," recognized as an outstanding minister and community leader.

HISTORY OF THE STATE CONGRESS BAND OF THE PROGRESSIVE MISSIONARY AND EDUCATIONAL BAPTIST STATE CONGRESS OF FLORIDA

Brother Charles T. Maxwell, Director

The State Congress Band was organized in the year 1974, and was the brainchild of the late Dr. James Carl Sams, who asked Brother Charles T. Maxwell, Director of Music of Second Missionary Baptist Church, Jacksonville, Florida, if he would organize and direct the group. The Band started with only three members: Sister Denise Mathis, Sister Cheryl Dawsey and Brother Carl Bryant; all of whom were members of the Second Missionary Baptist Church of Jacksonville, Dr. James Carl Sams, Pastor.

Thru the years, the Band has grown in numbers with participation from Sister Churches throughout the State. In the past, the nucleus of the Band has always come from the Second Missionary Baptist Church and the St. Joseph Missionary Baptist Church of Jacksonville, Dr. H. T. Rhim, Pastor, who has financed and encouraged the young people and some adults to participate in the group. The Band has participated in every Congress Session since 1974, the year that the first Congress was held in Tampa, Florida. They always received great encouragement from Dr. Sams, Dr, Rhim, Dr. A. H. Parker, Dr. Lovelace, Dr. Harper, and Deans Stephens and Sumpter. It became a tradition that the Band, along with the Congress Chorus, directed by Sister Mary Whitehurst, would furnish music for the daily re-assembly periods and especially during the President's Hour.

For the past two years, 1991 and 1992, the Band has become a part of the Youth Convention headed by Dr. Bass, and has continued to participate with the Congress during the President's Hour. Many Pastors are now becoming concerned and have begun to bring their talented young musicians to the convention to participate in the Congress Band.

During the class periods the members are taught music theory, performance discipline, the appropriateness of various kinds of sacred music to be played in the church, and solo, ensemble and full band performance techniques. The forms of music studied and performed are: hymns, spirituals, anthems, overtures, gospels, marches and other sacred selections. We endeavor to make this a rich and rewarding Christian Musical experience for our young people while allowing them to use their talents to the glory of God.

Endnotes

APPENDIX VII

1. Second Missionary Baptist Church, Jacksonville, Florida, Church Reports.

WORKS CITED

Books:

Bacon, F. D. *Women In the Church,* Lutterworth Press: London and Redhill, 1947.

Bennett, Charles E. *Twelve On the River St. Johns*. Jacksonville: University of North Florida Press, 1989.

Bentley, Altermese Smith. *History of the First South Florida Missionary Baptist Association, 1888–1988.* Chuluota, Florida: The Mickler House Publishers, 1988.

Bentley, Altermese Smith. *Centennial Celebration: History of the First South Florida Missionary Baptist Association, 1888–1988.* Sanford, Florida: The Celery City Press, 1989.

Corder, Lloyd. *Churches in Fellowship on Mission in Their Settings.* Atlanta: Associational Administration Service, Home Mission Board.

Cox, Merlin G. and J. E. Dovell. *Florida, from Secession to Space Age.* St. Petersburg: Great Outdoors Publishing Co., 1974.

Federal Writers Project. *Florida, A Guide to the Southernmost State.* New York: Oxford University Press, 1939.

Fishel, Leslie H. Jr., *The Negro American: A Documentary History.* Glenview, Illinois: Scott Foresman, 1967.

Fitts, Leroy. *A History of Black Baptists.* Nashville: Boardman Press, 1985.

Gibson, James L., John Ivavcevich and James H. Donnelly, Jr. *Organizations: Structure—Process and Behavior.* Dallas: Business Publications, Inc, 1973.

Hatcher, William E. *John Jasper: The Unmatched Negro Philosopher and Preacher.* New York: Fleming H. Revell Company, 1908.

Hughes, Langston and Meltzer Milton. *A Pictorial History of the Negro in America.* Third Revision by E. Eric Lincoln and Meltzer Milton. New York: Crown Publishers, 1973.

Johnson, James Weldon. *God's Trombones.* New York: The Viking Press, 1927.

Joiner, Edward Earl. *A History of Florida Baptists.* Jacksonville: Florida Convention Press, 1972.

McDonough, Gary W. Ed. *The Florida Negro: A Federal Writers' Project Legacy.* Jackson and London: University Press of Mississippi, 1993.

Marsh, Cecil E. *Developing Skills in Human Relations.* Nashville: Convention Press, 1971.

McKinney, George P. and Richard I. McKinney. *History of the Black Baptists of Florida, 1850–1985.* Miami: Florida Memorial College Press, 1987.

Morris, Allen. *The Florida Handbook, 1989–1990.* 22nd Biennial Edition. Tallahassee: The Peninsular Publishing Company, 1989.

Pius, N. H. *An Outline of Baptist History.* Nashville: National Baptist Publishing Board, 1911.

Quarles, Benjamin. *The Negro American.* Baltimore: Morgan State College, 1967.

Reynolds, William J. *Hymns of Our Faith.* Nashville: The Boardman Press, 1964.

Smith, J. Alfred and Charles O'Neal. *Baptists and Our Nation's Story: Condensed History of American Baptists, Southern Baptists and the National Baptists in America.* Fullerton, California: Christian Printing Service, 1976.

Smith, Julia Floyd. *Slavery and Plantation Growth in Antebellum Florida 1821–1860.* Gainesville: University Press of Florida, 1973.

Tebeau, Charlton. *A History of Florida.* Coral Gables: University of Miami Press, 1971.

Watson, E. C. *The Baptist Association.* Nashville: Convention Press, 1975.

Women of the Bible. Gastonia, North Carolina: Goodwill Publishers, 1969.

Woodson, Carter G. and Charles H. Wesley. *Negro Makers of History.* 6th edition—revised. Washington, D.C.: Associate Publishers, 1968.

Articles:

Ergood, Bruce. "The Female Protection And the Sun Light: Two Contemporary Negro Mutual Aid Societies," 50 *Florida Historical Quarterly* (July 1971), 25–38.

Kessel, Felicia. "The Fighting Black Clergy, The Evolution of the Black Ministry in America." *Crisis* (June/July 1990).

Raboteau, Albert J. "The Secret Religion of the Slave." 11 *Christian History:* 42–45.

Unpublished Materials:

Diggs, Paul. "Polk County Ushers Union," Florida Writers' Project, Lakeland Florida, November 25, 1938. P. K. Yonge Library, The University of Florida, Gainesville.

Diggs, Paul. "A Negro Community—Pierce, Florida," Florida Writers' Project, Lakeland, Florida, December 2, 1938. P. K. Yonge Library, The University of Florida, Gainesville.

Florida Writers Project. Baptist Church Associations, 1938–1939. Florida State Archives. Tallahassee, Florida.

Journals & Newspapers:

The Baptist Leader Adult Quarterly, 1983, 1986,

Crisis

The Liberator, 1987, 1988, 1993

Florida Watchman

The National Baptist Union Review, 1985, 1990.

The Weekly Challenger (St. Petersburg, Fl), May 14, 1988

Pamphlets, Reports and Church Records:

Brown, J. H. Historian's Report to the First South Florida Missionary Baptist, Association. November 1944.

Combined Minutes of the 46th Annual Session of the South Florida Missionary Baptist Association and Auxiliaries, November 22–26, 1961.

Combined Minutes of the Golden Jubilee Session of The Progressive Baptist State Convention of Florida, March 18–22, 1964.

Combined Minutes of the Sixty-Second Annual Session of the Progressive Baptist Missionary and Educational Baptist State Convention of Florida, 1976.

Combined Minutes of the Mt. Pilgrim Missionary Baptist Association, November 9–13, 1977.

Combined Minutes of the Seventieth Annual Session of the Progressive Missionary and Educational Baptist State Convention of Florida, Jacksonville, 1984.

Combined Minutes of the Seventy-Third Annual Session of the Progressive Missionary and Educational State Convention of Florida, March 17–22, 1987.

Combined Minutes of the Seventy-Fifth Annual Session of the Progressive Missionary and Educational State Convention of Florida, March 22–25, 1989.

Constitution of the Progressive Missionary and Educational Baptist State Convention.

Edwards, Isadore, Jr. "Foreign Mission Board's Doctrinal Statement."

Florida Baptist Academy Records.

The Florida Normal and Industrial Bulletin, 1943–44.

Florida Normal School Records

Foreign Mission Board of the National Baptist Convention of America, Inc.

Hargrett, Joseph F. Corresponding Secretary, Open letter, July 18, 1988.

Hargrett, Joseph F. "Brief History of the Progressive Missionary and Educational Baptist State Convention."

Historian's Annual Report of The Progressive Missionary and Educational Baptist Convention of Florida, March 1990.

Historian's Annual Report of The Progressive Missionary and Educational Baptist Convention of Florida, March 20, 1991.
Historical Information: East Florida and Bethany Baptist Association, by Herndon, Sessions, and Wilson, October, 1972.
M.A.B. Fuller's Christmas Offering, Pamphlet.
Minutes of the 37th Annual Session of the Progressive Baptist State Convention, March 20–25, 1951, Clearwater, Florida.
Minutes of the 49th Annual Session of the Progressive Baptist State BTU. Held with the Mt. Zion Progressive Baptist Church, St. Petersburg, Florida. Rev. L. S. McCree, Pastor, July 21–16, 1964.
Minutes of the Sixty-Ninth Annual Session of the Progressive Missionary and Educational Baptist State Convention, Ft. Lauderdale, 1983.
Minutes of the Seventy-Second Annual Session of the Progressive Missionary and Educational Baptist State Convention, Panama City, 1986.
Minutes of the Seventy-Eighth Annual Session of the Progressive Missionary and Educational Baptist State Convention of Florida, 1992.
Minutes of the State Sunday School and BYPU (Baptist Young People Union) Convention, held at Zion Hill Missionary Baptist Church, Sebring, Florida, July 19–23, 1951, Rev. C. Dean, Pastor.
Minutes of the First Session, Matron's Auxiliary.
Official Journal of the National Baptist Convention of America and Auxiliaries, 1985.
Official Journal National Baptist Convention of America and its Auxiliaries, 1986.
Official Journal National Baptist Convention of America and its Auxiliaries, 1987.
Official Journal of the Seventy-Sixth Annual Session of the Progressive Missionary and Educational Baptist State Convention of Florida, Inc. And Its Auxiliaries, 1990.

Open letter from the National Baptist Convention of America, Inc., dated July 15, 1988, signed by E. Edward Jones, President.

Program of the 43th Annual Session of the Progressive Baptist State Sunday School and BYPU Convention. To be held at the Harmony Baptist Church, Lakeland, Florida. Rev. J. J. McGriff, Pastor, July 23–27, 1958.

Program of the 51st Annual Session of the Progressive Baptist State Sunday School and BTU Convention.

Program of the 58th Annual Session of the Progressive Baptist State Sunday School and BTU Convention. St. John Missionary Baptist Church, Orlando, Florida. Rev. F. L. Maxwell, Pastor, July 17–22, 1973.

Progressive Missionary and Educational Baptist Convention of Florida, Inc., School of Christian Education 21st Annual Session, Lakeland, Florida, July 19, 1994, Banquet Awards Program.

Mrs. W. A. Smart, Annual Letter to the Ministers' and Deacons' Wives, March 23–27, 1980, Jacksonville, Florida. Sixty-Sixth Annual Session of the Progressive Missionary and Educational Baptist State Convention.

Smith, C. J. 1943 Report on the History of the Progressive Baptist State Convention.

Souvenir Program Golden Jubilee 50th Annual Session of the Progressive Baptist State Sunday School and BTU Convention.

Interviews and Personal Correspondence:

Altermese Smith Bentley interview with Mrs. Hazel Hall, November 1988.

Altermese S. Bentley Interview with Dr. Alex Harper, Sr., July 1992.

Altermese S. Bentley Interview with Reverend Lewis Lampley, July 1992.

Altermese Smith Bentley interview with Reverend L. E. McGee, 1987.
Altermese Smith Bentley interview with Dr. Richard I. McKinney, 1986.
Altermese S. Bentley Interview with Dr. Ned Saunders, July 1992.
Altermese Smith Bentley interview with Mrs. Lula Owens of Elizabeth Church, Arcadia, Florida, November 1988.
Fay Counts to Mrs. Altermese Bentley, March 13, 1986.
Isadore Edwards, Jr. to Mrs. Altermese Bentley, September 30, 1992.

Government Documents:
Warranty deed, Seminole County Florida, Official Records Book.
U.S. Department of Commerce, Bureau of the Census. Florida, 1910. Washington: U.S. Government Printing Office.

Miscellaneous Unpublished Materials:
Autobiography of Mrs. Mary H. Whitehurst, St. John Metropolitan Missionary Baptist Church, Sanford, Florida.
Church History of St. Paul Baptist Church, Dade City, Florida.
Church History of St. Luke, Kissimmee, Florida.
Church History of Bethel Baptist Church, Winter Park, Florida.
Church History of Mount Moriah Baptist Church, Winter Park, Florida.
Church History of Bethlehem Baptist Church, Winter Garden, Florida.
Church History of St. Mark Baptist Church, Port Tampa, Florida.
Church History of Bethel Baptist Church, Plant City, Florida.
Eulogistic Service Program for Agnes L. Dean, Kerney-Wilson Funeral Home, April 14, 1973, Sebring, Florida.

Funeral Program for Dr. Flagger G. Hilton, July 18, 1992.
Funeral Program for the Reverend Y. A. Roberts. March 23, 1922.
Historical Facts of the Women's Missionary and Educational State Convention of Florida.
Historical Sketch of Mt. Gilboa Baptist Church, Bartow in *Souvenir Program of the 92nd Anniversary of Mt. Gilboa Missionary Baptist Church, 1985.*
History of the St. John's First Baptist Church of Fort Myers, Florida.
History of the St. Matthew First Missionary Baptist Church, Clearwater, Florida.
The History of St. Paul Missionary Baptist Church, Dade City, Florida.
Obituary for Reverend Charles J. Smith.
Obituary for The Reverend Dr. James Carl Sams, July 24, 1985.
Unpublished History of the East Florida and Bethany Missionary Baptist Association.

ABOUT THE AUTHOR

ALTERMESE SMITH BENTLEY

Altermese Smith Bentley, a native of Sanford Florida, grew up in Bartow, where her father served as Pastor of Mt. Gilboa Baptist Church until 1934. She holds a B.S. degree from Shaw University, Raleigh, North Carolina, and an M.A. from Pepperdine University, Malibu, California.

She has studied at Howard University, Washington, D.C.; the University of Pennsylvania; and Temple University, Philadelphia, Pennsylvania. At Temple, she was enrolled for three years in the School of Religion and then transferred to Teachers College. After acquiring certification by the State of Pennsylvania, she taught in the School District of Philadelphia until her retirement on January 31, 1975. Before going to Philadelphia, she taught in the public schools of Florida and was Supervisor of Elementary Education in Columbia County, Lake City.

Altermese S. Bentley, who has been closely identified with the work of the First South Florida Missionary Baptist Association since early childhood, has wide experience in developing programs for Youth groups, Women's Mission Organizations, and Christian Education Departments. Presently she is Director Emeritus of the Workshop for the Senior Women's Convention; an auxiliary of the Progressive Missionary and Educational State Convention of Florida; reorganized the Senior Women's Mission Department of the Progressive Missionary and

Educational Baptist State Congress, and Historian for the Progressive Missionary and Educational State Convention of Florida. Most recently she attended the sixteenth Baptist World Congress in Seoul, Korea (August 1990), and the twelfth Baptist Youth World Conference, August 11–15, 1993, in Harare, Zimbabwe, South Africa.

On the 100th anniversary of the First South Florida Missionary Baptist Association (Clearwater, Florida), Mrs. Bentley initiated and organized a detailed historical exhibit of Central Florida's Black Churches which highlighted the institutions with the people who founded and served them and the Association. This effort was saluted by the Orange County Historical Society and the Orange County Historical Museum which sponsored the viewing of the exhibit from February 1 through April 1, 1989. In addition, Mrs. Bentley set up a display of information and archival materials on black life from 1870 through 1923 at the Seminole County School Student Museum.

As an active member, Mrs. Bentley served on the Pioneer Panel during the 1990 Community Involvement Conference, sponsored by the Afro-American Society of Seminole Community College, and as a major resource person for Seminole Community College's 1990 Governor's Program, the end-product of which was a historical video of Sanford's history. The title of the study, "*The Significance of Baked Cornbread*" was taken from the sayings of Mrs. Bentley.

Mrs. Bentley is the author of *The History of the First South Florida Missionary Baptist Association, 1888-1989* and *Georgetown: The History of a Black Neighborhood*.

Honors and recognition include The Martin Luther King, Jr. Community Award for Leadership in Civic and Educational Activities, City of Sanford, Florida; Youth Programs, Inc., Services to Disadvantaged Youth, Supreme Courts of Florida, Eighteenth Judicial Circuit; Seminole County Award, twice-cited for Service to Neglected and Abused Children; Young Men's Christian Association of Philadelphia and Vicinity, Award for Support Services; and Recognition for Historical Contributions by the Afro-American Society, Seminole Community College;

1991, National Distinguished Citizens Award, KAPPA ALPHA PHI NATIONAL FRATERNITY; Florida Memorial College, Miami, Florida—inducted into the President's Fountain of Excellence, February 20, 1994; the eleventh Annual Warren E. "Pete" Knowles Service Award Recognition for outstanding service to the City of Sanford, Florida, May 8, 1995; also, the Seminole County Branch of NAACP Community Service Award, in recognition of outstanding community involvement and contribution May 12, 1995. The Seminole County League of Women Voters selected her book, Georgetown, for the 75th Anniversary.

Altermese Smith Bentley is the mother of one daughter, the grandmother of three with one great grandchild. She is an active member of Saint Paul Missionary Baptist Church, Sanford, Florida; the Seminole County Historical Preservation Society; the Community Development Block Grant Advisory Board; Seminole County Health and Human Services Advisory Board; Board of Directors, Sanford Christian Sharing Center; Board of Directors, GoldenRule Housing & Community Development Corporation Inc., Sanford; past member of the City of Sanford Human Relations Advisory Board, and the City of Sanford Historical Preservation Advisory Board.